McDougal Littell

Biology

California Standards Review and Practice

McDougal Littell
A HOUGHTON MIFFLIN COMPANY
Evanston, Illinois • Boston • Dallas

McDOUGAL LITTELL BIOLOGY

Standards Review and Practice

Table of Contents
page

CALIFORNIA SCIENCE CONTENT STANDARDS

STANDARD SET 1: CELL BIOLOGY

STANDARD SET 2: GENETICS (MEIOSIS AND FERTILIZATION)

INTRODUCTION TO INVESTIGATION AND EXPERIMENTATION STANDARDS

STANDARD SET IE.1: INVESTIGATION AND EXPERIMENTATION

INTRODUCTION TO LIFE SCIENCE STANDARDS

Overview of California Standards and Tests

This workbook is your guide to the California Biology and Investigation Experimentation standards. Although all standards are covered in detail throughout the book, they are also listed here, beginning on page xi. In addition to the listed standards, you will see a chart that shows where each standard is covered in your textbook. Refer to these textbook pages if you need help with the concepts behind the standards.

3.2 Cell Organelles

KEY CONCEPT Eukaryotic cells share many similarities.

MAIN IDEAS
- Cells have an internal structure.
- Several organelles are involved in making and processing proteins.
- Other organelles have various functions.
- Plant cells have cell walls and chloroplasts.

VOCABULARY
cytoskeleton, p. 73
nucleus, p. 75
endoplasmic reticulum, p. 76
ribosome, p. 76
Golgi apparatus, p. 76
vesicle, p. 77
mitochondrion, p. 77
vacuole, p. 77
lysosome, p. 78
centriole, p. 78
cell wall, p. 79
chloroplast, p. 79

Section Opener

Standards listed in bold have primary focus in this section.

Standards in regular type are covered in the section but may be the main focus of another section.

Standards with an asterisk are untested but students are given an opportunity to learn them.

Standards labeled with two numbers and a letter (7.1.a) are Life Science standards from middle school for review.

CALIFORNIA STANDARDS

1.e **Students know** the role of the endoplasmic reticulum and Golgi apparatus in the secretion of proteins.

1.f *Students know* usable energy is captured from sunlight by chloroplasts and is stored through the synthesis of sugar from carbon dioxide.

1.g *Students know* the role of the mitochondria in making stored chemical-bond energy available to cells by completing the breakdown of glucose to carbon dioxide.

1.j *Students know* how eukaryotic cells are given shape and internal organization by a cytoskeleton or cell wall or both.

FIGURE 3.5 The cytoskeleton supports and shapes the cell. The cytoskeleton includes microtubules (green) and microfilaments (red). The blue area is the nucleus. (epifluorescence microscopy, magnification 750×)

components of the cytoskeleton

Connect Your body is highly organized. It contains organs that are specialized to perform particular tasks. For example, your skin receives sensory information and helps prevent infection. Your intestines digest food, your kidneys filter wastes, and your bones protect and support other organs. On a much smaller scale, your cells have a similar division of labor. They contain specialized structures that work together to respond to stimuli and efficiently carry out other necessary processes.

MAIN IDEA
Cells have an internal structure.

Like your body, eukaryotic cells are highly organized structures. They are surrounded by a protective membrane that receives messages from other cells. They contain membrane-bound organelles that perform specific cellular processes, divide certain molecules into compartments, and help regulate the timing of key events. But the cell is not a random jumble of suspended organelles and molecules. Rather, certain organelles and molecules are anchored to specific sites, which vary by cell type. If the membrane was removed from a cell, the contents wouldn't collapse and ooze out in a big puddle. How does a cell maintain this framework?

Each eukaryotic cell has a **cytoskeleton**, which is an extensive network of proteins that gives a cell its shape. Different types of protein subunits, including microtubules and microfilaments, assemble to form protein fibers. Just as bones in your skeleton are continually broken down and rebuilt by new cells, the cytoskeleton is also continually broken down and rebuilt. Its structure, shown in **FIGURE 3.5**, changes to meet the needs of the cell. The cytoskeleton serves many diverse and important functions.

- It supports and shapes the cell.
- It helps position and transport organelles.
- It provides strength.
- It assists in cell division.
- It aids cell movement.

Chapter 3: Cell Structure and Function **73**

California Standards Tests (CSTs) Two separate CSTs cover the California Biology and Life Science standards. All tenth grade students in California will take the California Life Science Standards Test. This test includes 60 multiple-choice items that assess high school Biology standards, selected middle school Life Science standards, and Investigation and Experimentation standards.

Upon the completion of your Biology course, you may also take a Biology/Life Science CST as part of the Standardized Testing and Reporting (STAR) Program in California. This test includes 60 multiple-choice items that assess Biology standards as well as Investigation and Experimentation standards.

Chapter Review
Small numbers indicate questions that address standards.

Standards-Based Assessment
Small numbers indicate which standards are addressed.

Biology/Life Sciences

Science Content Standards

CALIFORNIA STANDARD SET 1

Cell Biology

1 The fundamental life processes of plants and animals depend on a variety of chemical reactions that occur in specialized areas of the organism's cells. As a basis for understanding this concept:

1.a *Students know* cells are enclosed within semipermeable membranes that regulate their interaction with their surroundings.

1.b *Students know* enzymes are proteins that catalyze biochemical reactions without altering the reaction equilibrium and the activities of enzymes depend on the temperature, ionic conditions, and the pH of the surroundings.

1.c *Students know* how prokaryotic cells, eukaryotic cells (including those from plants and animals), and viruses differ in complexity and general structure.

1.d *Students know* the central dogma of molecular biology outlines the flow of information from transcription of ribonucleic acid (RNA) in the nucleus to translation of proteins on ribosomes in the cytoplasm.

WHAT IT MEANS TO YOU

All living things are made of one or more cells. In fact, your body is made of millions of cells that together carry out all of your life functions. As you read these words, muscle cells allow your eyes to scan the page, and nerve cells transmit chemical and electrical signals from your eyes to your brain.

STANDARD	CHAPTERS	PUPIL EDITION
1.a	3, 5	81–87, 134–137
1.b	2	54–56
1.c	3, 18	70–72, 544–545
1.d	8	239–242
1.e	3	73–79
1.f	4	103–112
1.g	4	113–121
1.h	2, 12	44–48, 368–371
1.i*	4	108–112, 117–121
1.j*	3	73–79

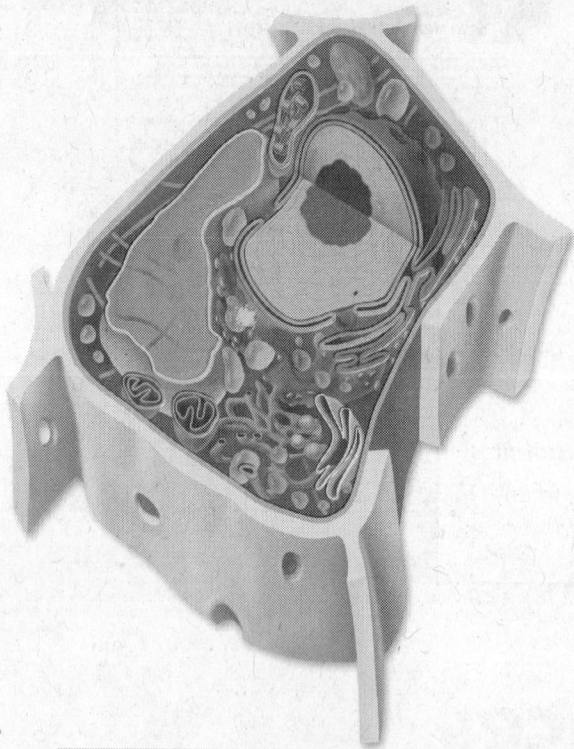

1.e *Students know* the role of the endoplasmic reticulum and Golgi apparatus in the secretion of proteins.

1.f *Students know* usable energy is captured from sunlight by chloroplasts and is stored through the synthesis of sugar from carbon dioxide.

1.g *Students know* the role of the mitochondria in making stored chemical-bond energy available to cells by completing the breakdown of glucose to carbon dioxide.

1.h *Students know* most macromolecules (polysaccharides, nucleic acids, proteins, lipids) in cells and organisms are synthesized from a small collection of simple precursors.

1.i* *Students know* how chemiosmotic gradients in the mitochondria and chloroplast store energy for ATP production.

1.j* *Students know* how eukaryotic cells are given shape and internal organization by a cytoskeleton or cell wall or both.

SAMPLE QUESTIONS

1. Cell membranes consist of a double layer of phospholipids. A variety of other molecules, including proteins, are embedded within the phospholipid layers. These proteins *most* likely function in `1.a`

   A helping material to cross the membrane.

   B producing DNA for the cell.

   C helping the cell to divide successfully.

   D converting energy into forms the cell can use.

2. Scientists are studying an enzyme that is involved in the breakdown of starch into simple sugars. Which of the following is *least* likely to affect the activity of this enzyme? `1.b`

   A raising the temperature

   B increasing the concentration of starch

   C changing the ionic conditions

   D lowering the pH

3.

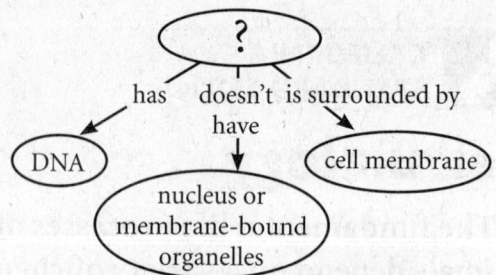

   Which of these *best* completes this concept map? `1.c`

   A animal cell

   B plant cell

   C prokaryotic cell

   D virus

4. Once proteins are produced, they generally move from the endoplasmic reticulum to the `1.e`

   A Golgi apparatus.

   B vacuoles.

   C nucleus.

   D mitochondria.

Answers: 1a, 2b, 3c, 4a

Genetics (Meiosis and Fertilization)

2 Mutation and sexual reproduction lead to genetic variation in a population. As a basis for understanding this concept:

2.a *Students know* meiosis is an early step in sexual reproduction in which the pairs of chromosomes separate and segregate randomly during cell division to produce gametes containing one chromosome of each type.

2.b *Students know* only certain cells in a multicellular organism undergo meiosis.

2.c *Students know* how random chromosome segregation explains the probability that a particular allele will be in a gamete.

2.d *Students know* new combinations of alleles may be generated in a zygote through the fusion of male and female gametes (fertilization).

2.e *Students know* why approximately half of an individual's DNA sequence comes from each parent.

2.f *Students know* the role of chromosomes in determining an individual's sex.

2.g *Students know* how to predict possible combinations of alleles in a zygote from the genetic makeup of the parents.

WHAT IT MEANS TO YOU

The moment that you were conceived, your entire genetic identity was formed. The process of meiosis produces sperm and egg cells, which have only one copy of each chromosome. So, when you were conceived, you received half of your DNA from your father and half from your mother.

STANDARD	CHAPTERS	PUPIL EDITION
2.a	6	173–176
2.b	6	168–171
2.c	6	183–187
2.d	6	189–191
2.e	6	173–176, 189–191
2.f	6	168–171
2.g	6	183–187

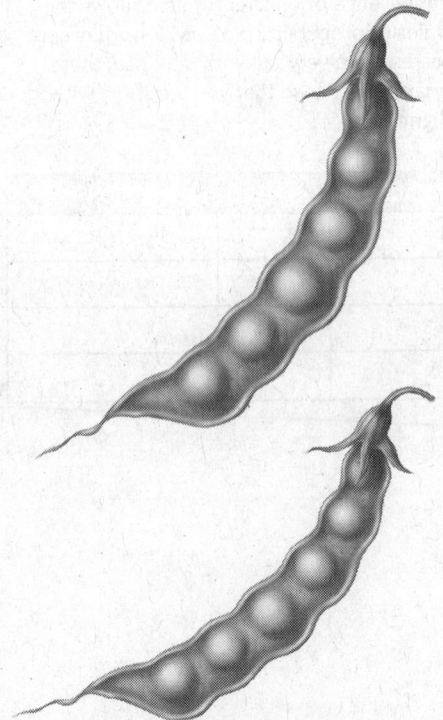

SAMPLE QUESTION

1. A female pea plant has a genotype of *RRYy*. Female gametes, or egg cells, are produced through meiosis. What are the possible genetic combinations that could be present in a single egg produced by this plant? **2.c**

   A *RR* only

   B *Yy* only

   C *Ry* and *rY*

   D *RY* and *Ry*

Answer: 1 d

Genetics (Mendel's Laws)

3   A multicellular organism develops from a single zygote, and its phenotype depends on its genotype, which is established at fertilization. As a basis for understanding this concept:

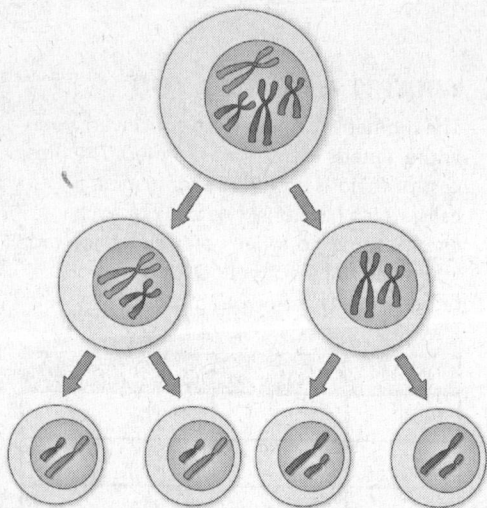

3.a *Students know* how to predict the probable outcome of phenotypes in a genetic cross from the genotypes of the parents and mode of inheritance (autosomal or X-linked, dominant or recessive).

3.b *Students know* the genetic basis for Mendel's laws of segregation and independent assortment.

3.c* *Students know* how to predict the probable mode of inheritance from a pedigree diagram showing phenotypes.

3.d* *Students know* how to use data on frequency of recombination at meiosis to estimate genetic distances between loci and to interpret genetic maps of chromosomes.

WHAT IT MEANS TO YOU

You may look more like one of your parents than the other, or you may be a perfect blend of both of your parents. If you've ever wondered why, the answers lie within Mendel's Laws. These laws explain how the inheritance of different traits follows the rules of probability. So even if both of your parents are very tall with dark hair, there may be a chance that you are short with light hair.

STANDARD	CHAPTERS	PUPIL EDITION
3.a	6, 7	183–187, 200–203
3.b	6	177–179, 183–187
3.c*	7	212–217
3.d*	7	209–211

SAMPLE QUESTIONS

1.

	F	f
f		
f		

Flower color in a certain plant species is determined by one gene with two alleles. The allele for pink flowers (*F*) is dominant and the allele for white flowers (*f*) is recessive. According to the parent genotypes in the Punnett square above, what is the probability of an offspring with white flowers?   **3.a**

A 25%

B 50%

C 75%

D 100%

2. Different gametes have different sets of chromosomes because homologous chromosomes are divided between gametes by   3.b

A genetic linkage.

B independent assortment.

C crossing over.

D external fertilization.

Answers: 1b, 2b,

Genetics (Molecular Biology)

4 Genes are a set of instructions encoded in the DNA sequence of each organism that specify the sequence of amino acids in proteins characteristic of that organism. As a basis for understanding this concept:

4.a *Students know* the general pathway by which ribosomes synthesize proteins, using tRNAs to translate genetic information in mRNA.

4.b *Students know* how to apply the genetic coding rules to predict the sequence of amino acids from a sequence of codons in RNA.

4.c *Students know* how mutations in the DNA sequence of a gene may or may not affect the expression of the gene or the sequence of amino acids in an encoded protein.

4.d *Students know* specialization of cells in multicellular organisms is usually due to different patterns of gene expression rather than to differences of the genes themselves.

4.e *Students know* proteins can differ from one another in the number and sequence of amino acids.

4.f* *Students know* why proteins having different amino acid sequences typically have different shapes and chemical properties.

WHAT IT MEANS TO YOU

If the DNA in each of your cells were stretched out end-to-end, it would measure more than two meters. A single DNA molecule is actually a chain of repeating units that carries a code that eventually controls protein production. Though there are only four different units in DNA, different combinations and sequences of these units produce the genetic diversity of all life as we know it.

STANDARD	CHAPTERS	PUPIL EDITION
4.a	8	243–247
4.b	8	243–247
4.c	8	252–255
4.d	8	248–251
4.e	2	44–48
4.f*	2, 8	44–48, 252–255

SAMPLE QUESTIONS

1. CCAGCAUAUGCC

A strand of messenger RNA contains the sequence shown above. How many amino acids are coded for in this sequence? `4.b`

A 3

B 4

C 6

D 12

2. A mutation is *least* likely to affect the phenotype of an organism if the mutation `4.c`

A involves a frameshift.

B exchanges one nucleotide for another.

C does not affect the resulting protein.

D occurs in a regulatory DNA sequence.

Answers: 1b, 2c

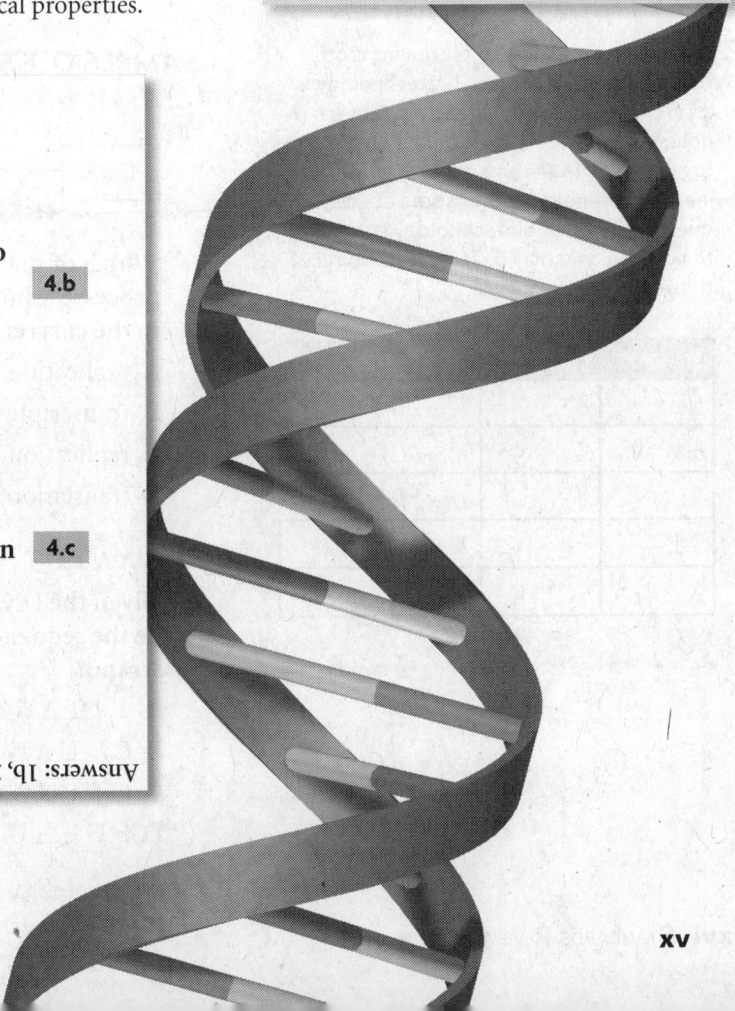

Genetics (Biotechnology)

5 The genetic composition of cells can be altered by incorporation of exogenous DNA into the cells. As a basis for understanding this concept:

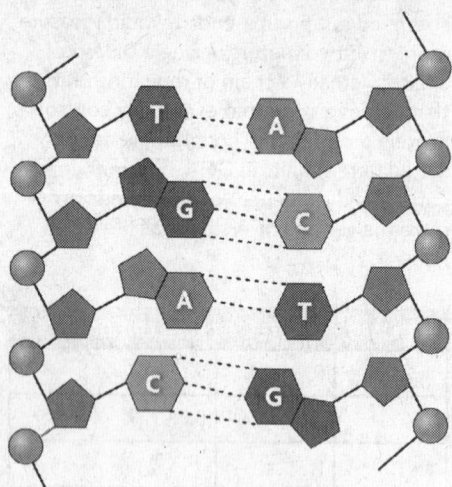

5.a *Students know* the general structures and functions of DNA, RNA, and protein.

5.b *Students know* how to apply base-pairing rules to explain precise copying of DNA during semiconservative replication and transcription of information from DNA into mRNA.

5.c *Students know* how genetic engineering (biotechnology) is used to produce novel biomedical and agricultural products.

5.d* *Students know* how basic DNA technology (restriction digestion by endonucleases, gel electrophoresis, ligation, and transformation) is used to construct recombinant DNA molecules.

5.e* *Students know* how exogenous DNA can be inserted into bacterial cells to alter their genetic makeup and support expression of new protein products.

WHAT IT MEANS TO YOU

From studying cancer to producing crops that are resistant to frost, biotechnology is an important part of our society. Biotechnology allows new genes to be added to an organism's DNA. As you can probably imagine, this technology poses some ethical questions. And as biotechnology continues to advance, you may be faced with some of these questions yourself.

STANDARD	CHAPTERS	PUPIL EDITION
5.a	8	226–233, 239–242
5.b	8	235–242
5.c	9	275–279
5.d*	9	264–267, 275–279
5.e*	9	275–279

SAMPLE QUESTIONS

1.

DNA →(1)→ (2) → RNA →(3)→ proteins

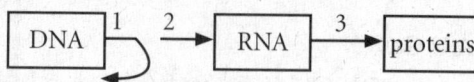

Which of the following identifies the processes shown in the flowchart above in the correct order?　　**5.a**

A replication, transcription, translation

B transcription, translation, replication

C replication, translation, transcription

D translation, replication, transcription

2. G A A T C T

Given the DNA sequence shown here, what would be the sequence of the complementary mRNA strand?　　**5.b**

A CTTAGA

B CUUAGA

C CTTUGU

D CUUAUA

Answers: 1a, 2b

Ecology

6 Stability in an ecosystem is a balance between competing effects. As a basis for understanding this concept:

6.a *Students know* biodiversity is the sum total of different kinds of organisms and is affected by alterations of habitats.

6.b *Students know* how to analyze changes in an ecosystem resulting from changes in climate, human activity, introduction of nonnative species, or changes in population size.

6.c *Students know* how fluctuations in population size in an ecosystem are determined by the relative rates of birth, immigration, emigration, and death.

6.d *Students know* how water, carbon, and nitrogen cycle between abiotic resources and organic matter in the ecosystem and how oxygen cycles through photosynthesis and respiration.

6.e *Students know* a vital part of an ecosystem is the stability of its producers and decomposers.

6.f *Students know* at each link in a food web some energy is stored in newly made structures but much energy is dissipated into the environment as heat. This dissipation may be represented in an energy pyramid.

6.g* *Students know* how to distinguish between the accommodation of an individual organism to its environment and the gradual adaptation of a lineage of organisms through genetic change.

WHAT IT MEANS TO YOU

You are part of an ecosystem, which includes all of the living and nonliving things in an area. Ecology is the study of interactions among these living and nonliving things. Most of your daily actions have some kind of effect on the ecosystems in which you live and those you visit. Some actions can even affect ecosystems on a global scale.

STANDARD	CHAPTERS	PUPIL EDITION
6.a	13	402–404
6.b	16	484–496
6.c	14	440–444
6.d	13	412–416
6.e	13	406–407, 408–411
6.f	13	408–411, 417–419
6.g*	10	298–301

SAMPLE QUESTION

1. Kudzu is a vine that was introduced to the United States from Japan in 1876 to help control erosion. It grew so quickly that it was declared a weed in 1972. Kudzu destroys forests by smothering trees and preventing access to sunlight. In this scenario, kudzu is *best* defined as a   **6.b**

   A predatory species.

   B emigrating species.

   C symbiotic species.

   D nonnative species.

   Answer: 1d

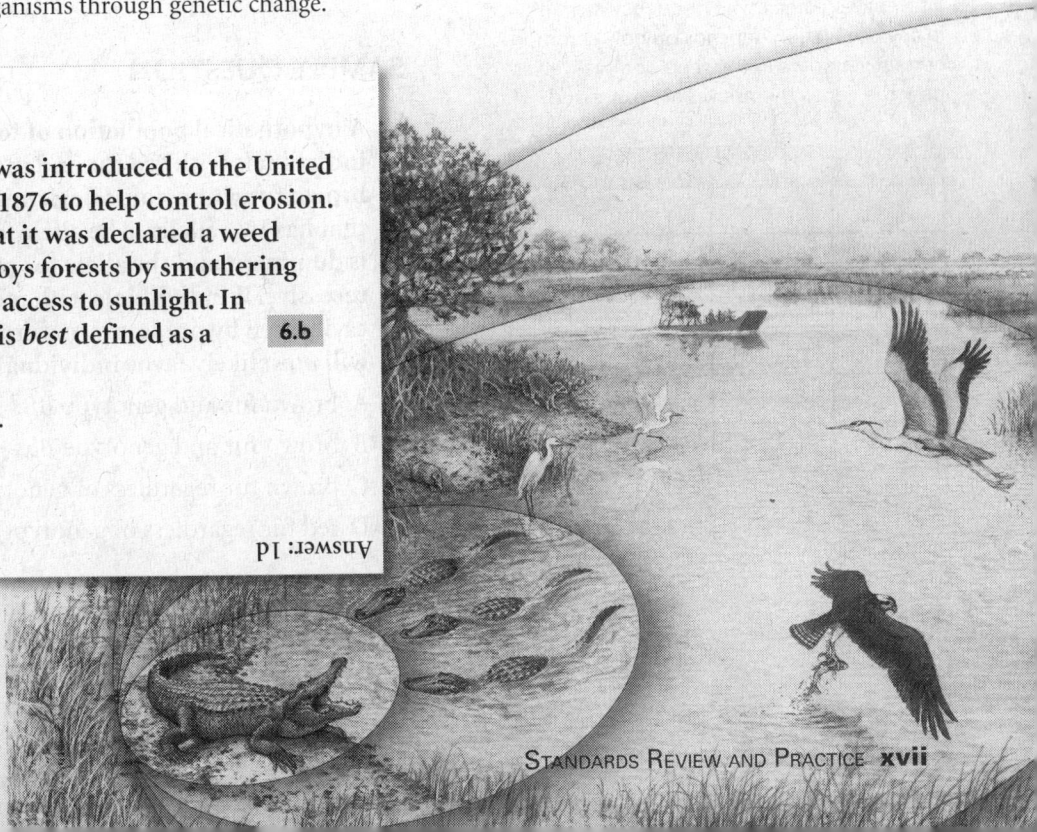

Evolution (Population Genetics)

7 **The frequency of an allele in a gene pool of a population depends on many factors and may be stable or unstable over time. As a basis for understanding this concept:**

7.a *Students know* why natural selection acts on the phenotype rather than the genotype of an organism.

7.b *Students know* why alleles that are lethal in a homozygous individual may be carried in a heterozygote and thus maintained in a gene pool.

7.c *Students know* new mutations are constantly being generated in a gene pool.

7.d *Students know* variation within a species increases the likelihood that at least some members of a species will survive under changed environmental conditions.

7.e* *Students know* the conditions for Hardy-Weinberg equilibrium in a population and why these conditions are not likely to appear in nature.

7.f* *Students know* how to solve the Hardy-Weinberg equation to predict the frequency of genotypes in a population, given the frequency of phenotypes.

WHAT IT MEANS TO YOU

Some traits are common among individuals, while others are quite rare. If you look around your classroom, you may notice many students with dark eyes. Perhaps only a few have red hair. The frequency of traits in any population depends on how common certain genes are in the gene pool, as well as how the genes themselves are expressed.

STANDARD	CHAPTERS	PUPIL EDITION
7.a	10	304–309
7.b	7, 11	200–203, 335–338
7.c	11	328–329
7.d	10, 11	304–309, 328–329
7.e*	11	340–343
7.f*	11	340–343

SAMPLE QUESTION

1. A hypothetical population of foxes includes individuals with red fur and individuals with brown fur. Fur color is determined by one gene that has two alleles. The allele for brown fur (*B*) is dominant and the allele for red fur (*b*) is recessive. If individuals with red fur are more easily seen by predators, natural selection will *most* likely favor individuals with   **7.a**

   A brown fur and genotype *BB*.

   B brown fur and genotype *Bb*.

   C brown fur regardless of genotype.

   D red fur regardless of genotype.

   Answer: 1c

Evolution (Speciation)

8 Evolution is the result of genetic changes that occur in constantly changing environments. As a basis for understanding this concept:

8.a *Students know* how natural selection determines the differential survival of groups of organisms.

8.b *Students know* a great diversity of species increases the chance that at least some organisms survive major changes in the environment.

8.c *Students know* the effects of genetic drift on the diversity of organisms in a population.

8.d *Students know* reproductive or geographic isolation affects speciation.

8.e *Students know* how to analyze fossil evidence with regard to biological diversity, episodic speciation, and mass extinction.

8.f* *Students know* how to use comparative embryology, DNA or protein sequence comparisons, and other independent sources of data to create a branching diagram (cladogram) that shows probable evolutionary relationships.

8.g* *Students know* how several independent molecular clocks, calibrated against each other and combined with evidence from the fossil record, can help to estimate how long ago various groups of organisms diverged evolutionarily from one another.

WHAT IT MEANS TO YOU

All of the organisms in your environment have adaptations that arose through natural selection. The wings of birds, the compound eyes of ants, and the shapes of leaves are all traits that are advantageous in certain environments. As traits such as these are selected for, and others are selected against, the genetic make-up of species changes over time.

STANDARD	CHAPTERS	PUPIL EDITION
8.a	10, 11	304–309, 330–333
8.b	12	376–378
8.c	11	335–338
8.d	11	344–346
8.e	11, 12	347–351, 365–367, 379–383
8.f*	17	524–528
8.g*	17	530–532

SAMPLE QUESTIONS

1. After the mass extinction that ended the Cretaceous period 65 million years ago, flowering plants radiated and became the dominant plant type on Earth's landmasses. Flowering plants that survived the mass extinction *probably* **8.a**

A were outcompeted by seedless plants.

B inherited advantageous traits.

C suffered increased predation.

D produced toxins that kept dinosaurs away.

2. Two populations of a particular bat species exist in separate caves on an island. Over many generations, these populations diverge into two distinct species. Which of the following *best* explains how this speciation event could have happened? **8.d**

A The populations became isolated after the main entrance to one of the caves became blocked.

B Gene flow between the two populations increased through immigration and emigration.

C Natural selection favors bats with thicker fur.

D Individuals from both populations began to eat a new type of fruit.

Answers: 1b, 2a

STANDARD	CHAPTERS	PUPIL EDITION
9.a	30, 32	910–931, 982–984
9.b	29	874–875, 885–894
9.c	29	891–901
9.d	29	876–879
9.e	29	876–890
9.f*	32	977–980
9.g*	32	986–991
9.h*	33	1006–1011
9.i*	29	896–901

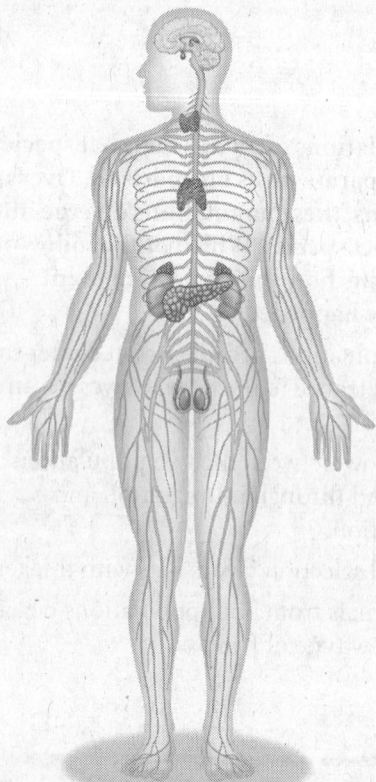

CALIFORNIA STANDARD SET 9

Physiology (Homeostasis)

9 As a result of the coordinated structures and functions of organ systems, the internal environment of the human body remains relatively stable (homeostatic) despite changes in the outside environment. As a basis for understanding this concept:

9.a *Students know* how the complementary activity of major body systems provides cells with oxygen and nutrients and removes toxic waste products such as carbon dioxide.

9.b *Students know* how the nervous system mediates communication between different parts of the body and the body's interactions with the environment.

9.c *Students know* how feedback loops in the nervous and endocrine systems regulate conditions in the body.

9.d *Students know* the functions of the nervous system and the role of neurons in transmitting electrochemical impulses.

9.e *Students know* the roles of sensory neurons, interneurons, and motor neurons in sensation, thought, and response.

9.f* *Students know* the individual functions and sites of secretion of digestive enzymes (amylases, proteases, nucleases, lipases), stomach acid, and bile salts.

9.g* *Students know* the homeostatic role of the kidneys in the removal of nitrogenous wastes and the role of the liver in blood detoxification and glucose balance.

9.h* *Students know* the cellular and molecular basis of muscle contraction, including the roles of actin, myosin, Ca^{2+}, and ATP.

9.i* *Students know* how hormones (including digestive, reproductive, osmoregulatory) provide internal feedback mechanisms for homeostasis at the cellular level and in whole organisms.

SAMPLE QUESTION

1. When a neuron is stimulated, an action potential moves down the axon of the neuron. But before the action potential can move to the next neuron, it must change from a(n)   **9.d**

   A magnetic impulse to an chemical signal.

   B chemical signal to an magnetic impulse.

   C electrical impulse to a magnetic impulse.

   D electrical impulse to a chemical signal.

Answer: 1d

Physiology (Infection and Immunity)

10 Organisms have a variety of mechanisms to combat disease. As a basis for understanding the human immune response:

10.a *Students know* the role of the skin in providing nonspecific defenses against infection.

10.b *Students know* the role of antibodies in the body's response to infection.

10.c *Students know* how vaccination protects an individual from infectious diseases.

10.d *Students know* there are important differences between bacteria and viruses with respect to their requirements for growth and replication, the body's primary defenses against bacterial and viral infections, and effective treatments of these infections.

10.e *Students know* why an individual with a compromised immune system (for example, a person with AIDS) may be unable to fight off and survive infections by microorganisms that are usually benign.

10.f* *Students know* the roles of phagocytes, B-lymphocytes, and T-lymphocytes in the immune system.

WHAT IT MEANS TO YOU

Your body has a variety of ways to fight off illnesses and infections. Your skin acts as a physical barrier to many types of microorganisms. If they do find their way into your body, specialized white blood cells produce antibodies. When you receive a vaccination, weakened microorganisms are injected into your bloodstream, which triggers your body to produce the appropriate antibodies.

STANDARD	CHAPTERS	PUPIL EDITION
10.a	31, 33	945–954, 1013–1015
10.b	31	945–954
10.c	18, 31	552–554, 955–956
10.d	18	563–565
10.e	31	960–963
10.f*	31	945–954

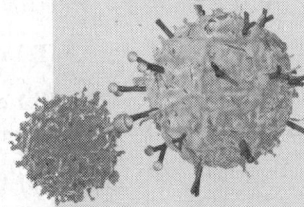

SAMPLE QUESTION

1. Your body has several lines of defense to protect you against pathogens. The skin provides protection in all of the following ways *except*
   10.a

   A acting as a physical barrier to pathogens by surrounding your body.

   B secreting oils and sweat that most pathogens cannot tolerate.

   C having openings lined with mucous membranes that help to trap pathogens.

   D releasing pathogen-specific hormones that help to fight off infection.

2. Children are generally vaccinated with the MMR vaccine around the age of one year. This vaccine is an immunization against measles, mumps, and rubella. Vaccinated individuals are protected against these diseases because the vaccine **10.c**

   A kills all living bacteria as well as viruses.

   B stimulates the immune system to produce antibodies.

   C prevents viruses from replicating in the body.

   D contains weak viruses that kill the stronger ones.

Answers: 1d, 2b

Investigation and Experimentation

IE.1 **Scientific progress is made by asking meaningful questions and conducting careful investigations. As a basis for understanding this concept and addressing the content in the other four strands, students should develop their own questions and perform investigations. Students will:**

IE.1.a Select and use appropriate tools and technology (such as computer-linked probes, spreadsheets, and graphing calculators) to perform tests, collect data, analyze relationships, and display data.

IE.1.b Identify and communicate sources of unavoidable experimental error.

IE.1.c Identify possible reasons for inconsistent results, such as sources of error or uncontrolled conditions.

IE.1.d Formulate explanations by using logic and evidence.

IE.1.e Solve scientific problems by using quadratic equations and simple trigonometric, exponential, and logarithmic functions.

IE.1.f Distinguish between hypothesis and theory as scientific terms.

IE.1.g Recognize the usefulness and limitations of models and theories as scientific representations of reality.

IE.1.h Read and interpret topographic and geologic maps.

IE.1.i Analyze the locations, sequences, or time intervals that are characteristic of natural phenomena (e.g., relative ages of rocks, locations of planets over time, and succession of species in an ecosystem).

IE.1.j Recognize the issues of statistical variability and the need for controlled tests.

IE.1.k Recognize the cumulative nature of scientific evidence.

IE.1.l Analyze situations and solve problems that require combining and applying concepts from more than one area of science.

IE.1.m Investigate a science-based societal issue by researching the literature, analyzing data, and communicating the findings. Examples of issues include irradiation of food, cloning of animals by somatic cell nuclear transfer, choice of energy sources, and land and water use decisions in California.

IE.1.n Know that when an observation does not agree with an accepted scientific theory, the observation is sometimes mistaken or fraudulent (e.g., the Piltdown Man fossil or unidentified flying objects) and that the theory is sometimes wrong (e.g., the Ptolemaic model of the movement of the Sun, Moon, and planets).

WHAT IT MEANS TO YOU

Learning how to think scientifically can help you in many aspects of your life. At some point, you'll likely want to read a scientific report to decide whether a certain product is safe or to help form an opinion about an issue during an election year. Understanding how to read scientific data and being familiar with scientific processes can help you to make informed decisions.

SAMPLE QUESTIONS

1. Scientists are studying how paramecia respond to different wavelengths of light. Which of the following sources of experimental error is *most* likely unavoidable? **IE.1.b**

   A genetic differences among the paramecia

   B using paramecia of several different species

   C conducting only one trial for each wavelength tested

   D changing temperature in the laboratory

2.

Set-up for Fertilizer Experiment		
Group	Number of Beans	Amount of Fertilizer
1	25	10 g
2	25	50 g
3	25	100 g
4	25	200 g

   A group of students decides to test the effects of a certain fertilizer on the growth of bean plants. The set-up of their experiment is shown above. Which of the following represents a flaw in their experimental design? **IE.1.c**

   A They used the same number of beans in each group.

   B Too much fertilizer was added to test group 4.

   C Too little fertilizer was added to test group 1.

   D There was no control group receiving no fertilizer.

3. A student wonders about how soil pH affects plant growth. She thinks that plants will probably grow the best in soil with a neutral pH. To find out if she is correct, she runs an experiment using three treatment groups: one with an acidic pH of 3, one with a neutral pH of 7, and one with a basic pH of 11. Her initial idea that plants will grow best in soil with a neutral pH *most closely* resembles a scientific **IE.1.f**

   A theory.

   B hypothesis.

   C conclusion.

   D law.

4.

   This diagram represents layers of rock at an excavation site. Paleontologists found a large fossil in layer A and a smaller fossil in layer C. Before performing radiometric dating on the fossils, the scientists are fairly certain of which fossil is the oldest. Which of the following statements *probably* describes the logic of these paleontologists? **IE.1.i**

   A The fossil in layer A is the oldest because it is the largest in size.

   B The fossil in layer A is the oldest because it was found in the uppermost layer of rock.

   C The fossil in layer C is the oldest because it is the smallest in size.

   D The fossil in layer C is the oldest because it was found in the deepest layer of rock.

5. Scientists are testing the effectiveness of a certain vaccine in preventing a viral infection in laboratory mice. The mice are randomly divided into two groups. One group is injected with the vaccine, and the other group is injected with water. What is the reason for injecting half of the mice with water? **IE.1.j**

   A to serve as a control group that the vaccinated mice can be compared against

   B to do something with them because the scientists did not make enough vaccine

   C to find out whether extra water could prevent the viral infection

   D to be used as the independent variable in the experimental design

Answers: 1a, 2d, 3b, 4d, 5a

Life Science Standards

The biology you learn in high school builds on the life science you have learned earlier. These Life Science standards will be assessed on the California Life Science Standards Test.

CELL BIOLOGY

7.1.c *Students know* the nucleus is the repository for genetic information in plant and animal cells.

7.1.d *Students know* that mitochondria liberate energy for the work that cells do and that chloroplasts capture sunlight energy for photosynthesis.

7.1.e *Students know* cells divide to increase their numbers through a process of mitosis, which results in two daughter cells with identical sets of chromosomes.

8.6.b *Students know* that living organisms are made of molecules consisting largely of carbon, hydrogen, nitrogen, oxygen, phosphorus, and sulfur.

8.6.c *Students know* that living organisms have many different kinds of molecules, including small ones, such as water and salt, and very large ones, such as carbohydrates, fats, proteins, and DNA.

GENETICS

7.2.a *Students know* the differences between the life cycles and reproduction methods of sexual and asexual organisms.

7.2.c *Students know* an inherited trait can be determined by one or more genes.

7.2.d *Students know* plant and animal cells contain many thousands of different genes and typically have two copies of every gene. The two copies (or alleles) of the gene may or may not be identical, and one may be dominant in determining the phenotype while the other is recessive.

7.2.e *Students know* DNA (deoxyribonucleic acid) is the genetic material of living organisms and is located in the chromosomes of each cell.

ECOLOGY

6.5.b *Students know* matter is transferred over time from one organism to others in the food web and between organisms and the physical environment.

6.5.c *Students know* populations of organisms can be categorized by the functions they serve in an ecosystem.

6.5.e *Students know* the number and types of organisms an ecosystem can support depends on the resources available and on abiotic factors, such as quantities of light and water, a range of temperatures, and soil composition.

EVOLUTION

7.3.a *Students know* both genetic variation and environmental factors are causes of evolution and diversity of organisms.

7.3.b *Students know* the reasoning used by Charles Darwin in reaching his conclusion that natural selection is the mechanism of evolution.

7.3.c *Students know* how independent lines of evidence from geology, fossils, and comparative anatomy provide the bases for the theory of evolution.

PHYSIOLOGY

7.5.a *Students know* plants and animals have levels of organization for structure and function, including cells, tissues, organs, organ systems, and the whole organism.

7.5.c *Students know* how bones and muscles work together to provide a structural framework for movement.

7.6.j *Students know* that contractions of the heart generate blood pressure and that heart valves prevent backflow of blood in the circulatory system.

INVESTIGATION AND EXPERIMENTATION

IE.6.7.c Construct appropriate graphs from data and develop qualitative statements about the relationships between variables.

IE.6.7.e Recognize whether evidence is consistent with a proposed explanation.

IE.7.7.c Communicate the logical connection among hypotheses, science concepts, tests conducted, data collected, and conclusions drawn from the scientific evidence.

IE.8.9.b Evaluate the accuracy and reproducibility of data.

IE.8.9.c Distinguish between variable and controlled parameters in a test.

Introduction to Biology Content Standards

The first section of this workbook focuses on the California science content standards for biology. Each standard has two pages devoted to it. The first page is a Review Page. This page will state the standard, and provide more details about the concepts covered in the standard. After reading the Review Page, you will be able to move on to the second page, a Practice Page. The Practice Page will have five multiple choice items that are related to the standard you just read about. This Practice Page will help you to determine whether you understand the content covered by the standard.

The pages are grouped by standard set. There are 10 standard sets that deal with content:
- Cell Biology
- Genetics (Meiosis and Fertilization)
- Genetics (Mendel's Laws)
- Genetics (Molecular Biology)
- Genetics (Biotechnology)
- Ecology
- Evolution (Population Genetics)
- Evolution (Speciation)
- Physiology (Homeostasis)
- Physiology (Infection and Immunity)

REVIEW

CALIFORNIA CONTENT
STANDARD 1.a

Cell Membranes

STANDARD Students know cells are enclosed within semipermeable membranes that regulate their interaction with their surroundings.

Read the summary and answer the questions on the next page.

Living cells depend on chemical reactions to carry out life processes. Therefore, cells must be able to regulate which molecules can enter and leave. The cell membrane allows the cell to control the movement of molecules into and out of the cell.

Membrane Structure

Cell membranes are composed of lipid molecules. Each molecule, called a phospholipid, has a polar, or charged, head and two nonpolar, or uncharged, tails. The phospholipids are arranged in layers that are two molecules thick. The polar heads are like the bread of a sandwich, facing either toward the environment or the cytoplasm. The two nonpolar tails make up the interior of the membrane, or what is between the "bread." Because the membrane is two molecules thick it is referred to as a **phospholipid bilayer.**

Embedded between the lipid molecules are proteins. These molecules move around the membrane like a ball floating in a pool of water. Because the arrangement of molecules is always moving and changing, the structure of the membrane is sometimes called a **fluid mosaic model.** The phospholipids and proteins prevent some molecules from entering or leaving the cell, which means the membrane is semipermeable. A **semipermeable membrane** is one that allows only some materials to enter or leave the cell.

Regulating Passage

There are three ways by which molecules can enter or leave a cell.

- **Diffusion** is the movement of molecules from an area of higher concentration to an area of lower concentration. Small molecules, such as oxygen and carbon dioxide gases, can pass between the lipid molecules and diffuse into or out of a cell.
- **Facilitated diffusion** is the movement of molecules from high concentration to low concentration, but, instead of diffusing between membrane lipids, the molecules pass through a protein embedded in the membrane. Facilitated diffusion is necessary for molecules that are too large to pass between phospholipids. These large molecules must go through a protein in the cell membrane to enter or leave the cell.
- **Active transport** is the movement of materials across a cell membrane that requires energy. As in facilitated diffusion, molecules pass through a membrane protein. However, this process requires energy because the cell moves the molecules from an area of lower concentration to an area of higher concentration, which is opposite to the direction of diffusion.

PRACTICE

CALIFORNIA CONTENT
STANDARD 1.a

Cell Membranes

DIRECTIONS: Choose the letter of the *best* answer.

1

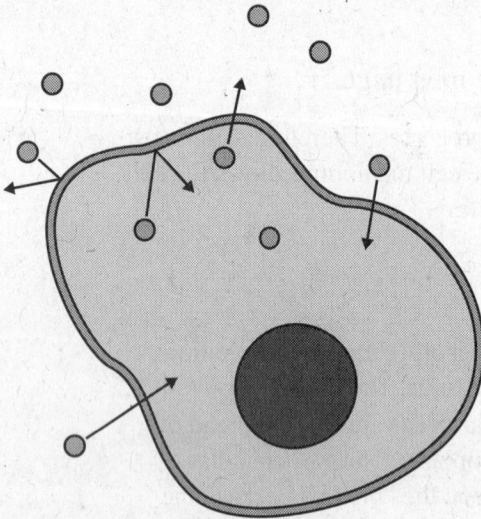

In the diagram above, some
molecules move across the cell
membrane, but other molecules
cannot cross the membrane. Some
molecules can cross, but others
cannot because the

A cell is alive.

B molecules are polar.

C membrane is semipermeable.

D cytoplasm is salty.

2 All cells are surrounded by
membranes. The *main* role of the
cell membrane is to

A regulate the cell's interactions with the
environment.

B release any type of molecule out of
the cell.

C arrange the cell's organelles in the
cytoplasm.

D prevent water from leaking out of the
cell.

3 What type of molecule embedded
in the cell membrane allows larger
molecules to pass through the
membrane by active transport?

A phospholipids

B proteins

C ATP

D carbohydrates

4 Osmosis is the movement of
water across a cell membrane. In
osmosis, water molecules move
between phospholipids and
toward areas that have a lower
concentration of water molecules.
Osmosis is a type of

A diffusion.

B facilitated diffusion.

C active transport.

D fluid mosaic model.

5 Some molecules embedded in
the cell membrane allow large
particles to enter or leave the cell.
If the embedded molecule does
not require energy to move a
particle across the membrane, it is
taking part in

A diffusion.

B facilitated diffusion.

C active transport.

D random movement.

REVIEW

CALIFORNIA CONTENT STANDARD 1.b

Enzymes

STANDARD Students know enzymes are proteins that catalyze biochemical reactions without altering the reaction equilibrium and the activities of enzymes depend on the temperature, ionic conditions, and the pH of the surroundings.

Read the summary and answer the questions on the next page.

Enzymes are proteins that reduce the amount of energy needed to start biochemical reactions within living cells, but enzymes are not used up in the process. Because enzymes depend on their physical structures to work properly, they require specific temperatures, ionic conditions, and pH.

What are Enzymes?

Each time a cell repairs DNA, breaks down sugar molecules to release energy, or builds proteins, enzymes are involved. **Enzymes** are proteins made by cells that act as catalysts in biochemical reactions. Biochemical reactions can build, split, or transform molecules, such as in the examples listed above, and they always involve changes in energy. Enzymes speed up chemical reactions by reducing the required activation energy, which is the amount of energy needed to start the reaction. Although enzymes participate in chemical reactions, they are not consumed in the process. Enzymes remain intact after the reaction is complete. Enzymes do not affect the reaction equilibrium, which means they do not change the direction of the reaction.

Enzyme Function

Enzymes have specific structures that help align certain reactants for a reaction to take place. The lock-and-key model illustrates this idea. Just as a key fits into a lock, a reactant fits into an enzyme. The three-dimensional structure of an enzyme is crucial to its function. If the enzyme's structure changes, the reactants will not be able fit, and the enzyme will not be able to speed up the chemical reaction.

Different environmental conditions can alter an enzyme's structure. These conditions include:

- **Temperature.** Enzymes usually work within a small range of temperatures, near the organism's normal body temperature.
- **Ionic Conditions.** Enzymes can stop functioning if they are exposed to inappropriate concentrations or types of salts.
- **pH.** Many enzymes function best at a nearly neutral pH. Some, however, such as digestive enzymes in the stomach, work best under acidic conditions.

STANDARD SET 1

PRACTICE

CALIFORNIA CONTENT
STANDARD 1.b

Enzymes

DIRECTIONS: Choose the letter of the *best* answer.

1 Proteins that reduce the amount of energy needed to start a chemical reaction are called

  A reactants.

  B ions.

  C sugars.

  D enzymes.

2 After the enzyme amylase breaks down a starch molecule, it can

  A not be reused.

  B break down more starch molecules.

  C change its shape to adapt to a different reactant.

  D alter equilibrium conditions.

3 Enzymes depend on their structure to function properly. Which of the following does *not* alter an enzyme's structure?

  A temperature

  B pH

  C concentration of reactants

  D ionic conditions

4

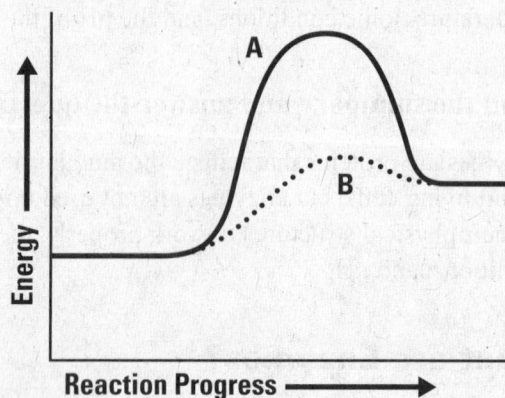

In the graph, which reaction is catalyzed by an enzyme?

  A A

  B B

  C both A and B

  D neither A nor B

5 In an experiment you find that high temperatures reduce enzyme activity. This result is most likely due to the effect of high temperatures on the

  A structure of the enzyme.

  B pH of the environment.

  C function of the reactants.

  D amount of activation energy required.

REVIEW

CALIFORNIA CONTENT STANDARD 1.c

Cell Types

STANDARD Students know how prokaryotic cells, eukaryotic cells (including those from plants and animals), and viruses differ in complexity and general structure.

Read the summary and answer the questions on the next page.

Based on their structures, all living cells can be categorized into two groups: prokaryotes and eukaryotes. Prokaryotes have no membrane-bound organelles. Eukaryotes have complex internal structures with membrane-bound organelles. In contrast, viruses are not living cells, but they do contain genetic material.

Prokaryotes and Eukaryotes

Prokaryotic cells are living cells that have proteins, ribosomes, DNA, and other molecules that float freely in the cells' cytoplasm. Although all prokaryotes have cell membranes, some also have cell walls. Common bacteria, such as disease-causing *E. coli* and salmonella, are prokaryotes. Other types of prokaryotes can live in diverse environments, including 76.7°C $(170^\circ$F) water, the guts of termites, and sewage!

Plants, animals, fungi, and other organisms are examples of eukaryotes. **Eukaryotic cells** are generally more complex than prokaryotes. Some eukaryotes are single-celled organisms, whereas others are multicellular. Eukaryotes have membrane-bound **organelles** within their cytoplasm. These organelles carry out specialized functions and chemical reactions within the cell. The nucleus is an organelle that stores DNA. Other organelles found in eukaryotes include mitochondria, which release energy from food molecules through cellular respiration, and lysosomes, which digest large molecules. Not all eukaryotic cells have identical organelles. Plant cells, for example, can contain chloroplasts, organelles in which photosynthesis takes place. Plant cells also have cell walls.

Viruses

Viruses, such as HIV and the chicken pox virus, are not cells. They are tiny particles that contain genetic material, either DNA or RNA, and are covered by a protein coat. Viruses are not considered to be alive because they cannot perform any functions on their own. For example, viruses do not have any organelles, and they cannot use energy to build proteins. Unlike eukaryotic and prokaryotic cells, which can undergo cell division, viruses cannot reproduce on their own. A virus must infect another cell in order to reproduce. The virus injects its genetic material into a cell and forces the cell to produce new viruses.

STANDARD SET 1

PRACTICE

CALIFORNIA CONTENT
STANDARD 1.c

Cell Types

DIRECTIONS: Choose the letter of the *best* answer.

1

DNA

The diagram above shows a cell that has a cell wall and free-floating DNA. What type of cell is this one *most* likely to be?

A prokaryotic

B eukaryotic

C viral

D animal

2 Eukaryotes and prokaryotes are similar in that they both have

A mitochondria.

B protein coats.

C nuclei.

D cell membranes.

3 In eukaryotes, thousands of chemical reactions are able to take part in separate compartments called

A prokaryotes.

B organelles.

C proteins.

D bacteria.

4 Suppose a team of researchers discovers a new particle, and they want to determine what it is. They perform experiments and find that the particle has no organelles and that the particles will only reproduce in the presence of other cells. The particle is probably a(n)

A animal cell.

B plant cell.

C virus.

D bacterial cell.

5 If you are looking at cells under a powerful microscope, what is the *best* way for you to tell the difference between prokaryotic cells and eukaryotic cells?

A Prokaryotic cells will always have cell walls, but eukaryotic cells will not.

B Prokaryotic cells will never have a cell membrane, but eukaryotic cells will.

C Prokaryotic cells will have either RNA or DNA, but eukaryotic cells will have both.

D Prokaryotic cells will not have membrane-bound organelles, but eukaryotic cells will.

REVIEW

CALIFORNIA CONTENT
STANDARD 1.d

Molecular Biology

STANDARD Students know the central dogma of molecular biology outlines the flow of information from transcription of ribonucleic acid (RNA) in the nucleus to translation of proteins on ribosomes in the cytoplasm.

Read the summary and answer the questions on the next page.

Living cells need to produce proteins to carry out different functions. Cells can produce proteins by using RNA to transcribe and translate the cells' DNA.

DNA and RNA

DNA, deoxyribonucleic acid, is the genetic material that contains the information necessary to produce proteins. DNA is made up of two long chains of molecules called nucleotides. The two chains are arranged so that the entire DNA molecule looks like a twisted ladder, as you can see in the diagram to the right. In plant and animal cells, DNA is found in the cell's nucleus.

Although DNA is found in the nucleus, a cell can only produce proteins in its cytoplasm. This means that the information stored in DNA must get out of the nucleus. But DNA itself cannot leave the nucleus. So a cell uses RNA. **RNA** is similar to DNA in that it is made up of nucleotides. However, unlike DNA, RNA is a single strand, and RNA can move out of the nucleus.

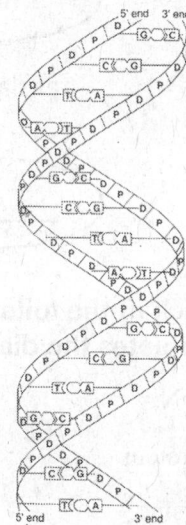

Transcription and Translation

In order to produce proteins, the information in DNA must get out of the nucleus and into the cytoplasm. For this to happen, RNA must get the information from the DNA. **Transcription** is the process of transferring information from DNA to RNA. In eukaryotes, transcription occurs in the nucleus. During transcription, enzymes separate the strands of DNA. The sequence of nucleotides from one DNA strand is transcribed onto a new RNA molecule. Then the single-stranded RNA molecule moves into the cytoplasm. Once in the cytoplasm, the RNA molecule is used to build proteins. The RNA moves to a tiny structure called a ribosome. The ribosome allows the cell to decode the RNA molecule and build proteins, a process called **translation.**

A set of three nucleotides in RNA is called a codon and corresponds to one of 20 molecules known as amino acids. The ribosome "reads" each group of three nucleotides and builds a chain of amino acids. The completed chain of amino acids is a protein. Although there are only 20 different amino acids used to build proteins, they can be assembled into thousands of different proteins.

PRACTICE

CALIFORNIA CONTENT
STANDARD 1.d

Molecular Biology

DIRECTIONS: Choose the letter of the *best* answer.

1

DNA

↓ transcribed by

RNA

↓ translated into

?

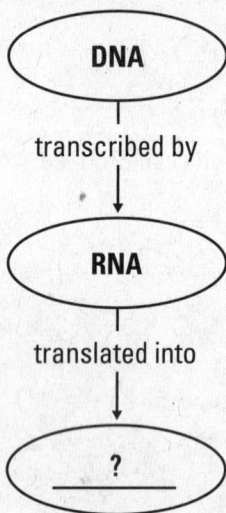

Which of the following terms *best* completes the diagram above?

A DNA

B protein

C lysine

D ribosome

2 **What is an important role of RNA during transcription?**

A to take DNA's information out of the nucleus

B to allow DNA to replicate itself

C to make DNA into a protein

D to stimulate DNA to produce amino acids

3 **DNA and RNA are both made up of nucleotides. However, the two are different because in eukaryotes DNA is found in the**

A ribosome.

B nucleus.

C cytoplasm.

D amino acid.

4 **During protein synthesis, information from DNA is transcribed into RNA. Once the RNA is in the cytoplasm, it goes to a ribosome. What is the role of the ribosome?**

A to put amino acids in the proper sequence for a protein.

B to build a copy of the original DNA strand.

C to gather the information to build more ribosomes.

D to produce a long chain of carbohydrates.

5 **Because proteins have different numbers and sequences of amino acids, cells can**

A change the properties of individual amino acids.

B build many different proteins from a limited set of amino acids.

C build identical proteins using different methods.

D transcribe information from RNA to DNA.

REVIEW

CALIFORNIA CONTENT STANDARD 1.e

Protein Secretion

STANDARD Students know the role of the endoplasmic reticulum and Golgi apparatus in the secretion of proteins.

Read the summary and answer the questions on the next page.

Living cells build proteins that carry out specific functions. But in order for those proteins to be useful, they must be modified and sent to the appropriate destination, either inside or outside of the cell. The endoplasmic reticulum and the Golgi apparatus are organelles that get proteins ready to go to their proper destinations.

Endoplasmic Reticulum

The **endoplasmic reticulum,** also called ER, is an organelle that is made up of folded membranes. There are two types of ER: rough and smooth. Both types help the cell produce finished proteins. Rough ER is a type of ER that has ribosomes along its edges. During translation, RNA enters ribosomes on rough ER. These ribosomes build a chain of amino acids. The ER takes this chain of amino acids and helps fold it into the shape of a specific protein. The folded protein then travels to the smooth ER, which lacks ribosomes. The smooth ER surrounds the protein, forming a sac-like structure called a vesicle. The vesicle then moves to the Golgi apparatus.

Golgi Apparatus

The **Golgi apparatus,** also called Golgi bodies or Golgi complex, is also a series of folded membranes. The Golgi apparatus acts like a cell's "post office," sorting and packaging molecules. The Golgi apparatus takes the protein from the vesicle. Once inside the Golgi apparatus, a protein might be modified by adding other molecules, such as lipids or carbohydrates. The Golgi apparatus also adds molecules that will direct the protein to its final destination. Like the ER, the Golgi apparatus ships proteins in vesicles.

Finished Proteins

Once the Golgi apparatus finishes the protein, it might travel to another organelle, such as a lysosome. Or it might leave the cell entirely through a process called secretion. For example, the protein insulin is packaged in a vesicle that travels to the cell membrane. The vesicle attaches to the cell membrane, becomes part of the cell membrane, and pushes its insulin contents out of the cell. This last step of secretion is known as exocytosis.

PRACTICE

CALIFORNIA CONTENT
STANDARD 1.e

Protein Secretion

DIRECTIONS: Choose the letter of the *best* answer.

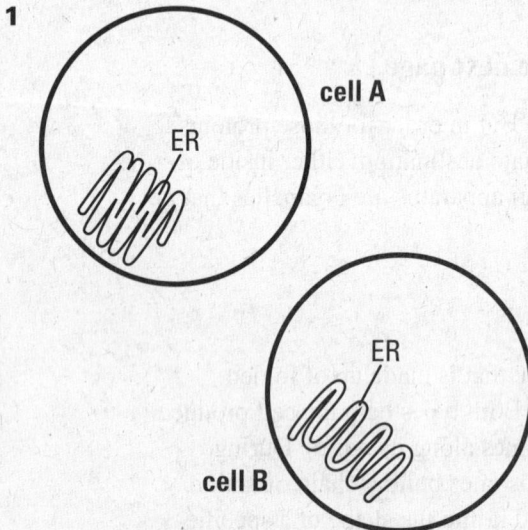

1

cell A

ER

ER

cell B

Cell A illustrates a cell taken from a healthy person. Cell A's endoplasmic reticulum (ER) is normal because the ER's membranes are tightly folded. Cell B is affected by a rare disease, in which the membrane of the ER is not properly formed. What might occur as a result of Cell B's abnormal ER?

A cannot complete mitosis

B disruption of DNA replication

C formation of incorrect proteins

D failure to absorb nutrients

2 Which of the following occurs in the endoplasmic reticulum?

A carbohydrate digestion

B exocytosis

C virus killing

D protein folding

3 There are two types of ER—rough and smooth. What is the *main* difference between the two types of ER?

A the presence of ribosomes

B the presence of a membrane

C the presence of Golgi apparatus

D the presence of mitochondria

4 Insulin is a protein that stimulates cells to remove glucose from the blood. After a person eats, an organ called the pancreas releases the protein into the blood so that glucose will not accumulate in the blood. Which cell structure is *most* directly involved in releasing insulin from cells in the pancreas?

A Golgi apparatus

B mitochondria

C nucleus

D cytoskeleton

5 Sometimes the Golgi apparatus is described as the cell's post office. This is because the Golgi apparatus

A holds molecules for organelles to pick them up.

B facilitates diffusion.

C sorts and packages proteins.

D stores carbohydrates in compartments.

REVIEW

CALIFORNIA CONTENT
STANDARD 1.f

Phototsynthesis

STANDARD Students know usable energy is captured from sunlight by chloroplasts and is stored through the synthesis of sugar from carbon dioxide.

Read the summary and answer the questions on the next page.

Photosynthesis occurs in a series of chemical reactions that use energy from sunlight, water, and carbon dioxide to produce sugars and oxygen. The process takes place in organelles called chloroplasts.

The Purpose of Photosynthesis

Essentially all energy used by organisms on Earth comes from sunlight. But humans and other animals cannot use energy directly from sunlight. **Photosynthesis** allows plants and other chlorophyll-containing organisms to capture energy from sunlight and store it in sugar molecules for future use. Plants use the stored chemical energy of sugars for all of their life functions. Humans and other animals that eat plants or animals that have eaten plants get energy from the sugars produced by photosynthesis.

The Process of Photosynthesis

Photosynthesis takes place through a series of chemical reactions. In general, carbon dioxide, water, and energy from sunlight are used to form sugar and oxygen. The process is summarized in the diagram.

In general,
carbon dioxide + water + light ⟶ sugar + oxygen

However, reactants act in unequal proportions,
$$6CO_2 + 6H_2O \longrightarrow C_6H_{12}O_6 + 6O_2$$

Photosynthesis occurs in two main stages, the light-dependent reactions and light-independent reactions.

Light-dependent reactions

First, a molecule called chlorophyll, which is found inside organelles called **chloroplasts**, absorbs energy from sunlight. The energy is transferred through structures called thylakoids. Water molecules are broken down and oxygen molecules are released. Energy is transferred to the light-independent reactions by energy-carrying molecules, such as ATP.

Light-independent reactions

The next stage of photosynthesis occurs in the chloroplast's liquid, called the stroma. Here, carbon dioxide is used to form a sugar molecule, usually glucose.

STANDARD SET 1

PRACTICE

CALIFORNIA CONTENT
STANDARD 1.f

Phototsynthesis

DIRECTIONS: Choose the letter of the *best* answer.

1

$\boxed{\text{Reactants}}$
(water, carbon dioxide)

go into the
↓

$\boxed{\text{Chloroplast}}$

which forms
↓

$\boxed{\text{Products}}$
(? ?)

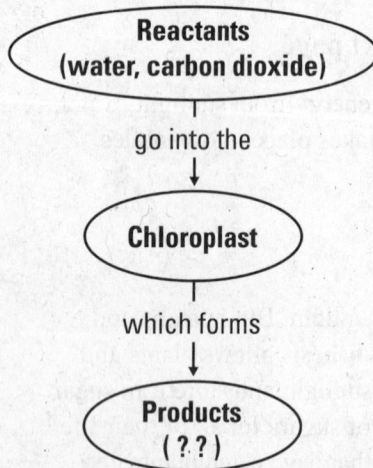

The diagram above illustrates photosynthesis occurring within a chloroplast. What products are formed by photosynthesis?

A carbon dioxide and energy

B water and oxygen

C chlorophyll and carbon dioxide

D sugar and oxygen

2 Plants are called producers because they have chloroplasts that

A release energy from sugars.

B produce heat needed to keep the plant warm.

C use oxygen to make water.

D use energy from sunlight to produce the plant's own food.

3 Which of the following is a true statement about how plants interact with their environment during photosynthesis?

A They release water into the atmosphere.

B They reflect all of the energy in sunlight into the atmosphere.

C They remove carbon dioxide from the atmosphere.

D They take oxygen out of the atmosphere.

4 During photosynthesis, plants use chloroplasts to convert energy in sunlight into a food source that organisms can use. The food source that is produced during photosynthesis is

A glucose.

B protein.

C stroma.

D oxygen.

5 Which of the following *best* describes the function of photosynthesis?

A to convert energy from sunlight into the stored chemical energy of sugar

B to release energy from sugar into the atmosphere

C to produce water for plants to use in photosynthesis

D to dispose of carbon dioxide that builds up by digesting food

REVIEW

CALIFORNIA CONTENT
STANDARD 1.g

Cellular Respiration

STANDARD SET 1

STANDARD Students know the role of the mitochondria in making stored chemical-bond energy available to cells by completing the breakdown of glucose to carbon dioxide.

Read the summary and answer the questions on the next page.

Eukaryotic cells, such as those found in plants, animals, and fungi, use cellular respiration. During cellular respiration, carbon-based molecules are broken down in the mitochondria to release the energy stored in the molecules. Cells use the energy for all of their processes.

The Function of Cellular Respiration

During photosynthesis, energy from sunlight is stored in molecules such as glucose. Cells release the energy stored in glucose to provide the energy needed for all cell functions. To release the energy, cells first break down glucose molecules in the cytoplasm through a process called glycolysis. Cellular respiration, which completes the break down of glucose, occurs in organelles called mitochondria. **Mitochondria** break down carbon-based molecules to release the energy that is stored in their bonds. In general, the more mitochondria found in a cell, the more energy that cell can produce.

The Process of Cellular Respiration

Cellular respiration is a process that uses oxygen to break down carbon-based molecules to release energy when oxygen is available to the cell. Cellular respiration releases usable energy (ATP), water, and carbon dioxide. The process of cellular respiration is described in the diagram below.

During cellular respiration,

sugar + oxygen   ⟶   carbon dioxide + water + energy

The chemical equation for cellular respiration is:

$$C_6H_{12}O_6 + 6O_2 \longrightarrow 6CO_2 + 6H_2O + energy$$

First, cells split glucose into two smaller molecules in the cytoplasm. In the mitochondria, these molecules are broken down further during a series of chemical reactions that releases carbon dioxide. The chemical reactions also produce energy-carrying molecules that are used to produce a large number of ATP molecules in the inner mitochondrial membrane. At the end of cellular respiration, oxygen enters the mitochondria and is used to produce water that is released as a waste product.

STANDARD SET 1

PRACTICE

CALIFORNIA CONTENT STANDARD 1.g

Cellular Respiration

DIRECTIONS: Choose the letter of the *best* answer.

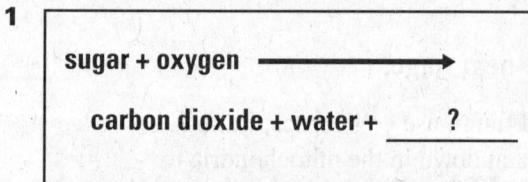

1

sugar + oxygen ⟶

carbon dioxide + water + _____?_____

The diagram above describes the process of cellular respiration. During this process, cells use sugar and oxygen to form carbon dioxide and water, and to produce a usable form of energy. What is the missing product in the equation above?

A mitochondria

B ATP

C sugar

D sunlight

2 Mitochondria are often called the cell's powerhouses because mitochondria

A release energy from sugars.

B pump oxygen around the cell.

C distribute electricity.

D direct the movement of the cell.

3 During cellular respiration, a series of chemical reactions produces which of the following molecules as a waste product?

A proteins

B carbon dioxide

C ATP

D oxygen

4 The heart is a muscle that pumps blood throughout the body. In order to perform its function, the heart requires a lot of energy. Which of the following would the heart need the *most* of in order to get the energy it needs to pump blood throughout the body?

A lysosomes

B mitochondria

C DNA

D endoplasmic reticulum

5 Carbon monoxide is a gas that has one carbon atom bonded with one oxygen atom (CO). When inhaled, carbon monoxide is deadly because it prevents red blood cells from carrying oxygen to other cells in the body. Without oxygen, cells cannot undergo

A cellular respiration.

B photosynthesis.

C DNA replication.

D passive transport.

REVIEW

CALIFORNIA CONTENT
STANDARD 1.h

Macromolecules

STANDARD Students know most macromolecules (polysaccharides, nucleic acids, proteins, lipids) in cells and organisms are synthesized from a small collection of simple precursors.

Read the summary and answer the questions on the next page.

Cells are constantly manufacturing and breaking down very large carbon-based molecules. Many of these large molecules, called macromolecules, are types of polymers. Polymers consist of many smaller molecules, called monomers, that are bonded together.

Macromolecules

All molecules are too small to be seen. But macromolecules are considered large when compared with other, smaller molecules. Many macromolecules, such as polysaccharides, nucleic acids, proteins, and lipids, contain smaller molecules that are bonded together.

As an analogy, consider the beads on a necklace. Each bead is a small unit, resulting in a large product, the necklace. In molecular terms, the beads represent smaller molecules, called **monomers.** The necklace is similar to a long chain of monomers, called a polymer. **Polymers** are molecules that are made of many monomers. Many macromolecules are polymers.

Examples of Macromolecules

There are four kinds of macromolecules that are common in cells.

- **Polysaccharides** are complex carbohydrates, made up of smaller repeating units called monosaccharides. A monosaccharide is a simple sugar, such as glucose. Starches and cellulose are polysaccharides. Cellulose is a straight, rigid molecule that makes up cell walls.
- **Nucleic Acids**, such as DNA and RNA, carry cells' genetic information in sequences of smaller repeating units called nucleotides. Each nucleotide is a monomer, linked together to form the nucleic acid polymer.
- **Proteins** are polymers made up of amino acid monomers. Only 20 amino acids make up all the proteins in our bodies. Different proteins are made of different amino acids in different orders. Different proteins have different functions. Some are enzymes that speed up reactions. Hemoglobin is a protein that carries oxygen in blood cells.
- **Lipids** include fats and oils that can be found in both plants and animals. Many lipids provide long-term energy storage. Many fats and oils contain smaller molecules called fatty acids, which can be either saturated or unsaturated.

PRACTICE

CALIFORNIA CONTENT
STANDARD 1.h

Macromolecules

DIRECTIONS: Choose the letter of the *best* answer.

1

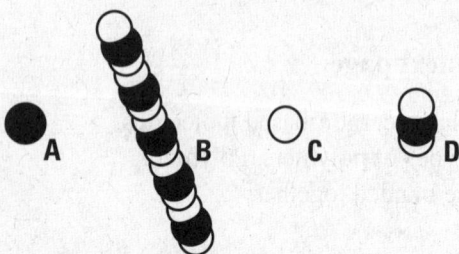

Each of the structures above represents a molecule. Which of the structures *best* represents a polymer or a macromolecule?

A Structure A

B Structure B

C Structure C

D Structure D

2 DNA is the genetic material that codes for a sequence of amino acids. Many amino acids make up a protein. Which is the monomer?

A cellulose

B protein

C amino acid

D DNA

3 Fats and oils are examples of

A lipids.

B proteins.

C nucleic acids.

D carbohydrates.

4 When you eat, enzymes work to break up the polysaccharides in your food into smaller pieces. If the polysaccharide is a polymer, what are the smaller units that are formed?

A proteins

B monosaccharides

C macromolecules

D amino acids

5 Which of the following *best* describes a macromolecule?

A a molecule that is part of a larger molecule

B a molecule that is a repeating subunit

C a molecule that is a much larger version of a polymer

D a molecule that is made up of smaller molecules

REVIEW

CALIFORNIA CONTENT
STANDARD 2.a

Meiosis

STANDARD Students know meiosis is an early step in sexual reproduction in which the pairs of chromosomes separate and segregate randomly during cell division to produce gametes containing one chromosome of each type.

Read the summary and answer the questions on the next page.

Sexually reproducing organisms get half of their DNA from each parent. The parents' DNA is divided in half during a process called meiosis.

Meiosis I

In sexual reproduction, a sperm cell fuses with an egg to create a new organism that is a genetic mixture of both parents. For the new organism to have the correct chromosome number, the egg and sperm cell—the gametes—need only half the usual number of chromosomes. Gametes are produced by **meiosis,** a process that divides a **diploid** cell that has two copies of each chromosome into genetically unique **haploid** cells that have only one copy of each chromosome. Meiosis involves two rounds of cell division, meiosis I and meiosis II.

At the start of meiosis, a diploid cell has already copied its DNA. As a result, each chromosome has two identical copies. These copies are called **sister chromatids,** and they are attached to each other at their center. Sister chromatids remain together throughout meiosis I and separate during meiosis II.

During prophase I, the nuclear membrane starts to break down, and chromosomes condense tightly. Homologous chromosomes pair up together. In metaphase I, these homologous pairs line up randomly along the middle of the cell. Each side of the cell has a mixture of 23 chromosomes, some from the organism's mother and some from the organism's father. In anaphase I, the homologous chromosomes separate from each other and move toward opposite sides of the cell. This random separation mixes up the combinations of chromosomes and helps maintain genetic diversity. Finally, during telophase I, the cell undergoes cytokinesis, forming two daughter cells with a haploid number of chromosomes.

Meiosis II

DNA does not replicate again before the start of meiosis II; however, the chromosomes in both daughter cells are still in their duplicated form. In meiosis II, these chromosomes line up along the middle of the cell, and the sister chromatids are separated from each other. In humans, the end result is a total of four haploid cells, each with a unique combination of 23, unduplicated chromosomes.

In addition to the random separation of chromosomes, a process called crossing over also helps create unique gene combinations during meiosis. **Crossing over** is the exchange of chromosome segments between homologous chromosomes. It takes place during prophase I of meiosis I when homologous chromosomes are paired closely together. Part of one chromatid from each homologous chromosome breaks off and reattaches to the other homologous chromosome. As a result, a chromosome from the mother may have a segment with genes from the father.

PRACTICE

CALIFORNIA CONTENT
STANDARD 2.a

Meiosis

DIRECTIONS: Choose the letter of the *best* answer.

STANDARD SET 2

1 **When chromosomes separate during meiosis, which of the following are produced?**

   A chromatids

   B gametes

   C zygotes

   D genes

2 **Meiosis has a very important role in sexually producing organisms. Which of the following *best* describes the important role meiosis plays in sexual reproduction?**

   A Meiosis allows chromosomes to condense.

   B Meiosis produces cells, with half the number of chromosomes.

   C Meiosis gets chromosomes to pair up along the cell equator.

   D Meiosis forms cells with sister chromatids.

3 **During meiosis, chromosome pairs are separated. Then each of the sister chromatids are pulled apart. Which statement *best* describes these processes?**

   A a subtle form of mitosis that keeps the cell healthy

   B a random event that does not affect reproduction in organisms

   C a type of cell division that produces zygotes in one parent

   D a way to produce cells with various combinations of chromosomes

4

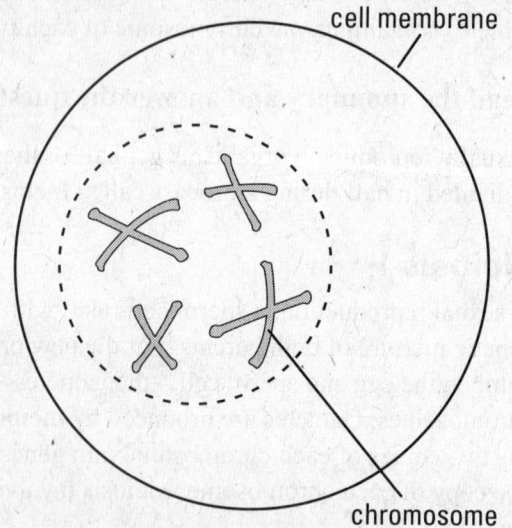

cell membrane

chromosome

Suppose that the cell in the diagram above is going to divide by meiosis. When the entire process of meiosis is completed, how many chromosomes will each of the new cells contain?

   A 1

   B 2

   C 3

   D 4

5 **A hypothetical organism has 18 chromosomes in its body cells. Which of the following *best* describes these chromosomes?**

   A They will result in offspring with 36 chromosomes.

   B They resulted when 9 chromosomes from each parent combined.

   C They were all originally found in the same gamete.

   D They had half as much genetic information as the parents' gametes.

REVIEW

CALIFORNIA CONTENT
STANDARD 2.b

Germ Cells

STANDARD Students know only certain cells in a multicellular organism undergo meiosis.

Read the summary and answer the questions on the next page.

Most of the cells in your body will never undergo meiosis. Only cells that will form gametes, or sex cells, will divide by meiosis.

Somatic Cells and Germ Cells

Meiosis is the process that causes cells to divide their DNA in half. However, not all cells undergo meiosis. The cells that make up most of your tissues and organs are called **somatic** cells. Somatic cells are specialized to perform specific body functions, or to become a particular set of body cells. Somatic cells only divide by mitosis. They contain a complete set of your DNA, but these cells cannot pass DNA on to offspring.

The only cells in your body that divide by meiosis are the **germ** cells. Germ cells are specialized diploid cells in the reproductive organs. They develop into the haploid **gametes**, or sex cells. The DNA inside gametes is passed on to offspring.

Gamete Production

There are two processes that produce gametes: spermatogenesis and oogenesis. **Spermatogenesis** occurs only in males. During this process, male germ cells in the testes undergo meiosis to form four identical haploid gametes. After meiosis, male gametes mature into streamlined, motile **sperm** cells. The round haploid cells produced by meiosis develop a whiplike flagellum and a connecting neck region packed with mitochondria. They lose most of their cytoplasm to form a compact head region containing tightly-packed DNA. Specialized proteins are added to the cell membrane that help the sperm cell recognize and fuse with the egg. These changes make it possible for the sperm cells to swim to an egg and fertilize it.

Oogenesis occurs only in females. During oogenisis, female germ cells in the ovary undergo meiosis to form one usable haploid egg, or oocyte, and two or three tiny **polar bodies**. The unequal division of cytoplasm between the oocyte and the polar bodies concentrates organelles, food, and molecules into one oocyte. The polar bodies contain little more than DNA and are eventually broken down.

Unlike spermatogenesis, oogenesis may have periods of active development and periods of inactivity. For example, in humans oogenesis begins before birth in the developing body of a female embryo. But the development of gametes stops partway through meiosis. An egg cell does not finish maturing until years later when it is fertilized by a sperm cell.

STANDARD SET 2

PRACTICE

CALIFORNIA CONTENT
STANDARD 2.b

Germ Cells

DIRECTIONS: Choose the letter of the *best* answer.

1 Suppose that a group of scientists want to manipulate the DNA in a corn plant so that the plant's offspring will have a mutation. They expose the plant to a chemical that changes some plant cells' DNA. Which cells *must* have the mutated DNA in order for the plant to pass it along to its offspring?

A cells that produce gametes

B cells that are found in the stem

C cells that can be added to a new plant

D cells that form the flower

2

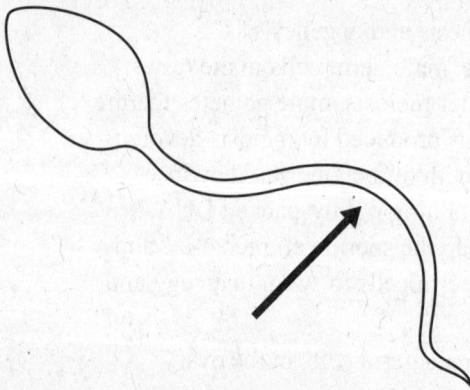

The diagram shows a sperm cell. What is the function of the part of the sperm cell indicated by the arrow?

A storing chromosomes

B making ATP

C detecting an oocyte

D moving the cell

3 Spermatogenisis and oogenisis are processes that form gametes in males and females. What kind of cells must undergo meiosis during these processes?

A somatic cells

B sperm cells

C polar body cells

D germ cells

4 In which of the following organs can you find cells that undergo meiosis?

A kidney

B brain

C ovary

D heart

5 Which of the following is true of cells that can be found in the finger?

A They will never undergo meiosis.

B They will undergo meiosis at different times of the organism's life.

C They will undergo meiosis only when they are stimulated.

D They will undergo meiosis after they have duplicated their DNA.

REVIEW

CALIFORNIA CONTENT
STANDARD 2.c

Chromosome Segregation

STANDARD Students know how random chromosome segregation explains the probability that a particular allele will be in a gamete.

Read the summary and answer the questions on the next page.

Meiosis is the process by which a cell's chromosome number is reduced by half. During meiosis, the cell's chromosomes are randomly separated so that each gamete that is produced has a different combination of chromosomes.

Chromosome Segregation

Each diploid germ cell contains pairs of homologous chromosomes. **Homologous chromosomes** are a pair of chromosomes that have the same sequence of genes, but each chromosome may have different **alleles**, or versions of those genes. One chromosome in each pair was inherited from the organism's mother; the other was inherited from its father. During meiosis the number of chromosomes is reduced by half, and homologous chromosomes separate independently. This process produces haploid gametes that each contain one copy of each chromosome in a unique combination from both parents. In humans, each gamete contains a unique combination of 23 chromosomes.

During meiosis I, spindle fibers randomly line up the homologous chromosome pairs along the middle of the cell. The result is that each side of the cell's equator contains some chromosomes that originated with the mother and some that came from the father. The division of the nucleus forms two haploid cells that each contain a unique combination of chromosomes from both parents. This process of **random chromosome segregation** mixes up chromosome combinations inside gametes and helps create and maintain genetic diversity. In humans, 23 pairs of chromosomes lining up and segregating independently can create gametes with about 2^{23}, or 8 million, different chromosome combinations.

Gene Segregation

Because chromosomes segregate randomly during meiosis, the genes they carry are also randomly segregated into gametes. Because these events are random, the mathematics of probability can be applied to calculate how likely it is that a particular allele or combination of alleles will be found in a gamete. Probability is the likelihood that a particular event will happen. It predicts the average number of times an event will occur, not the exact number of times.

Suppose an organism is **heterozygous** for a particular trait. All of its cells contain one chromosome with a dominant copy of the allele and one chromosome with a recessive copy of the allele (*Tt*). If a germ cell undergoes meiosis in this organism, a gamete could get either a dominant or a recessive allele. The probability that it will get a dominant allele is one out of two, or one-half. The probability that it will get a recessive allele is also one-half.

If an organism is **homozygous** for a trait, all of its cells contain two copies of the same allele (*TT* or *tt*). If a germ cell undergoes meiosis in this organism, all of the resulting gametes will get the same copy of the allele. The probability that it will get this allele is one out of one, or one.

PRACTICE

CALIFORNIA CONTENT
STANDARD 2.c

Chromosome Segregation

DIRECTIONS: Choose the letter of the *best* answer.

1 When a cell undergoes meiosis, it divides its genetic material in half. Which statement *best* describes the result of meiosis?

  A Chromosomes are randomly separated.

  B Chromosomes are larger in some cells.

  C Chromosomes are replicated.

  D Chromosomes are very organized.

2 Suppose a plant has an allele that gives it dark green leaves. When that plant reproduces, some of its offspring might have the allele that produces dark green leaves, but others might not. Which *best* explains this?

  A Some genetic material breaks down during meiosis.

  B Most genetic material is not represented in gametes.

  C All genetic material is divided randomly during meiosis.

  D Little genetic material actually codes for the dark green color.

3 During meiosis I, homologous chromosomes are randomly separated into different gametes. This process allows cells to produce large amounts of

  A genetic variation.

  B sister chromatids.

  C random chance.

  D live offspring.

4

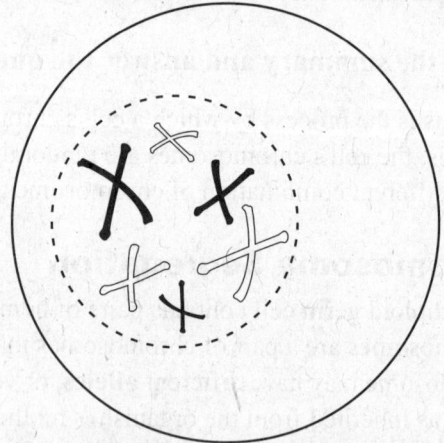

In the diagram above, the chromosomes that came from the mother are dark-colored and the chromosomes that came from the father are light-colored. The gametes produced by meiosis from this cell will contain

  A only chromosomes from the mother.

  B only chromosomes from the father.

  C an equal mix of chromosomes from the mother and the father.

  D a random mix of chromosomes from the mother and the father.

5 Human gametes can have one of more than 8 million combinations of chromosomes. Which of the following *best* explains how this is possible?

  A Chromosomes are randomly separated from one another during meiosis.

  B Chromosomes are changed when the cell produces gametes.

  C Chromosomes enter the gamete after meiosis has occurred.

  D Chromosomes are replicated at different rates in the gamete.

REVIEW

CALIFORNIA CONTENT
STANDARD 2.d

Fertilization

STANDARD SET 2

STANDARD Students know new combinations of alleles may be generated in a zygote through the fusion of male and female gametes (fertilization).

Read the summary and answer the questions on the next page.

The fusion of an egg cell and a sperm cell is called **fertilization**. Fertilization forms a single diploid cell, the first cell of a new individual with a unique combination of its parents' genes. This cell will develop into an adult organism with a unique phenotype that is a mixture of both parents' traits.

Meiosis Increases Variation

The process of meiosis plays an important role in creating new combinations of alleles in sexually reproducing species. Both the independent separation of chromosomes and crossing over events during meiosis I result in gametes with a unique combination of alleles. For example, independent segregation of the 23 chromosome pairs in a human genome during meiosis can produce gametes with about 2^{23}, or about 8 million, different chromosome combinations.

Fertilization Increases Variation

The process of meiosis forms gametes with half the number of chromosomes as are in the organism's other cells. Once gametes have been produced, they can join during sexual reproduction. This fusion is called fertilization. After the gametes join, their genetic material is combined. The result is a cell, called a **zygote**, that has the same number of chromosomes as are found in the parents' cells. Although the zygote has the same number of chromosomes as the parents' cells have, it has a very different combination of alleles.

Fertilization dramatically increases the number of possible chromosome combinations in a species. When a sperm cell containing one of those approximately 8 million chromosome combinations fuses with an egg cell that contains one of a different 8 million chromosome combinations, the result is one of more than 70 trillion chromosome combinations. Because the meeting of sperm and egg is random, each zygote contains a new combination of parental alleles.

PRACTICE

CALIFORNIA CONTENT
STANDARD 2.d

Fertilization

DIRECTIONS: Choose the letter of the *best* answer.

1

cell membrane

nucleus

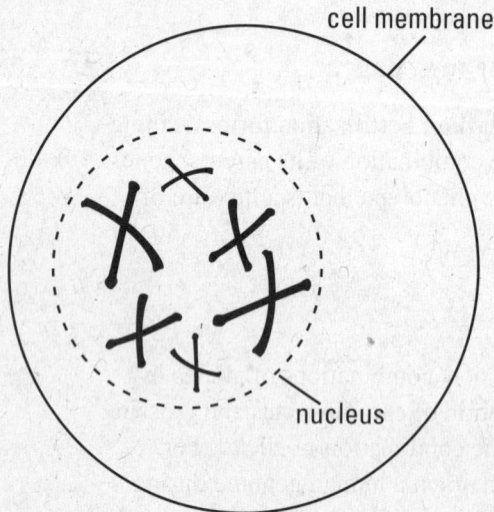

The cell in the above diagram resulted from fertilization. It has

A six chromosomes from its mother.

B six chromosomes from its father.

C three chromosomes from its mother and three from its father.

D four chromosomes from its mother and two from its father.

2 Which of the following *best* explains how fertilization contributes to genetic diversity?

A It allows parents' chromosomes to combine.

B It provides parents' chromosomes the time for crossing over.

C It produces gametes with different combinations of chromosomes.

D It stimulates zygotes to replicate the best chromosomes.

3 How do both fertilization and meiosis allow for genetic variation?

A They eliminate bad genes.

B They segregate and form different combinations of genes.

C They transfer the parents' genotypes of the offspring.

D They produce similar phenotypes in all of their cells.

4 Suppose two parent plants were crossed. One has two dominant alleles (*RR*), and the second has two recessive alleles (*rr*). If the two were to mate, they would produce offspring with

A Half of their alleles from each parent.

B Both alleles from their mother.

C Both alleles from their father.

D Uneven combinations of alleles from both parents.

5 A group of jellyfish in the Carribean release millions of gametes, which then undergo fertilization, into the water. Which type of cell is the *final* product of this reproductive event?

A sperm

B eggs

C polar bodies

D zygotes

REVIEW

CALIFORNIA CONTENT
STANDARD 2.e

Individual's DNA

STANDARD Students know why approximately half of an individual's DNA sequence comes from each parent.

Read the summary and answer the questions on the next page.

Meiosis produces gametes with half the number of chromosomes that are present in the organism's other body cells. When two gametes join during fertilization, their DNA combine. The result is a cell with half of its DNA from the mother and the other half of its DNA from the father.

Diploid and Haploid Cells

A chromosome is made up of a very long strand of DNA wrapped around a series of proteins that help to organize it. A **diploid cell** has two copies of each homologouos chromosome, whereas a **haploid cell** has only one copy of each homologous chromosome. **Homologous chromosomes** are pairs of chromosomes that are similar but not identical. In each pair, one chromosome comes from the mother and one comes from the father. Homologous chromosomes have the same sequence of genes, but each homologous chromosome can have different alleles, or alternate versions of those genes.

Your body cells are diploid. Each has 23 pairs of homologous chromosomès, for a total of 46 chromosomes. Your reproductive organs—the ovaries and the testes—have special diploid cells called **germ cells** that go through the process of meiosis. During meiosis, the two chromosomes in a homologous pair are separated from each other. As a result, meiosis forms daughter cells that have half the number of chromosomes as the original cell. That is, the daughter cells have one chromosome from each pair of homologous chromosomes. These haploid cells go through more processes to finally form **gametes,** or haploid sex cells.

Fertilization and Chromosomes

Fertilization is the fusion of gametes. Gametes—egg and sperm—are haploid. Their union produces a diploid cell. For example, you inherited one set of chromosomes from each of your parents. Your parents produced haploid egg and sperm cells by meiosis. The fusion of their gametes produced a diploid cell that went through many more rounds of cell division to make you.

By splitting up the homologous chromosome pairs, meiosis ensures that each gamete contains only one copy of each gene in an organism. The gamete contains half as much DNA as a normal body cell. This means that when an egg cell and a sperm cell fuse and combine their chromosomes into a single nucleus, they form a new individual with a normal number of paired homologous chromosomes—one set from the mother, the other set from the father.

Individual's DNA

DIRECTIONS: Choose the letter of the *best* answer.

1

cell membrane

nucleus

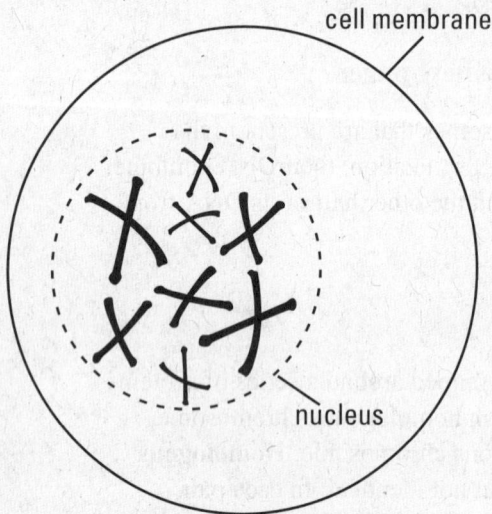

Suppose an organism has four pairs of chromosomes, as in the diagram. When two of these organisms mate, how many chromosomes will the mother contribute to the offspring?

A 1

B 2

C 4

D 8

2 How many chromosomes does an individual have compared to one gamete that formed that individual?

A one-fourth

B one-half

C the same

D twice as many

3 Before a cross, a male fish was fed carbon-15 that would appear on each of the fish's chromosomes in its sperm. How much of the zygote's DNA will contain carbon-15?

A none			**C** one-half

B one-fourth		**D** all

4 One parent in a test cross has a mutation on one of its chromosome pairs. After the cross, each of the offspring have one mutated chromosome, but none of them have two or no mutated chromosomes. Which of the statements *best* explains this?

A Offspring with no or two mutated chromosomes are not as fit.

B Offspring got some mutated chromosomes from each parent.

C Offspring experienced their own chromosomes mutate.

D Offspring received half of their DNA from the mutated parent.

5 In humans, males have XY sex chromosomes, and females have XX. Yet, there are normally no YY individuals. Which of the statements *best* explains this?

A Y chromosomes always segregate into polar bodies.

B Males are XY but have only one sex chromosome in their sperm.

C Males are XY and always carry both sex chromosomes in their sperm.

D X-inactivation destroys Y chromosomes.

STANDARD SET 2

REVIEW

CALIFORNIA CONTENT
STANDARD 2.f

Sex Determination

STANDARD SET 2

STANDARD Students know the role of chromosomes in determining an individual's sex.

Read the summary and answer the questions on the next page.

In humans, gender is determined by the sex chromosomes an individual has. Males have one X chromosome and one Y chromosome. Females have two X chromosomes. So the gender of offspring depends on whether the male's X or Y chromosome is present during fertilization.

Chromosomes and Fertilization

Humans are diploid organisms, which means they have two copies of each chromosome. However, the cells that join during fertilization are haploid, meaning they have only one copy of each chromosome. During fertilization, a male's sperm cell joins with a female's egg cell. When a sperm and an egg combine, they create a new diploid cell called a **zygote**. The zygote subsequently develops into a new individual of that species.

Sex Chromosomes

In many organisms, the zygote's sex is determined at fertilization by a set of **sex chromosomes** that control the development of sexual characteristics. Human cells contain 46 chromosomes, 22 pairs of homologous chromosomes that have no direct role in sexual development and one pair of sex chromosomes. In humans and other mammals, the two types of sex chromosomes, called **X** and **Y**, look very different. X chromosomes are large and contain a large number of genes, including many that are unrelated to sexual development. Y chromosomes are tiny and contain only a few genes, but these include the genes that direct the development of the testes.

Mammals inherit one sex chromosome from each parent. The combination of sex chromosomes offspring receive determines their sex, or gender. If the organism gets two X chromosomes, it will be female. If it gets one X and one Y chromosome, it will be male.

Sex Determination

The XY system of sex determination means that males are responsible for the sex of their offspring. Because females have a pair of homologous X chromosomes, every mature oocyte contains an X chromosome. In males, the nonhomologous X and Y chromosomes pair with one another during meiosis I. So, half of the developing sperm cells contain X chromosomes, and half contain Y chromosomes, as you can see in the diagram. The sex chromosome inside the sperm cell will determine whether an offspring is XX and female or XY and male.

	X	X
X	XX	XX
Y	XY	XY

PRACTICE

CALIFORNIA CONTENT
STANDARD 2.f

Sex Determination

DIRECTIONS: Choose the letter of the *best* answer.

1 Like mammals, birds' gender is determined by sex chromosomes. However, instead of X and Y chromosomes, birds have W and Z chromosomes. Birds with WZ sex chromosomes are female. Birds with ZZ sex chromosomes are male. The chromosome that determines the sex of the offspring is found in the

  A male's gamete.

  B female's gamete.

  C Z chromosome.

  D W chromosome.

2 In humans, males determine the gender of their offspring. Which of the following statements *best* explains why that is?

  A Females can only contribute X chromosomes.

  B Females do not prefer male or female offspring.

  C Females lose their Y chromosome during meiosis.

  D Female hormones determine their offspring's gender.

3 The X and Y chromosomes are considered a chromosome pair because

  A they are the same length.

  B they contain the same genes.

  C they are normally found in females.

  D they line up during meiosis I.

4

	X	X
X	XX	XX
Y	XY	XY

The diagram above shows a cross between two people. How many of their offspring will likely be female?

  A none

  B one-fourth

  C one-half

  D all

5 Although people usually have two sex chromosomes, occasionally people might have three: XXY. However, offspring never have XYY. Which statement *best* explains this?

  A Parents only have one Y chromosome, but they have three X chromosomes.

  B Parents with XYY are infertile and cannot produce offspring.

  C Parents that produce XYY offspring cannot keep these offspring alive.

  D Parents' two Y chromosomes are too weak to occur twice in one offspring.

REVIEW

CALIFORNIA CONTENT
STANDARD 2.g

Predicting Allele Combinations

STANDARD Students know how to predict possible combinations of alleles in a zygote from the genetic makeup of the parents.

Read the summary and answer the questions on the next page.

During meiosis, cells go through two nuclear divisions to form genetically unique haploid cells. If parental genotypes are known for a trait, you can use mathematics to predict how likely it is that one of the offspring will inherit a specific allele.

Allele Separation in Parents

Normal body cells are **diploid**: They contain two sets of **homologous chromosomes**. Homologous chromosomes are chromosomes that are similar but not identical. They contain the same sequence of genes, but each chromosome may have different **alleles**, or versions of those genes. In organisms that reproduce sexually, individuals use the process of **meiosis** to produce egg and sperm cells. Egg and sperm cells are **haploid**: They contain only one copy of each chromosome.

During meiosis, homologous chromosomes are separated and placed in different sex cells, or **gametes**. Each gamete contains only one allele for any particular trait. Because a diploid organism has two alleles for each trait, the mathematics of probability states that one allele will be found in half of the organism's gametes and the other allele will be in the other half. If the two alleles are the same, they are described as **homozygous**. If the two alleles are different, they are described as **heterozygous**. If the makeup of an individual's alleles for a trait, its **genotype**, is known, we can predict how likely it will be that those alleles will appear in its offspring.

Predicting Zygote Genotypes

Punnett squares are a convenient method of calculating genetic probabilities. The square is a grid of boxes that represent all of the possible genotypes the progeny of a particular cross may have. Parental alleles are placed by each box on the axes of the grid. In the diagram, both parents have one *R* allele and one *r* allele. To determine the possible allele combinations of their offspring, alleles from each parent are placed inside their corresponding grid boxes.

Because chromosome segregation and fertilization are random, the combinations of alleles in each box are equally likely. The number of squares with each genetic combination corresponds to the ratio of that genotypes in the offspring. In this example, one-fourth of the offspring would have *RR*; one-half of the offspring would have *Rr*; and the remaining one-fourth would have *rr*.

Parent 1

	R	r
Parent 2 R	**RR**	**rR**
r	**Rr**	**rr**

PRACTICE

CALIFORNIA CONTENT
STANDARD 2.g

Predicting Allele Combinations

DIRECTIONS: Choose the letter of the *best* answer.

1 In moths, the gene for dark wings (*D*) is dominant to the gene for light wings (*d*). If a homozygous dark moth (*DD*) is crossed with a heterozygous dark moth (*Dd*), which combination of alleles will be most common among the offspring?

A *DD*

B *Dd*

C *dd*

D *DD* and *Dd* are equally common.

2 The letters inside the grid boxes of a Punnett square represent the

A genotypes of the parents.

B phenotypes of the parents.

C genotypes of the offspring.

D phenotypes of the offspring.

3 The gene for brown eyes (*B*) is dominant to the gene for blue eyes (*b*). If a pair of individuals that are heterozygous for brown eyes (*Bb*) have children, what proportion of their children will have at least one *B*?

A 100%

B 75%

C 50%

D 25%

4

	T	*t*
T	*TT*	*tT*
t	**X**	*tt*

In the cross above, which combination of alleles will be found in the box marked X?

A *TT*

B *Tt*

C *tt*

D *TtTt*

5 In a Punnett square, the letters on the outside of the grid represent the

A parent's alleles.

B parent's traits.

C offspring's alleles.

D offspring's traits.

REVIEW

Predicting Phenotypes in a Genetic Cross

STANDARD Students know how to predict the probable outcomes of phenotypes in a genetic cross from the genotypes of the parents and mode of inheritance (autosomal or X-linked, dominant or recessive).

Read the summary and answer the questions on the next page.

When two organisms mate, they each donate half of their **alleles,** or copies of each gene, to their offspring. Because the parents' alleles are randomly separated into gametes, scientists use probability and Punnett squares to predict how likely it is that the offspring will inherit certain traits.

Calculating Probability of Inheritance

Every organism of a species has the same number of alleles. Half of these alleles come from one parent and half from the second parent. This collection of alleles makes up the organism's **genotype.** The traits an organism expresses make up its **phenotype.** A phenotype can be predicted if you know which trait is dominant and which is recessive.

Dominant and Recessive

Two alleles of the same gene interact to produce phenotypic traits. When one version of an allele is expressed over another, the expressed allele is called **dominant.** The allele that is not expressed is called **recessive**. Suppose you know that R is the dominant allele for a trait, and r is the recessive allele for the same trait. If an individual has *at least one* dominant allele (RR or Rr), that individual will express the dominant trait. Only individuals with two recessive alleles (rr) will express the recessive trait. Next, suppose you know that two parents both have the Rr genotype. Both of these individuals express the dominant trait. If they mate, about one-fourth of their offspring, shaded in gray in the Punnett square, will express the recessive trait. The remaining three-fourths will have at least one dominant allele, so they will express the dominant trait.

	R	r
R	RR	rR
r	Rr	rr

Genes on the sex chromosomes can also contribute to phenotype. Only males have a Y chromosome, so genes on the **Y chromosome** are only expressed in males. Both males and females have at least one X chromosome, so genes on the **X chromosome** affect traits in both sexes. Because females have two copies of the X chromosome, they inherit X-linked alleles in the same way as genes described above. Because males have only one X chromosome, all X-linked alleles—whether dominant (X) or recessive (X`)—are expressed in males. Females that have one recessive X-linked allele (X`X) will pass the recessive allele to half of their children, but only sons will express it, as the Punnett square shows.

	X	X'
X	XX	X'X
Y	XY	X'Y

STANDARD SET 3

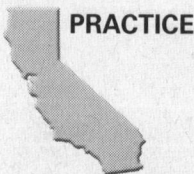

Predicting Phenotypes in a Genetic Cross

DIRECTIONS: Choose the letter of the *best* answer.

1 Which parent contributes an X chromosome to male offspring?

  A the father

  B the mother

  C either the father or the mother

  D both the father and the mother

2 Suppose you have two pea plants, one with green peas and one with yellow peas. After you cross the two plants, you find that all of the offspring have green peas. What can you conclude from observing these phenotypes?

  A The offspring have only dominant alleles.

  B The offspring have only recessive alleles.

  C The offspring have a dominant and a recessive allele.

  D The offspring have a mixture of their parents' traits.

3 Huntington's disease is a genetic disease that causes cells in the brain to die. Suppose it is caused by a dominant allele. If an affected (*Dd*) man and an unaffected (*dd*) woman have children, what percentage of their offspring are at risk for developing the disease?

  A none

  B one-fourth

  C one-half

  D all

4

	H	*h*
H		
h		

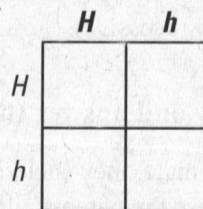

Suppose that the genotype *HH* produces an individual with a curly hair phenotype. *Hh* produces individuals with a curly hair phenotype. And *hh* produces individuals with a straight hair phenotype. If the two individuals represented in the Punnett square above were to mate, what percentage of their offspring will have straight hair?

  A 0%

  B 25%

  C 50%

  D 100%

5 The *sry* gene controls testicular development and is only found in males. Which chromosome is it most likely found on?

  A Y chromosome

  B X chromosome

  C both X and Y chromosomes

  D neither X nor Y chromosome

REVIEW

CALIFORNIA CONTENT STANDARD 3.b

Mendel's Laws

STANDARD Students know the genetic basis for Mendel's laws of segregation and independent assortment.

Read the summary and answer the questions on the next page.

Mendel's two laws state that: (1) each individual has two units for a trait, and the individual inherits one unit from each parent; and (2) each trait is passed independently of other traits.

Law of Segregation

Gregor Mendel determined that traits in an individual exist as a pair of units—one inherited from each parent—and that these units separate during gamete formation so that each gamete carries only one version of the trait. This deduction is called the **law of segregation**.

Today, we call Mendel's "units" **genes,** and we know that the patterns he observed were caused by the expression of alternate **alleles,** a term used to describe different versions of the same gene. Because organisms have two copies of each chromosome, they have two alleles for every gene—one on each chromosome. When two different versions of the allele are present, the **dominant** allele is expressed as a trait, and the **recessive** allele remains hidden.

Although Mendel did not know it, this is due to **meiosis.** When an organism's germ cells go through meiosis, its chromosomes are randomly separated into two sets. The resulting gametes have only one copy of each chromosome and, as a result, only one allele of each gene.

Law of Independent Assortment

Mendel also wanted to learn about how two different traits are inherited. For example, if a pea plan found that each trait is inherited independently of other traits. This means that traits are not inherited in pairs, and the presence of two characteristics together in a parent plant does not mean that those two characteristics will always occur in combination together. This observation is called the **law of independent assortment**.

The law of independent assortment is not always true. If two genes are very close together on the same chromosome, they can be inherited together. This is called **genetic linkage**. Mendel was very wise or very lucky in choosing many traits that were not on the same chromosomes and could move independently. He picked a few traits that shared a chromosome, but the genes for these traits were not physically close to one another. Because the genes were far apart on the chromosomes, they were separated by crossing over. **Crossing over** occurs when homologous chromosomes, those that are paired in a cell, line up by pairs and swap portions of their genetic material with each other, as shown in the diagram.

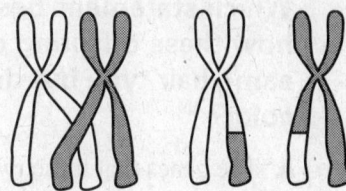

PRACTICE

CALIFORNIA CONTENT
STANDARD 3.b

Mendel's Laws

STANDARD SET 3

DIRECTIONS: Choose the letter of the *best* answer.

1 Individuals have two genes for each trait. Each parent contributes only one gene for each trait to offspring. Which term *best* describes these statements?

A crossing over

B law of segregation

C law of independent assortment

D genetic linkage

2 Suppose two dominant alleles (*PP*) are found in a pea plant that has smooth pods. This plant is crossed with a pea plant with wrinkled pods (*pp*). How many offspring will have more than one recessive allele (*p*)?

A 0%   C 50%

B 25%   D 100%

3 Suppose two parents have two children. One child has curly hair and brown eyes. The second child has curly hair and green eyes. Which statement *best* explains how these offspring can have the same hair type but different eye color?

A The genes that these two individuals have comes from different parents.

B The genes that codes for hair type and eye color is on sex alleles.

C The genes that codes for hair type and eye color are on linked genes.

D The genes that codes for hair type and eye color are on different chromosomes.

4 Which of the following *best* describes Mendel's conclusion about how multiple traits are passed to offspring?

A Traits are always passed in pairs.

B Traits get passed equally to offspring.

C Traits are passed independently of one another.

D Traits do not get passed to offspring.

5

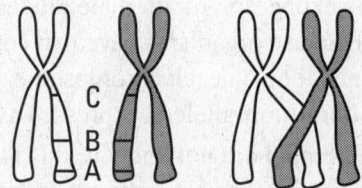

The figure above shows two chromosomes that have lined up during meiosis. The stripes on the chromosomes represent genes that code for different traits. When these chromosomes undergo crossing over, they will swap pieces of DNA. According to the diagram, which of the genes, (labeled A-C) will *most* likely follow Mendel's law of independent assortment after the crossing over occurs?

A A

B B

C C

D None of the genes will sort independently.

REVIEW

CALIFORNIA CONTENT
STANDARD 4.a

Translation: mRNA, tRNA, and Protiens

STANDARD Students know the general pathway by which ribosomes synthesize proteins, using tRNAs to translate genetic information in mRNA.

Read the summary and answer the questions on the next page

Although DNA stores the encoded information cells use to build proteins, it never leaves the cell's nucleus. Proteins are built, or synthesized, in the cell's cytoplasm. Messenger RNAs (mRNAs) transcribe the DNA code in the nucleus and carry the genetic information to the ribosomes, which translate the code into a series of amino acids that becomes a protein.

Ribosomes, tRNAs, and mRNAs

To build proteins, a cell needs mRNAs, ribosomes, and tRNAs.

- **mRNAs** are single strands of RNA nucleotides that are transcribed from the DNA molecule. Each three-nucleotide sequence in an mRNA is called a **codon**. Each codon codes for one amino acid or signals a ribosome to start or stop translation.
- **Ribosomes** are organelles made of RNA and protein. They consist of a small subunit that binds to mRNA molecules and a large subunit that binds for tRNA molecules.
- **tRNAs** are folded RNA molecules. One end of the molecule binds a specific amino acid, and the other end has three exposed nucleotides called an **anticodon**. The anticodon binds to the complementary codon on the mRNA strand.

Translation and Building a Protein

Once the mRNA leaves the nucleus, the cell begins **translation**, or the process of building proteins using the information carried by mRNA. During translation, a ribosome binds to the mRNA molecule. The first codon, or mRNA's sequence of three nucleotides, is exposed and binds to tRNA's anticodon. The amino acid carried by the tRNA is removed and added to the chain of amino acids that will form the completed protein. This process is described in more detail below.

1. The small ribosomal subunit binds to an mRNA molecule.
2. A complementary tRNA carrying an amino acid binds to the start codon. .
3. The ribosome pulls the mRNA strand through itself one codon at a time. As the strand moves, the first bound tRNA moves with it.
4. When a new codon is exposed, another tRNA molecule with a complementary anticodon binds to it.
5. The ribosome attaches the amino acids to one another and breaks the bond between the second tRNA and its amino acid.
6. When the ribosome pulls the mRNA strand again, exposing another codon, another tRNA with a matching anticodon attaches.
7. In the meantime, the first tRNA is released.
8. This pattern of reading new codons and adding new amino acids continues until the ribosome reaches a stop codon on the mRNA. At this point the ribosome releases the new protein.

STANDARD SET 4

PRACTICE

CALIFORNIA CONTENT
STANDARD 4.a

Translation: mRNA, tRNA, and Protiens

DIRECTIONS: Choose the letter of the *best* answer.

1 During translation, the information in mRNA codons is used to build a protein. What molecules carry amino acids and have the anticodons that match the mRNA codons?

A rRNAs

B DNA

C tRNAs

D ribosomes

2

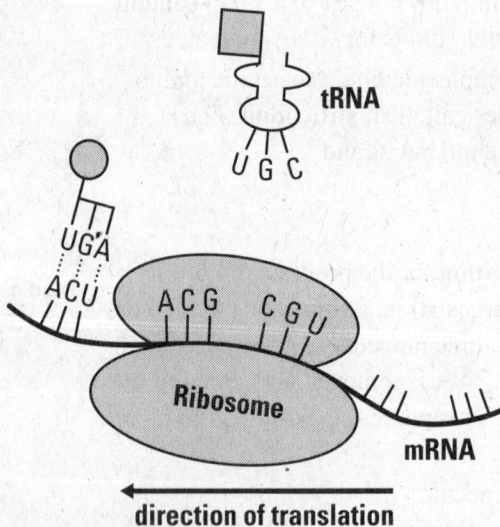

The above diagram shows a ribosome in the process of translation. Which of the following events will happen next?

A The ribosome will add another amino acid to the protein.

B The ribosome will release the protein.

C The ribosome will pull the mRNA through itself.

D The ribosome will bind a tRNA to the start condon.

3 Which is responsible for exposing codons and binding amino acids together?

A anticodons

B ribosomes

C mRNA

D tRNA

4 Suppose you isolate the following nucleotide sequence in DNA: TACTAATAACAA. How many amino acids are coded for by this DNA sequence?

A 2 amino acids

B 4 amino acids

C 6 amino acids

D 12 amino acids

5

A. tRNA binds to codon.

B. tRNA detaches from the mRNA.

C. Ribosome binds two amino acids.

D. Ribosome pulls mRNA through.

Here are steps that occur during translation. Which of the following puts them in order?

A A; D; C; B

B A; B; D; C

C A; C; D; B

D A; B; C; D

STANDARD SET 4

REVIEW

CALIFORNIA CONTENT STANDARD 4.b

Decoding mRNA and tRNA

STANDARD Students know how to apply the genetic coding rules to predict the sequence of amino acids from a sequence of codons in RNA.

Read the summary and answer the questions on the next page.

Only four DNA nucleotides store the codes for all of the proteins in a cell, and only 20 different types of amino acids are used to build the proteins. Reading DNA sequences can allow you to determine the amino acids that the DNA codes for.

Complementary Bases

Messenger RNA (mRNA) transcribes DNA in the nucleus. Complementary mRNA nucleotides bind to the DNA nucleotides. As the chart shows, if the DNA nucleotide is an A, the complementary RNA nucleotide is a U. A T in DNA binds with a complementary A of RNA, and so on. When the mRNA leaves the nucleus and translation begins, complementary nucleotides on a tRNA molecule must bind to the mRNA. And tRNA, just as mRNA, contains U instead of T. Therefore, in mRNA and tRNA, U binds with A and G binds with C.

Base-Pairing Rules

DNA	mRNA	tRNA
A →	U →	A
T →	A →	U
C →	G →	C
G →	C →	G

The Amino Acid Code

Most three-nucleotide sequences in the genetic code are translated into one of 20 amino acids. The three-nucleotide sequence in an mRNA molecule is called a **codon**. During translation, complementary tRNA molecules that have three-nucleotide sequences called **anticodons** bind to an mRNA molecule that is bound to a ribosome. Each tRNA molecule carries a specific amino acid.

Using a chart, such as the one shown here, you can determine the amino acids that are coded for by mRNA nucleotides. (In this chart, mRNA bases are found along the perimeter, and the amino acids they code for are found in the middle.) Suppose the mRNA has the sequence CAA.

1. The first base in the sequence is C. Look to the left of the chart, and find the row marked C next to the title "First Base."

2. Then find A column under the title "Second Base." Determine where the C row and A column intersect.

3. Finally, look to the right, and find A. Follow along that row. In this case, the amino acid is *gln*, or glutamine.

Codons in mRNA

First Base	Second Base U	C	A	G	Third Base
U	Phe	Ser	Tyr	Cys	U
U	Phe	Ser	Tyr	Cys	C
U	Leu	Ser	Stop	Stop	A
U	Leu	Ser	Stop	Trp	G
C	Leu	Pro	His	Arg	U
C	Leu	Pro	His	Arg	C
C	Leu	Pro	Gln	Arg	A
C	Leu	Pro	Gln	Arg	G
A	Ile	Thr	Asn	Ser	U
A	Ile	Thr	Asn	Ser	C
A	Ile	Thr	Lys	Arg	A
A	Met	Thr	Lys	Arg	G

PRACTICE

CALIFORNIA CONTENT
STANDARD 4.b

Decoding mRNA and tRNA

DIRECTIONS: Choose the letter of the *best* answer.

1 Suppose you have an mRNA molecule that has the following nucleotide sequence: AUA GGU CCC. Which of the following *best* represents the complementary tRNA anticodons ?

   A TAT CCA TTT

   B GAG TTC UUU

   C ATG CCA AAA

   D UAU CCA GGG

2 Which of the following *best* describes a difference between mRNA and tRNA?

   A tRNA is only found in the nucleus, but mRNA is found in the nucleus and the cytoplasm.

   B tRNA transports amino acids during translation, but mRNA is bound to a ribosome.

   C tRNA has the nucleotide T, but mRNA has U instead.

   D tRNA has nucleotides that join together to form proteins, but mRNA does not.

3 Suppose an mRNA molecule has the following sequence CCUGACAACGCGUUUGUG. How many amino acids are coded for by this sequence?

   A 2 amino acids

   B 3 amino acids

   C 4 amino acids

   D 6 amino acids

4 Codons are sequences of three nucleotides in an mRNA molecule. Each codon codes for one

   A amino acid.

   B protein.

   C gene.

   D lipid.

5   **Base-Pairing Rules**

DNA	mRNA	tRNA
A →	U →	A
T →	A →	U
C →	G →	C
G →	C →	G

A strand of mRNA contains the sequence AUGAGGUGU. Which of the following amino acid sequences does this code for?

   A Met – Arg - Trp

   B Ile – Ser - Cys

   C Met – Arg – Cys

   D Ile – Arg - Cys

STANDARD SET 4

REVIEW

CALIFORNIA CONTENT
STANDARD 4.c

Mutations and Gene Expression

STANDARD Students know how mutations in the DNA sequence of a gene may or may not affect the expression of the gene or the sequence of amino acids in the encoded protein.

Read the summary and answer the questions on the next page.

A **mutation** is any permanent change to the sequence of nucleotides in an organism's DNA. Some mutations can cause changes in a protein. Other mutations do not affect the amino acid sequence in a protein.

Types of Mutations

The DNA sequence can be changed in many different ways, from single nucleotide substitutions to large movements of parts of chromosomes.

- **Point mutations** are caused when one nucleotide is substituted for another. When these mutations occur during DNA replication, they are usually caught and corrected by DNA polymerase. If they are not caught, the daughter cells and the daughter cells of those cells, and so on will inherit the mutation.

- **Frameshift mutations** are caused by insertions or deletions of nucleotides in DNA. The mutation shifts the sequence of codons that follows by one or more nucleotides.

- **Gene duplication** is a chromosomal mutation caused by errors in crossing over during meiosis. If homologous chromosomes do not align with each other, crossing over may exchange segments of unequal length. When this happens, one chromosome will have duplicate copies of the same gene and the other will not have the gene.

- **Translocation** is a chromosomal mutation caused when two nonhomologous chromosomes exchange segments of DNA during meiosis. Each chromosome gets a set of genes that did not previously exist on that chromosome.

Effects of Mutations

Many mutations within a gene do not affect an organism's phenotype because most amino acids are represented by more than one specific codon. For example, four different codons (GUU, GUC, GUA, GUG) all code for the amino acid valine. Suppose the genetic code for a protein included the sequence GUC, and a mutation changed the C to A (GUA). Even though the genetic code is changed, the amino acid sequence of the protein it produces is the same, because both GUC and GUA code for the same amino acid.

Proteins that are changed by mutations are likely to be nonfunctional. Chromosomal mutations may break up genes or result in hybrid genes with new functions. Frameshift mutations can change large segments of a protein by changing all of the code after the mutation. These mutations can completely change the amino acid sequence of the protein downstream from the mutation, or even cut the protein short if a stop codon appears in the new sequence. Improvements in function occasionally occur and may be favored by natural selection.

Mutations are only passed to offspring if they occur in the organism's gametes. These mutations are the underlying source of genetic variation among organisms. However, mutations in body cells affect only that organism.

STANDARD SET 4

PRACTICE

CALIFORNIA CONTENT
STANDARD 4.c

Mutations and Gene Expression

DIRECTIONS: Choose the letter of the *best* answer.

1 A dairy cow is exposed to radiation that changes the DNA sequence for a milk protein in her milk-producing cells. It is not possible for the cow to

  A continue to make a normal milk protein.

  B produce milk for its offspring.

  C make a milk protein that functions better than the normal version.

  D pass these mutations on to offspring through its gametes.

2 Suppose a gene in a plant leaf cell undergoes a mutation. In the original gene, the nucleotide sequence was GCCTATCCA. The mutated sequence is GCCATCCA. This new sequence will *most* likely

  A cause the production of an incorrect protein.

  B give the plant an advantage over other plants in its environment.

  C be passed on to its offspring.

  D kill the plant before the mutation is passed on to its offspring.

3 Suppose a particular gene has four codons. If one of the bases in the sequence is replaced by a different one, how many codons will be affected by this mutation?

  A one

  B two

  C three

  D four

4 Why do some mutations not affect the amino acid sequence of a protein?

  A Many amino acids are coded for by more than one codon.

  B Many ribosomes will recognize mutations and not translate them.

  C Many cells can produce the correct proteins out of habit.

  D Many mutations are ignored during translation.

5

Codons in mRNA

Second Base

First Base	U	C	A	G	Third Base
U	Phe	Ser	Tyr	Cys	U
	Phe	Ser	Tyr	Cys	C
	Leu	Ser	Stop	Stop	A
	Leu	Ser	Stop	Trp	G
C	Leu	Pro	His	Arg	U
	Leu	Pro	His	Arg	C
	Leu	Pro	Gln	Arg	A
	Leu	Pro	Gln	Arg	G
A	Ile	Thr	Asn	Ser	U
	Ile	Thr	Asn	Ser	C
	Ile	Thr	Lys	Arg	A
	Met	Thr	Lys	Arg	G
G	Val	Ala	Asp	Gly	U
	Val	Ala	Asp	Gly	C
	Val	Ala	Glu	Gly	A
	Val	Ala	Glu	Gly	G

Suppose a strand of mRNA has the codon GCG. What is *most* likely to happen if a mutation occurs, and the third base is replaced with A?

  A Ala will still be the amino acid in the protein.

  B Glu will replace Ala in the protein.

  C Met will replace Val in the protein.

  D Asp will replace Ala in the protein.

STANDARD SET 4

REVIEW

Gene Expression

STANDARD Students know specialization of cells in multicellular organisms is usually due to different patterns of gene expression rather than to differences of the genes themselves.

Read the summary and answer the questions on the next page.

All body cells in a multicellular organism have the same DNA. However, different types of cells in a multicellular organism have different structures and functions. These differences occur because cells only express some of the genes in their DNA.

Gene Expression

Every body cell in a multicellular organism has the same DNA, yet multicellular organisms have specialized cells with different structures and functions. The cells differ from one another because different genes are transcribed and translated to make different proteins in different cells. Whether or not a gene is transcribed in a cell is called **gene expression.**

Regulating Gene Expression

Gene expression contributes to cell specialization. Cells can regulate gene expression by controlling which genes are transcribed and when. Transcription is controlled by specific nucleotide sequences that are located before the nucleotides that make up a gene. In prokaryotes, the region of DNA that includes a gene and all of the sequences that control its expression is called an **operon**. Operons include a promoter, an operator, and a gene. The **promoter** is a DNA segment that helps RNA polymerase find the start of the gene. The **operator** is a DNA segment that turns the transcription of a gene "on" or "off." Operators interact with molecules in the cell to either block or enhance the action of RNA polymerase.

Gene expression is regulated in more complex ways in eukaryotic organisms.

- **Promoters** in most eukaryotic cells have a 7-nucleotide sequence called the TATA box. As in prokaryotes, the promoter helps RNA polymerase find the start of a gene.
- **Enhancers** are nucleotide sequences that, when active, speed up the rate of transcription of a gene.
- **Silencers** are nucleotide sequences that, when active, slow down the rate of transcription of a gene.

After transcription, an mRNA is processed to remove noncoding segments of nucleotides called **introns** from the part of the gene that codes for protein. The function of introns is unclear. They may regulate gene expression, or allow the same sequence of nucleotides to be cut in different ways to produce different proteins.

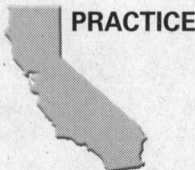

PRACTICE

CALIFORNIA CONTENT
STANDARD 4.d

Gene Expression

DIRECTIONS: Choose the letter of the *best* answer.

1 Insulin is only made by the ß-cells in the pancreas. Which statement *best* explains why?

  A ß-cells are the only cells that express the insulin gene.

  B ß-cells attack any other cells that express the insulin gene.

  C ß-cells secrete proteins that stop other cells from expressing the insulin gene.

  D ß-cells have the gene to make insulin, but no other cell has it.

2 Suppose a specialized cell produces a protein *A* that binds to particular locations on a DNA strand. When protein *A* binds to DNA, the cell is stimulated to produce other proteins that the cell needs to function. Protein *A* controls the expression of certain genes by regulating

  A mRNA tails.

  B intron removal.

  C translation.

  D transcription.

3 Which of the following terms *best* describes cells in the same organism that have different structures and functions?

  A prokaryotic

  B mutated

  C genetic

  D specialized

4 cell 1

cell 2

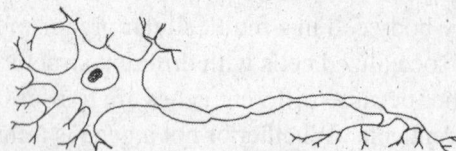

The two cells in the diagram above were taken from the same animal. Which of the following statements *best* describes the reason why these two cells look differently?

  A The cells have different DNA that gives them specialized structures.

  B The cells produce different proteins that give them different structures.

  C The cells are adapted to live in different parts of the body.

  D The cells will change their structures to fit the activities they have to do.

5 Genes in a cell's DNA allow the cell to produce

  A carbohydrates.

  B lipids.

  C energy.

  D proteins.

STANDARD SET 4

Differences Between Proteins

STANDARD Students know proteins can differ from one another in the number and sequence of amino acids.

Read the summary and answer the questions on the next page.

Organisms have thousands of proteins. Each of these proteins has a different number and sequence of amino acids.

Protein Structure

Amino acids are **monomers,** or small units that can be bonded together to form large molecules called **polymers.** Amino acids are bonded together into a long chain called a protein. The number of amino acids in a protein is determined by the gene that codes for the protein. All living things use the same set of 20 different amino acids to build all of their proteins. However, the different amino acids within the chain might form bonds between each other, giving a protein a three-dimensional structure. Therefore the structure of a protein is determined by the specific sequence of amino acids.

All amino acids are made up of an amino group, a carboxyl group, and a unique side chain. When amino acids are joined in a chain, covalent bonds, called peptide bonds, are formed between the amino group of one amino acid and the carboxyl group of the next amino acid.

The unique side chain, or "R" group, in amino acids define each amino acid's chemical properties. When amino acids are linked together, these side chains interact, causing the entire molecule to fold into a particular shape. This process gives each protein a unique, complex, three-dimensional shape.

Protein Function

Proteins are the functional units of the cell. Even the simplest organism makes many different proteins. Proteins may be enzymes, hormones, transport molecules, antibodies, or the structural components of cells and tissues. Every protein has a function that is dictated by its shape. This is because when a protein is folded, only some R groups are exposed and available to form bonds with other molecules. If the shape changes, other R groups might become exposed, and the protein might not be able to make the bonds it would have made otherwise.

PRACTICE

CALIFORNIA CONTENT
STANDARD 4.e

Differences Between Proteins

DIRECTIONS: Choose the letter of the *best* answer.

1 **What is the maximum number of *different* amino acids that might be present in a protein?**

A 20   **C** 2,000

B 200   **D** 20,000

2 **Human red blood cells contain a protein called hemoglobin. Hemoglobin has a specific shape that allows it to bind to oxygen. Hemoglobin is different from other proteins because its**

A sequence of its amino acids is different.

B amino acids in its chain are smaller than other amino acids.

C chain has as many as 50 unique amino acids.

D number of amino acids in its monomers differs from other proteins.

3 **Amino acids have three parts. Two of those are the same for every amino acid. The third part is different for every one, and it is called an "R" group. Which of the following *best* describes the role of R groups in a protein?**

A They help give the protein its structure.

B They help the protein to build amino acids.

C They help the protein decode DNA during translation.

D They help the protein to change its function.

4

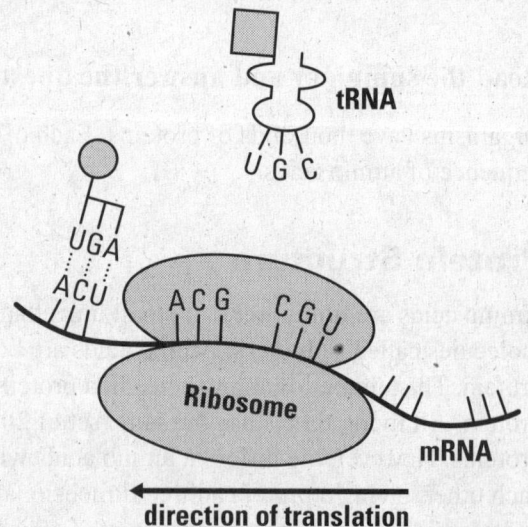

direction of translation

Above, a protein that functions as an enzyme is being built. Suppose a mutation in the DNA results in a protein with an incorrect amino acid. Which statement *best* explains why the mutated enzyme might not function?

A The new amino acid has changed the shape of the active site.

B The new amino acid blocked the active site.

C The new amino acid replaces the substrate in the active site.

D The new amino acid replaces the product in the active site.

5 **A protein's function is very closely related to its structure. Which of the following contributes the *most* to protein structure and function?**

A number and sequence of amino acids

B different properties of one amino acid

C rate of change of an R group in an amino acid

D length of polymers within the amino acids

STANDARD SET 4

REVIEW

CALIFORNIA CONTENT
STANDARD 5.a

DNA, RNA, and Proteins: Structure and Function

STANDARD Students know the general structures and functions of DNA, RNA, and protein.

Read the summary and answer the questions on the next page.

Three biological polymers, DNA, RNA, and protein, are the main players in molecular biology. Each molecule's structure is related to its function.

Similarities between DNA and RNA

DNA and RNA are both nucleic acids, long polymers built of monomers called **nucleotides**. Each nucleotide has three parts: a phosphate group, a ring-shaped sugar built of five carbons, and one nitrogen-containing base. There are five bases: adenine (A), guanine (G), cytosine (C), thymine (T), and uracil (U). However, T is only found in DNA, and U is only found in RNA.

DNA

DNA is a double-stranded molecule that looks like a twisted ladder, with alternating sugar and phosphate groups making up each side and paired bases forming its "rungs." The strands are held together by hydrogen bonds between pairs of bases. Bases always pair the same way: adenine (A) to thymine (T) and cytosine (C) to guanine (G). This makes the two strands complementary—they fit together and are the opposite of one another.

   DNA is an information-storing molecule. Its sequence of bases stores coded instructions for making all of the RNAs and proteins in an organism, although each cell can only make a small number of them at a time.

RNA

RNA is a single-stranded molecule that takes information from DNA and uses this information to build proteins. Three different forms of RNA work to do this.

   Messenger RNA (mRNA) is a long, polymer that is the complement of a gene. mRNA does not have thymine (T), so it matches uracil (U) to adenine (A) instead. mRNA acts as a link; it is the template that carries the code for a protein from DNA in the nucleus to ribosomes in the cytoplasm. **Transfer RNAs (tRNAs)** are folded molecules that bind to amino acids and bring them to ribosomes during protein synthesis. **Ribosomal RNA (rRNA)** forms one part of ribosomes, the sites of protein synthesis.

Proteins

Proteins are polymers built out of a series of amino acids. Each amino acid has an amino group (NH_2), carboxyl group (COOH), and a unique side chain. Covalent bonds, called polypeptide bonds, form between the amino and carboxyl groups to produce a polypeptide. Each protein has a unique amino acid sequence which determines its three-dimensional structure. Its function in the organism depends on the specific properties of its shape. Proteins may be enzymes, hormones, transport molecules, antibodies, or the structural components of cells and tissues.

PRACTICE

CALIFORNIA CONTENT
STANDARD 5.a

DNA, RNA, and Proteins: Structure and Function

DIRECTIONS: Choose the letter of the *best* answer.

1 Suppose you're working in a laboratory, and you find a molecule you did not expect to see. In your analysis, you determine that it is a type of polymer that has the bases adenine (A), guanine (G), cytosine (C), and thymine (T). Which of the following *best* describes the molecule you have found?

  A DNA

  B mRNA

  C tRNA

  D protein

2 One type of polymer is responsible for taking genetic information from the nucleus and delivering this information into the cytoplasm. What molecule in the cell performs this task?

  A DNA

  B mRNA

  C tRNA

  D protein

3 Proteins are polymers that can have one of many different roles in the body. Some proteins function as enzymes and others give cells a specific structure. Proteins' roles are often determined by their

  A shape.

  B bases.

  C cells.

  D sugars.

4 In the cytoplasm, molecule 1 carries amino acids to the ribosome. At the ribosome, these amino acids are joined together to form molecule 2. Which of the following statements *best* describes the identity of molecule 1?

  A Molecule 1 is rRNA.

  B Molecule 1 is tRNA.

  C Molecule 1 is mRNA.

  D Molecule 1 is DNA.

5

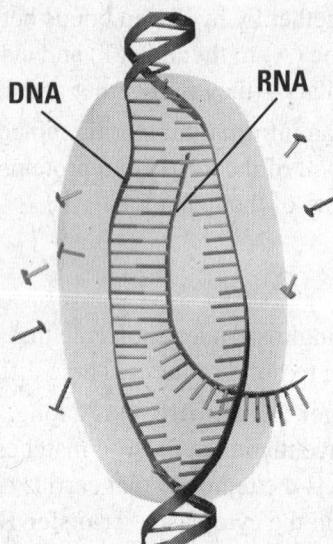

DNA   RNA

The diagram above shows how DNA matches up with a type of RNA. These two molecules can match up because they both have

  A complementary bases.

  B two strands of nucleotides.

  C ribose sugars.

  D phosphate groups.

REVIEW

**CALIFORNIA CONTENT
STANDARD 5.b**

Base-Pairing Rules

STANDARD Students know how to apply base-pairing rules to explain precise copying of DNA during semiconservative replication and transcription of information from DNA into mRNA.

Read the summary and answer the questions on the next page.

DNA is an information-storing molecule. It contains coded instructions for building RNA and proteins in an organism. Its structure permits it to accurately copy itself into new DNA molecules and serve as a template to build RNA molecules.

DNA Structure and Base-Pairing Rules

DNA is a long, molecule that is made up of many smaller molecules called **nucleotides.** Nucleotides are themselves made of three parts: a phosphate, a sugar, and a base. The nucleotides are bound together into two long strands and form a twisted ladder, a shape called a double helix. Alternating sugar and phosphate molecules make up the sides of the ladder. Each "rung" of this ladder is made up of two bases that are held together by hydrogen bonds. DNA has only four types of bases: adenine (A), thymine (T), cytosine (C), and guanine (G). In DNA, each base can only bond with one other base. A must bind to T, and C must bind to G. These strict pairing rules, shown in the diagram, are called the base-pairing rules.

Semiconservative Replication

During replication, proteins separate the two strands of DNA and hold them apart. Then complementary nucleotides pair with the exposed bases. An enzyme helps bind together the nucleotides in the new strand of DNA. The result is two new DNA molecules, each containing a parent strand and a new, complementary daughter strand. Because one parent strand is present in each DNA molecule, the process is called **semiconservative replication**.

```
DNA           DNA
 A ......... T
 T ......... A
 C ......... G
 G ......... C
              RNA
 A ......... U
 T ......... A
 C ......... G
 G ......... C
```

Transcription and Base-Pairing Rules

Transcription is the first step a cell takes in building proteins. During transcription, the cell builds a single stranded messenger RNA (mRNA) molecule. Like DNA, RNA is a nucleic acid and follows the base-pairing rules. In RNA, however, uracil (U) pairs with A, and T is not present, as you can see in the diagram. The process of transcription shares many similarities with replication.

1. Enzymes separate the strands of DNA, exposing the bases.
2. Free-floating nucleotides pair up with nucleotides in that segment of the DNA.
3. Enzymes binds the nucleotides together, forming a new mRNA molecule.

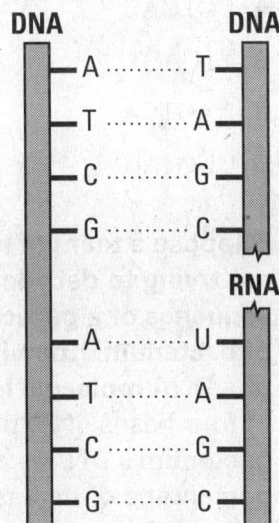

PRACTICE

CALIFORNIA CONTENT
STANDARD 5.b

Base-Pairing Rules

DIRECTIONS: Choose the letter of the *best* answer.

1 When DNA replicates, its two strands separate. Then bases are added to each strand. When the process is complete, there are two new DNA molecules, and each has one strand from the original molecule. The term that *best* describes this is

  A semiconservative replication.

  B semicommemorative replication.

  C semiconstructive replication.

  D semiconductive replication.

2 In a DNA molecule, if the sequence of bases in one strand of the molecule is GGACTG, what will be the sequence of bases in the complementary strand?

  A CCTGAC

  B TTCAGT

  C AAGTCA

  D UUGTAU

3 Suppose a team of researchers are trying to decode the genetic sequence of a particular species of bacterium. Knowing that all of a DNA molecule is comprised of four bases, if 20 percent of the bacterium's DNA is adenine, what percentage of its bases would be cytosine?

  A 10 percent

  B 20 percent

  C 30 percent

  D 40 percent

4 Suppose a strand of mRNA has the base sequence UGCCAGUCA. What was the DNA sequence that this mRNA was built from?

  A CATTGACTG

  B GUAACUGAG

  C TUGGAUTGA

  D ACGGTCAGT

5

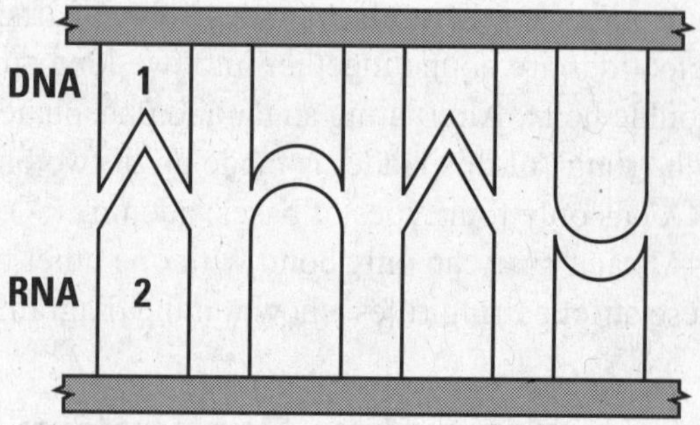

The diagram above shows an RNA sequence matching to a DNA sequence. In this case, base 1 on the DNA matches to base 2 on the RNA. What statement *best* describes the possible identities of these two bases?

  A Base 1 is uracil (U), and base 2 is guanine (G).

  B Base 1 is adenine (A), and base 2 is thymine (T).

  C Base 1 is cytosine (C), and base 2 is guanine (G).

  D Base 1 is uracil (U), and base 2 is thymine (T).

REVIEW

CALIFORNIA CONTENT
STANDARD 5.c

Biotechnology

STANDARD Students know how genetic engineering (biotechnology) is used to produce novel biomedical and agricultural products.

Read the summary and answer the questions on the next page.

Scientists have developed methods to take genes from one organism and move them to another. This process, called genetic engineering, allows scientists to produce medical and agricultural products that we would not be able to produce otherwise.

Manipulating DNA

Genetic engineering is the process of manipulating organisms' DNA. Suppose a scientist wants to make a type of lettuce plant that is not affected by a certain fungus. The scientist has identified a gene in a corn plant that makes it resistant to the same fungus. The scientist can now remove the gene from the corn plant's DNA and insert it into the lettuce plant's DNA. The result is **recombinant DNA,** or DNA that has genes from more than one organism. The process of how scientists alter DNA is described below.

1. **Separating DNA Strands.** Once researchers have identified a gene that codes for a trait of interest, they use restriction enzymes to remove it from the DNA strand. These enzymes cut DNA molecules at specific nucleotide sequences. This produces a fragment of DNA with tails of free bases at the cut, as shown in the diagram.

2. **Combining DNA.** The ends of the freshly cut DNA are called "sticky ends" because they will immediately connect to any other piece of DNA with complementary bases. Just as in DNA replication, A binds to T and C binds to G.

3. **Copying the new DNA.** Scientists can then take the new strand of DNA and make billions of copies using polymerase chain reaction (PCR).

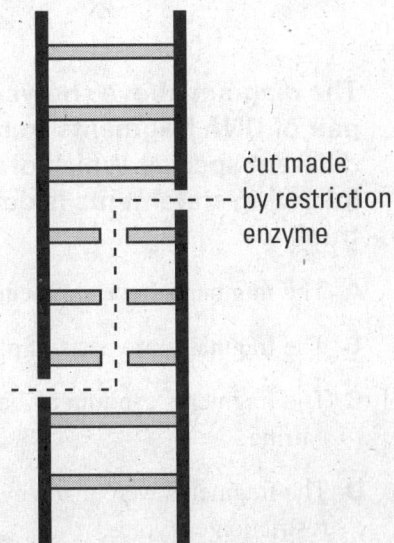

cut made by restriction enzyme

Inserting New DNA into an Organism

Bacterial plasmids allow scientists to take the newly formed DNA and insert it into a different organism. **Plasmids** are tiny, independently replicating rings of DNA. Scientists cut the plasmid with restriction enzymes and insert the new piece of DNA, which quickly binds to the "sticky ends" of the plasmid. Then, bacteria take up the plasmid. Once the plasmid is inside the bacteria, it will express the new gene. Transgenic bacteria can make proteins, such as human insulin and human growth hormone, in large quantities.

Transgenic bacteria can also be used to modify plants. After a new gene is inserted into bacteria as described above, the bacteria infect a plant. Once infected, the new gene may become part of the plant's DNA and get expressed like any other gene. This technique has created plants with increased resistance to frost, diseases, herbicides, and insect pests.

STANDARD SET 5

PRACTICE

CALIFORNIA CONTENT
STANDARD 5.c

Biotechnology

DIRECTIONS: Choose the letter of the *best* answer.

1

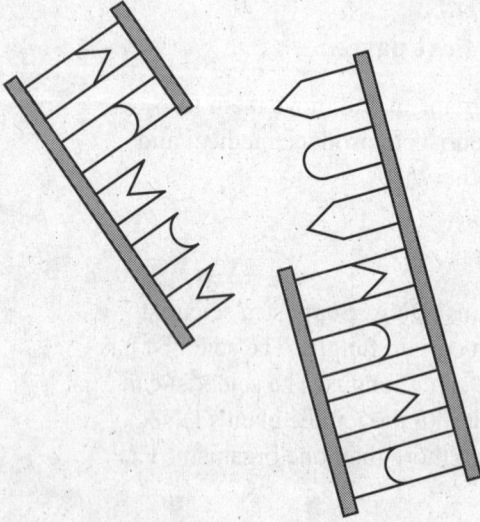

The diagram above shows a pair of DNA fragments from two different species. Which of the following statements is definitely true?

A The fragments have blunt ends.

B The fragments are parts of plasmids.

C The fragments can join by base pairing.

D The fragments were made by different restriction enzymes.

2 Which of the following *best* describes a plasmid?

A a virus that infects bacteria

B a self-replicating ring of DNA

C a piece of chromosomal RNA

D a small bacterial protein

3 Which of the following would scientists use polymerase chain reaction (PCR) to do?

A add DNA into a virus

B insert plasmids into a bacterium

C produce many copies of a piece of DNA

D cut DNA into small pieces

4 It takes several steps to make a transgenic plant. If you arranged the following steps in order, which would be second?

A Remove a gene from an organism with restriction enzymes.

B Insert the plasmid into a bacterium.

C Infect the plant with the transgenic bacterium.

D Insert the gene into a plasmid.

5 Humans with Type 1 diabetes must inject a hormone called insulin into their bloodstream to survive. The insulin they use comes from genetically modified bacteria. These bacteria produce the same human insulin that healthy people produce. Which of the following explains how bacteria can produce human insulin?

A The bacteria evolved to produce human insulin.

B The bacteria express the gene for human insulin.

C The bacteria cure Type 1 diabetes by producing human insulin.

D The bacteria get their gene for human insulin from pigs.

REVIEW

CALIFORNIA CONTENT STANDARD 6.a   *Biodiversity*

STANDARD Students know biodiversity is the sum total of different kinds of organisms and is affected by alterations of habitats.

Read the summary and use the diagram to answer the questions on the next page.

Biodiversity refers to the collection and variety of living things within a geographic area. The degree of biodiversity in a habitat depends on factors such as geography, temperature, moisture, and other species present. Habitat changes, such as climate change and invading species, can threaten biodiversity. The more diverse an ecosystem is, the more stable it is.

Biodiversity and Variety

The term **biodiversity** refers to the variety of living things, or biota, in an ecosystem. Biodiversity is not affected by the number of organisms in a population, only the number of species in an area. Areas with a large assortment of species have a high level of biodiversity. Areas with low biodiversity contain relatively few species.

The amount of biodiversity in an area depends on its living, biotic, and nonliving, abiotic, factors and tends to vary by region and habitat. A **habitat** is the area where an organism lives and all of the biotic and abiotic factors affecting the organism. Biodiversity generally is greatest in tropical regions and lowest in polar regions, and temperate regions are somewhere between the two extremes in terms of biodiversity.

Challenges to Biodiversity

Alterations to habitats through natural disasters and human-made disturbances can have major effects on local biodiversity. For example, natural disasters, such as volcanic eruptions, could kill hundreds of organisms. Likewise, if humans cut down parts of a forest to build a shopping mall, many organisms might not be able to survive in this new, fragmented environment. Tropical rain forests are one of several habitats across the globe referred to as hot spots—areas rich in biodiversity, but threatened by human activities, such as deforestation.

The amount of biodiversity in an ecosystem determines its stability and resilience. Stability is a measure of the ecosystem's resistance to change. Resilience reflects its ability to recover after a disturbance. Ecosystems with a high degree of biodiversity are more stable and resilient than those in which biodiversity is low.

PRACTICE

CALIFORNIA CONTENT
STANDARD 6.a

Biodiversity

STANDARD SET 6

DIRECTIONS: Choose the letter of the *best* answer.

1

Ecosys-tem	Number of species	Total population
Rainforest	3,507	25,459
Tundra	123	4,987
Scrubland	1,309	27,023
Woodlands	1,015	6,320

The table above comes from a hypothetical census of organisms living in four regional ecosystems. Which ecosystem has the most biodiversity?

A Rainforest

B Tundra

C Scrubland

D Woodlands

2 Which of the following *best* describes the term biodiversity?

A the number of organisms inhabiting tropical rainforests

B the range of habitats within a geographic area

C the variety of species living in an ecosystem

D the abiotic and biotic factors in an ecosystem

3 Compared with ecosystems that have less biodiversity, ecosystems high in biodiversity have more

A rainfall.

B stablility.

C abiotic factors.

D human disturbances.

4 Which term *best* describes the area where an organism lives and all of the biotic and abiotic factors affecting it?

A community

B population

C biodiversity

D habitat

5 Elephants are considered an important species in east Africa. During droughts, they dig deep holes in dry riverbeds, and the holes fill up with water. These holes are then used by all other animals in the area. Which of the following *most* accurately describes how the loss of elephants would affect this ecosystem?

A Biodiversity would increase, as more species evolved.

B Biodiversity would remain the same, but population sizes would increase.

C Biodiversity would decrease, since few species could tolerate living with less available water.

D Biodiversity would not change, though there would be increased predation by lions.

REVIEW

CALIFORNIA CONTENT
STANDARD 6.b

Analyzing Ecosystem Changes

STANDARD Students know how to analyze changes in an ecosystem resulting from changes in climate, human activity, introduction of nonnative species, or changes in population size.

Read the summary and answer the questions on the next page.

Ecosystems change over long periods of time. However, human activities can cause these normally slow changes to occur much more quickly.

Observing Change

Researchers study changes in ecosystems so that they can learn to predict the consequences of a change. Researchers notice change through observation, experiments, and modeling. They observe the present condition. Then they experiment, observing whether a change occurred. If they find patterns, they can use these patterns to model, or predict, whether what they learned can be applied to different situations.

Ecosystems change naturally. For example, a change in the amount of rainfall can have an effect on which organisms will survive. Natural changes can be predictable because the changes occur over many years, and similar changes might have been observed before. It is much more difficult to predict the outcome if changes occur quickly, and researchers do not have time to observe, experiment, and model the effects of the change.

Human Influence

Ecosystem changes caused by human activity are difficult to predict for several reasons: First, human activities have an immediate effect; second, they have a large scale effect; and third, humans have not likely observed the same changes previously, so they could not suspect they would occur. However, these changes can have great effects on ecosystems. The rapid destruction of habitat through land clearing or pollution, or the introduction of new species occurs too quickly for the ecosystem to respond. As a result, the ecosystem can quickly destabilize. Here are some of the ways human activities alter ecosystems.

- **Invasive Species.** Sometimes, by accident or on purpose, humans take one species from its natural habitat and introduce it into a completely different ecosystem. Introduced species might outcompete native species for resources and cause the population of native species to crash. Also, unlike native species, introduced species do not have natural predators in their new ecosystem.

- **Habitat Destruction.** Clearing forests, filling wetlands, and polluting air, land, and water threatens habitats and the organisms that live in them. Habitat destruction, such as clearing a forest or dumping large quantities of poisonous chemicals into a river, can occur far too rapidly for the ecosystem to adjust.

- **Climate Change.** Climate change due to fossil fuel burning is difficult to predict because it is on a global scale. Humans have not existed long enough to have observed anything like it, and so, we must use computer models to predict what might happen if the Earth's average temperature rises.

PRACTICE

CALIFORNIA CONTENT
STANDARD 6.b

Analyzing Ecosystem Changes

DIRECTIONS: Choose the letter of the *best* answer.

1 Compared to ecosystem changes resulting from human activity, most natural changes in ecosystems are predictable because they

A evolve over a long time.

B are random in their effect.

C affect population size but not resource availability.

D occur on a seasonal basis.

2

Species	Low (°C)	High (°C)
A	–7	21
B	–15	29

The table above shows the range of temperatures that two different species of hypothetical trees can live in. Suppose the trees are in an area where temperature ranges from 15°C to 20°C and that Species A is more common than Species B. Which of the following would most likely occur if the temperature increased by 5°C?

A Species A will become more abundant, but Species B will go extinct.

B Species A will go extinct, but Species B will become more abundant.

C Species A will become less common, but Species B will become more abundant.

D Species A will become more abundant, but Species B will become less common.

3 Unexpected changes in ecosystems resulting from human activities are most likely to

A increase predation rates.

B destabilize the ecosystem.

C lessen interspecific competition.

D improve water quality and availability.

4 The zebra mussel is a freshwater organism from Europe. However, some were accidentally brought into the Great Lakes by shipping vessels. Which statement *best* explains how these mussels could threaten the ecosystems in the Great Lakes?

A They will provide a new food source to other animals in the Great Lakes.

B They can encourage other animals in the Great Lakes to evolve more quickly.

C They have no natural predators to limit their population, so they might outcompete native animals.

D They can actually stabilize the ecosystem by increasing the resources available.

5 Using observed patterns to predict what will happen if there is a change is called

A observing.

B experimenting.

C sampling.

D modeling.

REVIEW

CALIFORNIA CONTENT
STANDARD 6.c

Population Fluctions

STANDARD Students know how fluctuations in population size in an ecosystem are determined by the relative rates of birth, immigration, emigration, and death.

Read the summary and answer the questions on the next page.

Changes in population size result from four factors: immigrations, births, emigrations, and deaths. Immigration and birth increase population size, but emigration and death decrease it.

Population Change

A **population** is all of the organisms of a species that live in the same area. Population size may change due to the number of immigrations, births, emigrations, and deaths. These four factors are affected by the availability of food, water, and shelter.

Population Growth. When resources are plentiful, populations may grow. Birth rates may increase because organisms have more nutrients or better nesting sites. Immigration, or movement of individuals into a population, may increase because resources attract other organisms to an area. Population size also can rise because increased resources produce a reduced death rate and rate of emigration. The rate of population growth can be gradual or very quick. For example, if a resource becomes suddenly available, growth will be very fast. If the resource becomes available gradually, the population will increase slowly.

Population Decline. If resources are in short supply, population size may decline. With less food and shelter, more organisms will die, and others will leave the area in search of a new habitat—a process called emigration. Also, fewer individuals will be born, and fewer organisms will immigrate into a population when resources are difficult to get. The rate of population decline generally follows the rate at which one or more critical resources are lost. If a resource diminishes over a long period, population size may decrease slowly. A sudden decrease in resources, as may occur after a natural disaster, may cause a population crash—a dramatic drop in population size in a short timeframe.

Net Population Change

Population size is always changing. The change in a population over time is determined by comparing birth and immigration rates with death and emigration rates.

Net population size = (births + immigration) – (deaths + emigration)

Though immigration and births bring more individuals into a population, decreased emigration or a lower death rate can produce a net increase. On the other hand, though emigration and deaths remove individuals from a population, the net decrease in population size in a given period can result from a decreased birth rate or lower rate of immigration.

PRACTICE

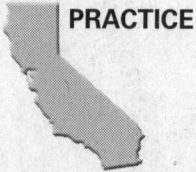

CALIFORNIA CONTENT
STANDARD 6.c

Population Fluctions

DIRECTIONS: Choose the letter of the *best* answer.

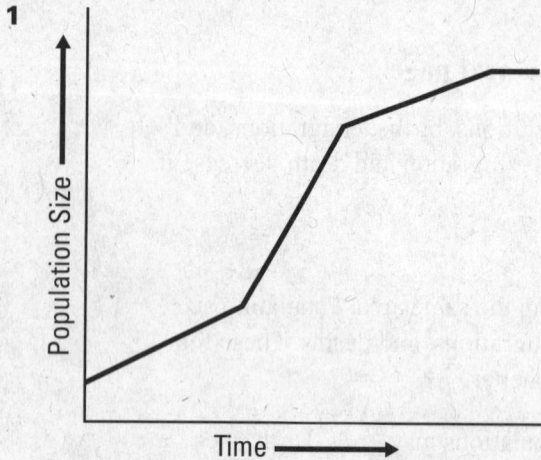

1

Population Size

Time ⟶

The chart above shows an increase in population over time. Which of the following could *best* explain this increase?

A decreased resource rate

B decreased growth rate

C decreased death rate

D decreased immigration rate

2 In many cities, parks have signs asking people to not feed pigeons. The *most* likely reason for decreasing the birds' food supply is that it may

A increase the birds' death rate.

B force them to emigrate.

C make it unnecessary for park employees to clean up after pigeons.

D replace pigeons with songbirds.

3 In a given area, a population is a group of organisms of the same

A family.   C habitat.

B ecosystem.   D species.

4 Many lakes in the United States have received large amounts nutrients, such as nitrogen and phosphorus, as a result of pollution from farms and industry. This pollution causes rapid and massive increases in some lakes' algae population. This gradually depletes lakes' oxygen supply, killing many organisms. What is the *most* logical explanation for the rapid growth of algae?

A The increased nutrients led many organisms to emigrate.

B The increased nutrients supported the population growth of algae.

C The increased nutrients allowed algae to outcompete other species.

D The increased nutrients caused algae to immigrate.

5 Suppose the deer population in a local forest preserve is much larger than last year. There have been no major changes in food supply, and hunting is forbidden. Which of the following *best* accounts for the population increase?

A increased emigration and increased birth rate

B decreased emigration and increased death rate

C increased immigration and increased birth rate

D increased immigration and increased death rate

REVIEW

CALIFORNIA CONTENT
STANDARD 6.d
Chemical Cycles

STANDARD Students know how water, carbon, and nitrogen cycle between abiotic resources and organic matter in the ecosystem and how oxygen cycles through photosynthesis and respiration.

Read the summary and answer the questions on the next page.

Elements move through ecosystems through chemical cycles. Organisms take in nutrients and break them down into elements that are used for life processes. When an organism dies, these elements are recycled into the environment and can be re-used in nutrient cycles again. The most important cycles for living things are those of water, nitrogen, carbon, and oxygen.

Abiotic and Biotic

All living things require nutrients, or molecules that allow organisms to function. In general, nutrients can be found in either abiotic or biotic resources. **Abiotic** resources are those that are nonliving, such as the soil or the air. **Biotic** resources are those that are living, such as any organism. Nutrients such as water, nitrogen, carbon, and oxygen move between biotic and abiotic resources by chemical cycles.

Chemical Cycles

Nutrients are present on Earth in a limited supply, so there must be a way for them to be taken in and recycled from abiotic resources and dead organic matter into living organisms. Below are discussions of how important nutrients cycle between biotic and abiotic resources.

Water Cycle. Water enters ecosystems as precipitation. When organisms drink the water, it becomes part of their tissues. Water reenters the abiotic resources in three ways: evaporation, transpiration in plants, and respiration in animals.

Nitrogen Cycle. Bacteria take gaseous nitrogen and convert it to forms that plants can use. Nitrogen is passed through the food chain as consumers eat plants or other consumers. When organisms die, decomposers return the nitrogen to the soil again. Then, plants may take up the nitrogen, or bacteria may release it into the atmosphere.

Carbon Cycle. Carbon enters the biotic resources when plants convert carbon dioxide gas (CO_2) into sugar during photosynthesis. The sugars in plants are passed to consumers who eat plants. Carbon is returned to the atmosphere as CO_2 during decomposition, respiration, and fossil fuel burning.

Oxygen Cycle. Oxygen cycles through ecosystems via photosynthesis and respiration. Plants and other producers release oxygen as a byproduct of photosynthesis. Non-photosynthetic organisms take in oxygen from the atmosphere and release carbon dioxide through respiration.

PRACTICE

CALIFORNIA CONTENT
STANDARD 6.d

Chemical Cycles

DIRECTIONS: Choose the letter of the *best* answer.

STANDARD SET 6

1

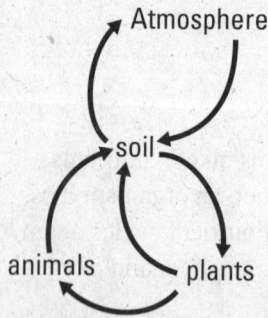

The diagram above shows the nitrogen cycle. Which of the following *best* describes an abiotic resource where nitrogen in stored?

A in the animals

B in the atmosphere

C in tree roots

D in leaf cells called stomates

2 Which of the following *best* traces the path of a carbon atom from the air a cow?

A carbon dioxide ➡ photosynthesis ➡ grass ➡ cow

B methane ➡ chemosynthesis ➡ grass ➡ cow

C methane ➡ photosynthesis ➡ grass ➡ cow

D carbon dioxide ➡ eutrophication ➡ algae ➡ cow

3 How does nitrogen get from one biotic factor to another?

A by moving through photosynthesis

B by moving through the food chain

C by moving through the water cycle

D be moving through precipitation

4 Scientific evidence suggests that there is more carbon dioxide in the atmosphere today than there was a hundred years ago. Some scientists theorize that because fossil fuels, such as oil and coal, have carbon in them, fossil fuel burning has caused the increase of carbon in the atmosphere. Which of the following *best* describes the movement of carbon in this case?

A Carbon trapped in abiotic resources, such as fossil fuels, moved into the atmosphere.

B Carbon was moving from fossil fuels into the atmosphere before humans started burning them.

C Carbon moved from the atmosphere into biotic factors through respiration.

D Carbon stays in fossil fuels and the atmosphere because it only moves between abiotic factors.

5 How do the processes of respiration and photosynthesis help cycle oxygen?

A Photosynthesis takes in oxygen, and respiration takes in oxygen.

B Photosynthesis releases oxygen, and respiration releases oxygen.

C Photosynthesis releases oxygen, and respiration takes in oxygen.

D Photosynthesis takes in oxygen, and respiration releases oxygen.

REVIEW

Producers and Decomposers

STANDARD Students know a vital part of an ecosystem is the stability of its producers and decomposers.

Read the summary and answer the questions on the next page.

The ability of an ecosystem to get energy and recycle nutrients depends on producers and decomposers. Producers, such as plants, use energy from sunlight to manufacture food that supports the entire ecosystem. Decomposers, such as fungi or bacteria, break down dead or waste organic matter. By breaking organic matter into simpler compounds, these compounds become available to other organisms.

Producers

All ecosystems depend on producers. Producers provide the basis for the ecosystem's energy, which is why they're found at the bottom of the energy pyramid. A **producer** is an organism that uses energy from nonliving resources to manufacture food. Plants, algae, seaweed, and photosynthetic microorganisms are different types of producers.

Producers that contain chlorophyll—plants, algae, and cyanobacteria, for example—use energy from sunlight to convert carbon dioxide and water into sugars and carbohydrates. Chemosynthetic producers—usually bacteria—use chemical energy to produce carbohydrates. When other organisms eat producers, they use the carbohydrates as an energy source. This is how producers make food for an entire ecosystem.

Decomposers

A **decomposer** is an organism that breaks down organic matter into simpler compounds. While doing this, the decomposer gets energy it needs to live. Fungi, bacteria, and some worms and insects are decomposers. Decomposers are important to the stability of an ecosystem because they take vital nutrients, such as nitrogen and carbon, out of dead organic matter and return these nutrients to the environment, where they can be picked up and used again by other organisms.

Nutrient Cycling and Ecosystem Stability

Energy flows through an ecosystem in one direction—from producers to consumers. The stability of any ecosystem depends on the presence of producers, since they convert the sun's energy into food for the entire ecosystem. Ecosystems generally have more than one type of producer—the more producers, the more food available, the more stable the ecosystem.

Nutrients cycle from the environment to organisms and back to the environment. Decomposers are responsible for cycling nutrients between dead and living organisms. If decomposers were not present in an ecosystem, dead matter would not be removed and would pile up rapidly. Furthermore, nutrients would not be cycled back into the environment, and so nutrients would gradually become unavailable for other organisms. Without the proper flow of nutrients, the ecosystem would become unbalanced.

PRACTICE

CALIFORNIA CONTENT
STANDARD 6.e

Producers and Decomposers

STANDARD SET 6

DIRECTIONS: Choose the letter of the *best* answer.

1

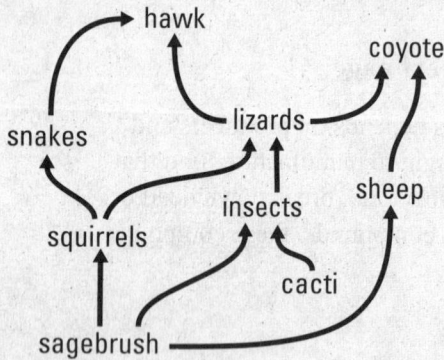

In the diagram above of a hypothetical ecosystem, which species are likely to be producers?

A cacti and insects

B cacti and sheep

C cacti, insects, and lizards

D cacti and sagebrush

2 The *most* accurate description of a producer is an organism that

A gets its energy from nonliving resources to produce its own food.

B uses energy from burning sugars to produce the oxygen we breathe.

C uses sunlight as an energy source to produce nitrogen for an ecosystem.

D breaks down hydrogen sulfide during chemosynthesis to produce sulfuric acid.

3 Which of the following *best* describes the role of decomposers in an ecosystem?

A use energy from the Sun to produce food

B remove nutrients from dead matter and return it to the soil

C convert energy from chemicals into glucose

D use nutrients from dead matter to synthesize sugars

4 A stable ecosystem requires that

A organisms have the ability to consume plants and animals.

B producers use chemicals for photosynthesis.

C nutrients cycle through it.

D consumers are more common than producers.

5 What is the role of producers in a stable ecosystem?

A to manufacture food if the decomposers begin to die out

B to supply the ecosystem with an energy source

C to remove nitrogen to form glucose and dead organic matter

D to filter wastes out of the environment

REVIEW

CALIFORNIA CONTENT STANDARD 6.f

Food Webs and Energy Pyramids

STANDARD   Students know at each link in a food web some energy is stored in newly made structures but much energy is dissipated into the environment as heat. This dissipation may be represented in an energy pyramid.

Read the summary and answer the questions on the next page.

An energy pyramid shows how energy is distributed in a community, and food webs show the feeding relationships of organisms in a community. As one organism consumes another, some energy is gained, but almost 90 percent of the energy is lost as heat. An energy pyramid is a visual representation showing how energy decreases as you move up the food chain.

Food Webs

A group of different species in the same area is called a **community.** Organisms in a community may compete with one another for energy. Food webs show feeding relationships between these organisms. All food webs begin with producers.

Producers, such as plants or bacteria, use photosynthesis or chemosynthesis to manufacture their own food. Producers are eaten by consumers. Consumers may be herbivores, carnivores, or omnivores. Herbivores are called primary consumers because they eat only producers. Carnivores eat other consumers. Carnivores that eat herbivores are called secondary consumers. Omnivores are types of consumers that eat both producers and consumers.

Energy Pyramids

While feeding relationships are shown in a food web, the flow of energy through a community is shown in an energy pyramid. An **energy pyramid** is a diagram that compares energy gained by producers, primary consumers, and other organisms. Each division of the pyramid represents a different **trophic level**, or amount of energy gained from consuming one food item. Producers—which manufacture their own food—gain the greatest amount of energy. Consumers at the next higher trophic level get comparatively less energy per meal. So each trophic level receives much less energy than the level below it.

As energy flows up the energy pyramid, a small amount is converted to biomass at each trophic level. That is, when an organism eats food, a small amount of the food's energy is incorporated into that organism's biomass; the remaining energy is lost as heat. The dissipation, or loss, of energy between trophic levels may be as much as 90 percent; this means that only 10 percent of the energy at one trophic level can be transferred to the next trophic level. Because energy is lost at each stage of a food chain and energy pyramid, the longer the chain is, the more energy is lost overall.

PRACTICE

CALIFORNIA CONTENT
STANDARD 6.f

Food Webs and Energy Pyramids

DIRECTIONS: Choose the letter of the *best* answer.

1

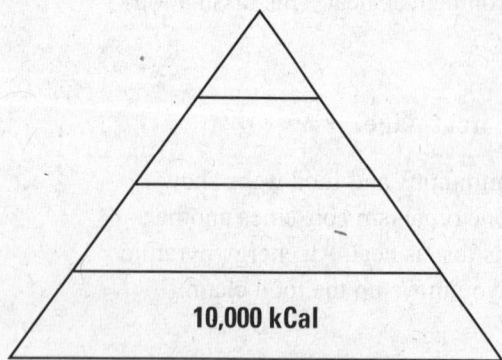

10,000 kCal

The flow of energy between organisms of a community is represented by an energy pyramid. A pyramid is used because its triangular shape shows that there

A are always many tertiary consumers.

B is less and less energy transferred between trophic levels.

C cannot be any more producers in a community.

D should always be omnivores in a community.

2 Almost 90 percent of the energy transferred up the food chain is lost as heat between trophic levels. The energy that is *not* lost as heat is

A recycled by decomposers.

B recycled back to producers.

C incorporated as biomass at each level.

D used to provide energy for chemosynthesis.

3 Which of the following *best* illustrates the feeding relationships between organisms in a community?

A energy pyramid

B decomposer

C Hardy-Weinberg equilibrium

D food web

4 Producers are always at the base of a food chain or food web. The *best* explanation for this is

A producers are stronger than consumers.

B producers manufacture the food that supports the entire ecosystem.

C producer populations are less important than consumer populations.

D producers grow on the ground or on the sea floor.

5 Each level of the energy pyramid represents an amount of energy that organisms can get by eating food sources on lower levels. What is the term that is used to refer to these levels?

A trophic

B consumer

C energy

D omnivorous

REVIEW

CALIFORNIA CONTENT
STANDARD 7.a

Phenotype Vs. Genotype

STANDARD Students know why natural selection acts on the phenotype rather than the genotype of an organism.

Read the summary and answer the questions on the next page.

Natural selection is a theory that states that the individuals that are best adapted to their environment will survive and reproduce most successfully. Natural selection acts on physical traits and not on an individual's genes.

Phenotype and Genotype

In biology, a trait is a characteristic or feature of an individual. Some traits, such as height or leaf shape, are morphological and easily viewed by other organisms. Traits also may be biochemical or behavioral—blood type and wood pecking are two examples, respectively.

The physical expression of a trait in an individual is called its **phenotype**. A phenotype is usually produced through the interaction of the alleles of several genes with each other and with the environment. For example, height in humans is influenced by several genes, as well as environmental factors such as nutrition.

However, organisms don't inherit "traits." Instead, they inherit genes that code for the traits. The group of alleles that interact and that code for a given trait is called a **genotype**.

Natural selection works on phenotype rather than on genotype because it is the physical expression of a trait that can allow individuals to better survive and reproduce. Furthermore, environmental influences, such as nutrition, can affect individuals living in the same environment differently.

Natural Selection in Populations

Natural selection works on individuals, but it is populations that evolve over time. Natural selection acts on different phenotypes in a population. To have different phenotypes, a population must have genetic variation. Environmental factors determine whether a phenotype is favorable regardless of the arrangement of genes for that trait. Genetic variation increases the chance that some members of a population will be able to adapt to their environment.

STANDARD SET 7

PRACTICE

CALIFORNIA CONTENT
STANDARD 7.a

Phenotype Vs. Genotype

DIRECTIONS: Choose the letter of the *best* answer.

1

Genotype	Phenotype
SS	spotted skin
Ss	spotted skin
ss	solid skin

In the hypothetical frog population shown above, the allele for spotted skin (*S*) is dominant to the allele for solid (*s*) skin. Frogs with spotted skin blend in with their surroundings better and are unable to be seen by predators. Which of the following would natural selection "select" in this environment?

A frogs with at least one *S* allele in a genotype

B frogs with a heterozygous phenotype

C frogs with a spotted skin phenotype

D frogs displaying the solid-skin genotype

2 The group of alleles that interact and that code for a given trait is called a(n)

A genotype.

B adaptation.

C phenotype.

D mechanism.

3 Natural selection is the theory that individuals that are best adapted to an environment will survive and produce more offspring than the individuals that are less well adapted. What does natural selection act on?

A genotypes

B phenotypes

C alleles

D environment

4 Which of the following best describes the difference between phenotype and genotype?

A All phenotypes are acquired, while genotypes are inherited.

B A phenotype is the way a trait is expressed, while a genotype is the combination of alleles that codes for it.

C A phenotype is a physical trait, while a genotype can be a biochemical or behavioral trait.

D A phenotype is inherited only under favorable conditions, whereas a genotypes can be inherited under any conditions.

5 A physical trait is part of an individual's

A allele.

B adaptation.

C phenotype.

D variation.

REVIEW

CALIFORNIA CONTENT
STANDARD 7.b

Genetic Disease

STANDARD Students know why alleles that are lethal in a homozygous individual may be carried in a heterozygote and thus maintained in a gene pool.

Read the summary and answer the questions on the next page.

Some alleles cause death or severe illness in individuals. A homozygous individual, or one that carries two copies of a lethal allele, will be affected negatively. A heterozygous individual will not be affected by a lethal allele if the allele is recessive, but when the individual reproduces, its offspring might receive the allele. Thus, heterozygous individuals might contribute lethal recessive alleles to a gene pool.

Genetic Disease in Individuals

Each individual has two copies of alleles, one from its mother and one from its father. An individual's collection of alleles is called a genotype. For this discussion, suppose that there are two alleles for a certain trait: a dominant *R* allele, and a recessive *r* allele. Genotypes are either homozygous or heterozygous. **Homozygous** genotypes contain two identical alleles. These can be either two dominant alleles *(RR)* or two recessive ones *(rr)*. But **heterozygous** genotypes have two different alleles, one dominant and one recessive *(Rr)*. Together, these alleles produce an individual's phenotype, or the physical expression of that trait. If an individual's genotype has at least one copy of a dominant allele *(Rr or RR)*, the dominant allele will express the trait, and the recessive allele will not contribute to the phenotype. If an individual has two copies of a recessive allele *(rr),* these alleles will produce the trait.

Alleles that produce a genetic disease or cause death are called lethal alleles. If the lethal allele is recessive, it will only be expressed in individuals that are homozygous recessive for the allele *(rr)*. This means that individuals that are heterozygous *(Rr)* or homozygous dominant *(RR)* will not get the disease because the dominant allele is expressed.

Genetic Disease in Gene Pools

The **gene pool** is the collection of all of the alleles in a population. Although lethal recessive alleles might prevent a homozygous recessive individual from reproducing, these alleles can remain in the gene pool because heterozygous individuals may pass the allele to their offspring without expressing the negative phenotype.

Suppose that a recessive allele *(r)* is lethal. If an individual expresses the disease, the individual will die and not reproduce successfully. By not reproducing, that individual will not pass along any genetic information to offspring. However, recall that only homozygous *(rr)* individuals will express a recessive phenotype. If an individual has a heterozygous *(Rr)* genotype, it will not get the lethal disease despite having the recessive allele. However, when this individual reproduces, it might pass on the recessive allele to its offspring. These individuals are called **heterozygous carriers** because, although they do not express the lethal trait, they carry the allele that causes it and might pass the allele on to their offspring.

STANDARD SET 7

Name   Period   Date

Genetic Disease

DIRECTIONS: Choose the letter of the *best* answer.

1

Alleles	Genotypes
GG	homozygous dominant
Gg	heterozygous
gg	homozygous recessive

The table above displays the
genotypes for Tay-Sachs disease,
a recessive disorder in which a
substance called GM2 builds up in
the brain, causing severe seizures.
Most individuals with Tay-Sachs
do not survive past age four. The
Tay-Sachs allele is *most* likely
maintained in a gene pool through
matings involving

A homozygous dominants.

B heterozygous recessives.

C homozygous recessives.

D heterozygous carriers.

**2 Which statement *best* describes the
difference between homozygous and
heterozygous genotypes?**

A Homozygous genotypes have
recessive alleles; heterozygous
genotypes have dominant alleles.

B Homozygous genotypes are lethal;
heterozygous individuals remain
healthy but carry the lethal trait.

C Homozygous genotypes contain a
pair of identical alleles; heterozygous
genotypes contain a pair of different
alleles.

D Homozygous genotypes are found
in reproductive cells; heterozygous
genotypes are found in all cells.

**3 Why aren't lethal recessive traits
expressed in heterozygotes?**

A The lethal recessive allele is masked
by the dominant allele.

B The dominant allele is masked by the
lethal recessive allele.

C Heterozygotes are too healthy to be
affected by the recessive allele.

D Heterozygous individuals have higher
fitness than recessives.

4 A gene pool includes all of the

A individuals in a population.

B mating pairs in a population.

C alleles in a population.

D families in a population.

**5 Heterozygotes for the sickle cell
allele have sickle cell trait (SCT).
They produce some abnormal
hemoglobin, but are generally
normal. These persons are immune
to malaria, a disease caused
by parasites that thrive on red
blood cells. SCT is prevalent in
areas where malaria infection
is very common. Because of
this correlation some scientists
hypothesize that the sickle cell
allele remains prevalent in the
gene pool due to**

A natural selection.

B founder effect.

C gene flow.

D genetic drift.

STANDARD SET 7

REVIEW

CALIFORNIA CONTENT
STANDARD 7.c

Mutation

STANDARD Students know new mutations are constantly being generated in a gene pool.

Read the summary and answer the questions on the next page..

A **mutation** is a change in the coding region of a gene. Mutations alter the way the gene's nucleotide sequence is translated. In some cases this forms new alleles. Mutations in reproductive cells can be passed on to offspring, thereby increasing genetic variation in the population. Because there are many genes in each individual and many individuals in a population, new mutations form constantly in the gene pool.

Mutations and the Genetic Code

In some cases, a mutation will form a new allele, introducing variation in the population. But most mutations do not affect fitness because some changes in DNA will still code for the same amino acid. For example, there are six different codons that will produce the amino acid arginine. If a mutation produces the same amino acid, the same protein will be produced during translation, and there will be no affect on the organism.

A small number of mutations are beneficial. Changing the nucleotide sequence of a gene may improve the stability of a protein product, or have another positive effect. Mutations are a source of genetic variation in populations. However, some mutations can be harmful. Changing a single base in a nucleotide sequence could have an enormous negative effect. Most harmful mutations are removed from the population by natural selection.

Types of Mutations

There are three main types of mutations: substitutions, additions, and deletions.

- **Substitutions** occur when one base in a nucleotide sequence is replaced by another. This is sometimes called a point mutation.
- **Additions** occur when one or more bases are added to a nucleotide sequence. Bases might be added to a sequence because of an error in transcription, or when a piece of chromosome breaks off and then reinserts itself incorrectly.
- **Deletions** are mutations that occur when one or more bases are removed from a nucleotide sequence. Deletions may occur during recombination or by chromosome breakage.

Mutations and Variation

Genetic variation is stored in a population's **gene pool**—the combined alleles of all of the individuals in a population. Since each individual has many genes, and a population has many members, new mutations form frequently in a population's **gene pool**. Alleles associated with favorable phenotypes increase in frequency. Unfavorable mutations are generally removed from the gene pool by natural selection, while advantageous ones tend to get passed to offspring.

PRACTICE

CALIFORNIA CONTENT
STANDARD 7.c

Mutation

DIRECTIONS: Choose the letter of the *best* answer.

1

1	2	3	4	5	6
GAU	GAU	UAG	UGA	GAU	AGA
GAU	GAC	UAG	CGA	GAU	AGA

Suppose a researcher is trying to modify a corn plant so it can grow in a dry environment. In the table above, sequence 1 is the control plant, and sequence 2 is the strand the researcher was trying to modify. In which codons did the researcher successfully produce mutations?

A 1 and 5

B 2 and 4

C 3 and 6

D None contain mutations.

2 Which of the following *best* explains why a mutation might be harmless?

A A mutation involves only small portions of the genome.

B A mutation makes DNA too big to fit in the nucleus.

C A mutation might not change the amino acid produced.

D A mutation requires large amounts energy to maintain.

3 Some mutations occur when one nucleotide is replaced by another. What type of mutation is this?

A a substitution

B a deletion

C a frameshift

D an addition

4 Unfavorable mutations are generally removed from the gene pool by natural selection. Why might this occur?

A Unfavorable mutations arise too rapidly to become adaptive.

B Unfavorable mutations do not improve an individual's fitness.

C Unfavorable mutations require too much energy to maintain.

D Unfavorable mutations are less important than favorable ones.

5 What is the *best* reason why new mutations are generated frequently in a population's gene pool?

A Organisms in a population have a higher mutation rate than isolated individuals.

B Alleles associated with favorable phenotypes increase in frequency.

C Environmental factors are more favorable for mutations in groups than for individuals.

D Individuals have many genes, and a population contains many individuals.

Genetic Variation: Within a Species

STANDARD Students know variation within a species increases the likelihood that at least some members of a species will survive under changed environmental conditions.

Read the summary and answer the questions on the next page.

Natural selection acts on variation that already exists in a population. This means that many different traits already exist, and when environmental conditions change, one of these pre-existing traits may be more beneficial than the others. The most advantageous trait will be selected for. The more variation between individuals in a population, the more likely that some individuals will have an advantageous trait and survive changes in the environment.

Heritability and Variation

Variation describes the differences in traits between individuals in a population. If a population has great variation, the population has many different traits. In order for natural selection to work, these traits must be heritable. A **heritable** trait is one that is produced by an allele and can be passed from one generation to another through reproduction.

There is generally more variation in sexually reproducing species than in asexual species. In asexual reproduction, a single parent produces offspring that are genetically identical to itself. In sexual reproduction two parents contribute genes to each offspring through gamete production and recombination. Sexual reproduction allows new combinations of genes to come together, producing many different traits and greater variation.

Selection and Species Survival

Variation is important for natural selection because natural selection works on traits that already exist. If there are six different skull shapes in a population, and something happens so that only individuals with one type of skull can obtain food, these individuals will survive and reproduce, but the others will not. The measure of an individual's ability to survive and reproduce is called **fitness.** The more advantageous traits an individual has, the more fit the individual is.

As long as environmental conditions select for the beneficial trait, it will be passed on to successive generations and become more common in the population. If the environment changes, different traits may become beneficial, and the individuals with those traits will become more common. The greater the variation in traits, the more likely it is that some individuals of a population can survive in a changing environment.

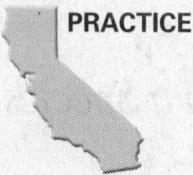

PRACTICE

CALIFORNIA CONTENT
STANDARD 7.d

Genetic Variation: Within a Species

DIRECTIONS: Choose the letter of the *best* answer.

1 When the environmental conditions change, natural selection will select individuals that

A mutate in response to changing conditions.

B have the traits that are most beneficial.

C move to a different environment.

D join members of another species in the area.

2 Which statement *best* describes how variation is important for the survival of a species that exists in a changing environment?

A Variation rates increase due to new selective pressures.

B Heritable variation increases as a result of environmental changes.

C The amount of variation increases due to increased mutation rates.

D Variation increases the likelihood that some individuals will survive.

3 A scientist observes a hypothetical plant species and finds that when there is little rain, only some individuals can survive. The scientist hypothesizes that if the climate changed, and there was less rainfall, the individuals that can survive in drought would out compete the ones that cannot. This is an example of how natural selection works on

A new mutations.

B population fitness.

C redundant alleles.

D existing traits.

4 The collection of different traits within a population is called

A variation.

B heritability.

C fitness.

D selection.

5

 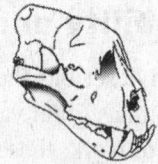

type 1   **type 2**

In a hypothetical population, most jaguars *(type 2)* have medium-sized teeth and jaws that are well adapted to eating small mammals. Fewer jaguars *(type 1)* have larger jaws and teeth, enabling them to feed on shelled reptiles as well small mammals. If the small mammals in the area go extinct, the *type 2* jaguars will not be able to survive. Eventually only *type 1* jaguars will be in the population. Which of the following statements would be true?

A *Type 1's* fitness will be greater than *type 2's.*

B *Type 2's* fitness will be greater than *type 1's.*

C The relative fitness between the types remains unchanged.

D The fitness of both groups increases equally.

REVIEW

CALIFORNIA CONTENT
STANDARD 8.a

Natural Selection: Fitness

STANDARD Students know how natural selection determines the differential survival of groups of organisms.

Read the summary and answer the questions on the next page.

Organisms with beneficial traits can outcompete and produce more offspring than individuals with less beneficial traits. Over time, this natural selection can cause major changes in the gene pool of a population.

Principles of Natural Selection

Natural selection is a process by which individuals with certain traits survive and produce more offspring than individuals without these traits. Natural selection is based upon four principles: overproduction, variation, adaptation, and descent with modification. As long as environmental conditions continue to favor the trait, it will become more common in the population over time.

- Overproduction occurs when some organisms, such as mice, produce more offspring than can survive, given the limits to natural resources. The individuals will compete for resources, and some individuals will survive to reproduce.

- Variation in a population's genes leads to different traits. Variation for a given trait can arise through a mutation or through recombination.

- Adaptations are variations that are beneficial. Individuals with beneficial adaptations have an increased chance of survival and reproductive success.

- Descent with modification is a principle which states that for natural selection to occur, the beneficial trait must be heritable. A **heritable** trait is one that is genetic and can be passed to and expressed in offspring.

Environmental Change and Fitness

Natural selection acts on phenotypes, or physical traits, rather than on genetic material itself. This is because natural selection relies on individual differences within a population. For some traits, all phenotypes provide an equal chance of survival. If environmental conditions change, one phenotype may become more adaptive. Individuals with this adaptation are more likely to survive, and they tend to have relatively high **fitness**. In biology, fitness is a measure of reproductive success—individuals with higher fitness produce more offspring than other individuals; these offspring will in turn pass on the adaptation to their own offspring. Such changes can have major effects on how a population looks and behaves.

However, fitness and differential survival depend on the environmental circumstances that favor it. Traits that are adaptive in one environment may lose their benefit or even become harmful if environmental conditions change.

STANDARD SET 8

PRACTICE

CALIFORNIA CONTENT
STANDARD 8.a

Natural Selection: Fitness

DIRECTIONS: Choose the letter of the *best* answer.

1

Bird A

Bird B

In the diagram above, bird A thrives on a diet of large, thick-shelled nuts. Bird B feeds exclusively on insects. Which feature could most likely be considered an adaptation of these birds to their diet?

A skull shape

B beak size

C visual keenness

D toe length

2 In terms of evolution, the ability of an organism to produce more offspring relative to other members of its population is a measure of its

A fertility.

B heritability.

C variation.

D fitness.

3 A feature that allows an organism to better survive in its environment is called a(n)

A allele.   **C** adaptation.

B mutation.   **D** variation.

4 Overproduction is a reproductive strategy in which some animals have many offspring. With more offspring, it's more likely that some will survive to reproduce. Overproduction is a principle of

A adaptation.

B natural selection.

C evolution.

D mutation.

5 A storm destroys the tall shade trees in a hypothetical forest. In the following days, increased sunlight reaches the forest's floor. Although individuals of shade-intolerant plant population die, some individuals survive. Which of the following *best* explains this?

A A trait that already existed in the population became favorable when the environment changed.

B The loss of shade caused a mutation in some individuals.

C Individuals that preferred the light outcompeted individuals that preferred shade.

D Individuals that survived the loss of shade were healthier than the individuals that died.

STANDARD SET 8

REVIEW

CALIFORNIA CONTENT
STANDARD 8.b
       Diversity and Survival

STANDARD Students know a great diversity of species increases the chance that at least some organisms survive major changes in the environment.

Read the summary and answer the questions on the next page.

The more different species present in an environment, the more likely that some of those species will survive a change in the environment.

Diversity Between Different Species

Variation among species is critical for the long-term survival of different groups of organisms. Remember that **natural selection** states that individuals that are best adapted to their environment will survive and reproduce more successfully. Natural selection occurs in part because individuals are in competition for resources. Each individual tries to obtain the resources it needs to survive and successfully reproduce. Organisms of different species may also be in competition with one another for the same resources. If the environmental conditions change, some of those species might be better adapted to the new environment. Those species will reproduce more successfully than species that are less adapted for the new environmental conditions. A high level of diversity between different species increases the chance that at least some species will survive a major change.

For example, trees share many traits that distinguish them from other plants. Yet within the group of organisms we call "trees" are many subgroups distinguished by certain traits, such as different leaf characteristics. Deciduous trees, like maples and oaks, have broad leaves adapted to catch as much sunlight as possible. The needles of conifers, such as pine and fir trees, are actually modified leaves whose shape limits water loss. These leaf characteristics are adaptations to their environments: Maples and oaks grow in thick forests where light is limited; conifers grow in dry climates where precipitation is minimal.

Species Survival

Suppose the climate on Earth becomes very dry, even in areas that were previously rainy. The decreased precipitation and humidity would select for individuals with traits that enabled them to thrive under dry conditions.

Under such circumstances, oak and maple trees might not survive. If no tree types were adapted to survive dry conditions, all forms of trees would become extinct. However, most conifers would probably survive and reproduce. In producing offspring, they would pass on all of their genes to future generations—genes unique to conifers as well as those shared with all trees. In this sense, "trees" as a group would not be lost.

PRACTICE

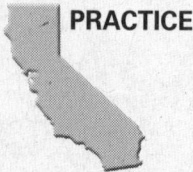

CALIFORNIA CONTENT
STANDARD 8.b

Diversity and Survival

DIRECTIONS: Choose the letter of the *best* answer.

1 According to natural selection, which kind of species will *most* likely survive environmental changes?

  A the smallest organisms

  B the least mutated

  C the best adapted

  D the most important

2

Group	Shell	Habitat
clams	yes	burrow
oysters	yes	rocks
octopi	no	swim
mussels	yes	rocks
snails	yes	plants
slugs	no	plants
squid	no	swim
cuttlefish	no	swim

Mollusks that live in warmer water usually don't have shells. If ocean temperatures increase, which of the groups listed above would *most* likely survive?

  A octopi, slugs, clams, and cuttlefish

  B snails, slugs, oysters, and mussels

  C mussels, snails, squid, and slugs

  D slugs, squid, octopi, and cuttlefish

3 Natural selection works on phenotypes that are already

  A mutating.   **C** existing.

  B adapting.   **D** adjusting.

4 There are many theories about what caused the dinosaurs to go extinct. Some scientists hypothesize that temperatures decreased below the level that reptiles, such as dinosaurs, could tolerate. However, some reptiles survived. According to this theory, what is the *most* likely reason that some reptiles survived?

  A Because there were many species of reptiles, some had adaptations that allowed them to survive cooler temperatures.

  B Because only dinosaurs dislike cold weather, they were the only reptile group that went extinct.

  C Because most non-dinosaur reptiles were so small, they avoided the cold temperatures.

  D Because other reptiles produced more offspring than dinosaurs, they did not go extinct.

5 The fossil record shows that two-thirds of burrowing lizard species survived a mass extinction. What is the *best* conclusion one could draw from this event?

  A The surviving species found new ways to survive the change in circumstances.

  B Diversity among lizard species' behaviors increased the chance that some species would survive.

  C Some species went extinct because they couldn't compete for resources.

  D Lizards generally had many advantages over other groups when circumstances

STANDARD SET 8

REVIEW

CALIFORNIA CONTENT
STANDARD 8.c

Genetic Drift

STANDARD Students know the effects of genetic drift on the diversity of organisms in a population.

Read the summary and answer the questions on the next page.

Small populations are vulnerable to **genetic drift,** which is the process by which chance events in a population change the allele frequencies in that population. Genetic drift leads to a loss of genetic diversity in the population.

Random Chance

In large populations, allele frequencies change due to natural selection. An allele that produces an advantageous trait will become more common, while a gene that does not increase fitness will be selected against. In small populations, allele frequencies are more likely to be affected by chance events such as disease, predation, or natural disasters. Changes in allele frequencies that result from chance events are called **genetic drift.** Genetic drift causes a loss of genetic diversity in a population's **gene pool**, the combined alleles of all of the individuals in a population.

Genetic drift is similar to sampling error. If a small number of individuals is separated from a larger population, characteristics of the smaller group may differ from those in the large group simply because of random chance. In populations, a chance event will produce a random shift in allele frequencies. For example, if a population has ten individuals, and a flood reduces the population to three individuals, the alleles the seven that had died are lost from the population. Due to chance alone, alleles in the three survivors will have a higher frequency than those alleles had before the flood. Because these alleles are more frequent, there is a greater chance that these alleles will be passed to more offspring and that these alleles will become fixed. A fixed allele is one that is present in every individual, and therefore cannot be removed from the population by natural selection. In genetic drift, the change in allele frequency does not occur because the allele produces an advantageous trait.

Bottlenecks and Founder Effects

Two processes cause populations to become small enough for genetic drift to occur: the bottleneck effect and the founder effect.

- The bottleneck effect occurs when an event, such as flood, fire, or overhunting, greatly reduces the size of a population.
- The founder effect occurs after a small number of individuals move into a new area.

With only a few individuals in the resulting populations, many of the alleles that were present in other individuals are no longer available in the gene pool. Even if these smaller populations increase in size, the new population will have only a fraction of the alleles that the initial population had. In both scenarios, the genetic variation in the smaller population would be severely reduced.

PRACTICE

CALIFORNIA CONTENT
STANDARD 8.c

Genetic Drift

DIRECTIONS: Choose the letter of the *best* answer.

1   **Initial Population**

New Population

Each of the patterns in the diagram above represents a different allele for the same trait. Which of the following statements *best* describes what causes changes in allele frequencies in the new population?

A chance

B selection

C variation

D adaptation

2 Populations that undergo genetic drift have

A increased gene flow.

B higher growth rates.

C decreased genetic diversity.

D increased selection.

3 Changes in allele frequencies resulting from chance alone are called genetic drift. Which of the following factors is *most* likely to result in drift?

A increased emigration

B decreased genetic variation

C small population size

D maladaptive allele

4 Genetic disorders that are rare in the general population often are common in populations that were established by a small group of individuals. This is an example of a

A bottleneck effect.

B point mutation.

C gene pool.

D founder effect.

5 The Florida panther has been overhunted for decades. Current population size is estimated to number around 80 individuals. If the species receives protection and does not become extinct, it will be able to breed again; however, it will probably have lost most of its genetic diversity. Which of the following *best* describes this situation?

A bottleneck effect

B alternation of generations

C founder effect

D adaptive radiation

STANDARD SET 8

Speciation

STANDARD Students know reproductive or geographic isolation affects speciation.

Read the summary and answer the questions on the next page.

If two populations of the same species stop mating with one another, the flow of genes between the two populations stops. Once this happens, the populations become isolated. With time, isolated populations become more and more genetically different.

Isolation

If gene flow between two populations stops, the populations are said to be isolated. Over time, these isolated populations will adapt to their environments. The gene pools, or sum of alleles in a population, will change as phenotypes that are best suited to their environments will become increasingly common. As the isolated populations adapt to different environments and conditions, they will become more and more genetically different. Eventually they will reach the stage of reproductive isolation. **Reproductive isolation** occurs when members of different populations can no longer mate successfully with one another. If organisms cannot mate and produce fertile offspring, they are different species. For this reason, reproductive isolation is the final step in becoming separate species. The rise of two or more species from one existing species is called **speciation.**

Barriers to Mating

In order for speciation to occur, members of one species have to form separate populations and stop mating with one another. Several kinds of barriers can isolate populations and prevent mating.

- **Behavioral isolation** is caused by differences in courtship or mating behaviors. Chemical scents, courtship dances of birds, and courtship songs of frogs are sexual signals used to attract mates. Changes in these signals can prevent mating between populations, and may arise through natural selection or genetic drift.

- **Temporal isolation** occurs when timing prevents reproduction between populations. Increased competition for mates during the annual mating season may lead some members of a population to show signs of courtship at different times. This can gradually lead to reproductive seasons at a different time of the year or day.

- **Geographic isolation** involves physical barriers that divide a population into two or more groups. Natural physical barriers include mountains, rivers, lakes, and so forth. However, many human-made barriers such as highways and shopping malls can isolate members of a population from each other.

At some point, isolated populations will have so many changes in their DNA that attempts at mating would only produce a sterile or otherwise nonviable offspring. This signals that reproductive isolation is complete, and the two isolated groups may now be considered as two distinct species.

PRACTICE

CALIFORNIA CONTENT
STANDARD 8.d

Specitation

DIRECTIONS: Choose the letter of the *best* answer.

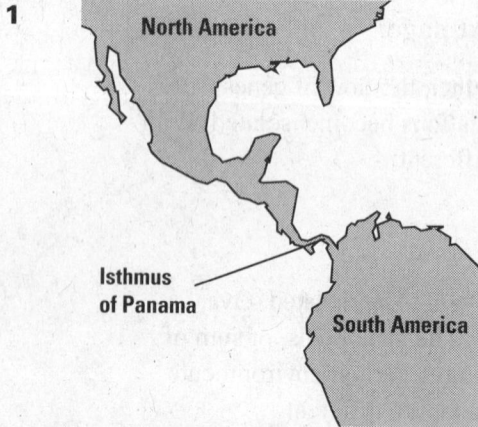

1

North America

Isthmus
of Panama

South America

Formation of the Isthmus of Panama prevented marine organisms to cross from the Atlantic to the Pacific Ocean and vice versa. Snapping shrimp in the Atlantic and Pacific oceans look similar but are distinct species. Males and females from opposite sides of the isthmus will not mate when they come into contact. The Atlantic and Pacific species most likely underwent speciation as a result of

A   geographic isolation.

B   behavioral isolation.

C   temporal isolation.

D   sympatric speciation.

2   **Speciation occurs when two populations of the same species become so genetically distinct that they can no longer produce fertile offspring. Which of the following leads to speciation?**

A   allopatric speciation

B   reproductive isolation

C   behavioral accomodation

D   postzygotic barriers

3   **Two hypothetical apple tree species are closely related. However tree A produces fruit in August, while tree B begins fruiting in November and continues into the winter. Which of the following barriers *best* describes how these two species arose?**

A   geographic isolation

B   behavioral isolation

C   temporal isolation

D   postzygotic barriers

4   **Male and female fireflies produce patterns of flashes that attract mates of their own species. Suppose Species 1 firefly emits one flash every second, Species 2 firefly emits one flash every two seconds, and species 3 firefly produces a double flash every five seconds. All three evolved from the same parent species. Which of the following is the *most* likely reason that these three species evolved?**

A   geographic isolation

B   temporal isolation

C   behavioral isolation

D   allopatric isolation

5   **Which of the following is a critical factor in preventing reproductive isolation?**

A   genetic drift   C   mutation

B   natural selection   D   gene flow

REVIEW

Fossil Evidence

STANDARD Students know how to analyze fossil evidence with regard to biological diversity, episodic speciation, and mass extinction.

Read the summary and answer the questions on the next page

The fossil record contains evidence of the major events in the history of life. The fossil record shows a repeating pattern of long periods of stability punctuated by relatively short bursts of evolutionary activity.

Biological Diversity Over Time

Researchers can observe major events in the history of life by looking at the fossil record. Analysis of fossils and the rocks that hold them provides information about where and when a species lived. Fossils also give clues to environmental conditions and other circumstances surrounding major events.

The fossil record supports the idea that natural selection can have an effect on evolution over many generations. Species can shape each other over time through coevolution. Coevolution occurs when species evolve in response to changes in each other. Evolution toward similar characteristics in unrelated species is called convergent evolution. Analogous structures, such as wings on birds and insects, are evidence of this. The evolution toward different directions from a single species is called divergent evolution. Divergent species, such as the red fox and kit fox, often appear very similar, but they are actually different species.

Extinction and Speciation

The elimination of a species from Earth is called **extinction**. A **mass extinction** is a rare event in which many species throughout the world die. The boundaries between the major geologic eras are defined by mass extinction events. There have been at least five mass extinctions in the last 600 million years.

Fossil evidence shows that evolutionary activity does not happen at a steady pace. Instead, the fossil record shows a repeating pattern in which many new species seem to appear at once followed by long periods with relatively little change. This pattern forms the basis for the theory of punctuated equilibrium.

Extinction and speciation events appear sporadically in the fossil record. Most mass extinctions generally coincided with a major environmental event, such as an asteroid impact or continental drift. Most mass extinction events are then followed by large-scale adaptive radiation. This process marks the rapid diversification of one ancestral species into a wide array of descendent species. The loss of species through a mass extinction event opens a wide variety of empty niches. This provides unique ecological opportunities for other species to adapt to. Speciation also occurs in episodic bursts. Major episodes of speciation generally follow the evolution of a novel characteristic, such as feathers, but also occur after mass extinctions.

STANDARD SET 8

Name   Period   Date

PRACTICE

CALIFORNIA CONTENT
STANDARD 8.e

Fossil Evidence

DIRECTIONS: Choose the letter of the *best* answer.

1

descendent species

ancestral species

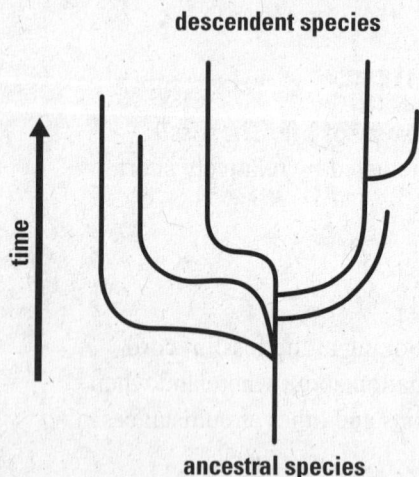

Suppose the diagram above illustrates the evolution of six species of apple trees that descended from one ancestor. Which of the following terms *best* describes the result in this diagram?

A mass extinction

B speciation

C analogous traits

D equilibrium

2 Suppose scientists study ancient plants. The scientist discovers that none of the ancient plants that he studies are present at a more recent time in the fossil record. In fact, many of the organisms he had observed in earlier fossils were no longer there. The scientist hypothesizes that there might have been a(n)

A mass extinction.

B divergent evolution.

C adaptive radiation.

D coevolution.

3 The fossil record displays a pattern in which short bursts of extinction and speciation alternate with long periods of stability in which no evolutionary activity takes place. Which theory describes this observation?

A natural selection

B punctuated equilibrium

C adaptive radiation

D convergent evolution

4 According to the fossil record, the appearance of a novel characteristic, such as wings, generally leads to a burst of

A mating activity.

B speciation.

C coevolution.

D extinction.

5 Some plants produce poisonous chemicals to discourage herbivores from eating them. However, over time, natural selection might favor herbivores that do not react to the poison. These herbivores can eat the plants without feeling the effects of the chemicals. In return, natural selection might eventually favor plants that can produce different or stronger chemicals. This is an example of

A adaptive radiation.

B convergent evolution.

C divergent evolution.

D coevolution.

82 STANDARDS REVIEW AND PRACTICE

REVIEW

CALIFORNIA CONTENT STANDARD 9.a

Homeostasis

STANDARD Students know how the complementary activity of major body systems provides cells with oxygen and nutrients and removes toxic waste products such as carbon dioxide.

Read the summary and answer the questions on the next page.

The chemical reactions that take place in the human body can occur only within a narrow range of temperatures, pH levels, and salt concentrations. The organ systems of the body must work together to maintain these internal conditions to keep a person functioning and alive. By regulating the flow of incoming nutrients and the removal of wastes, cells can maintain a consistent internal environment despite changes in the external environment. Maintenance of a stable internal environment is called **homeostasis.**

Transporting Nutrients and Wastes

Several different organ systems are responsible for bringing nutrients into and removing wastes from the body. The lungs of the respiratory system, for example, take in oxygen and release carbon dioxide. The small intestine in the digestive system breaks down and absorbs glucose and other nutrients. The bladder of the excretory system eliminates urine. However, these organs cannot distribute oxygen or collect liquid waste on their own. They rely on the circulatory system to do this for them.

The circulatory system transports nutrients to and carries wastes away from cells. Nutrients such as oxygen and glucose are essential to cellular respiration. Oxygen enters the respiratory system and diffuses into the circulatory system. Glucose and other products of digestion diffuse from the digestive system into the circulatory system. These nutrients move through the bloodstream and into the cells where they undergo cellular respiration to form ATP. Waste products from cellular respiration, such as carbon dioxide and water, move into the circulatory system and exit the body through the respiratory and excretory systems.

Regulating Nutrient and Waste Levels

The organ systems in your body work together to make sure that your cells have a constant flow of nutrients. Internal receptors monitor the blood level of critical molecules such as glucose and carbon dioxide. When these receptors detect small changes from set values, they trigger responses in the nervous and endocrine systems either to remove or store molecules in the body. For example, when carbon dioxide builds up in the blood, the nervous system stimulates the lungs to take a breath and exchange carbon dioxide for oxygen. After a meal, glucose levels increase, and the endocrine system releases hormones that signal liver cells to store excess glucose. In this way, organ systems work together to maintain homeostasis.

PRACTICE

CALIFORNIA CONTENT
STANDARD 9.a

Homeostasis

DIRECTIONS: Choose the letter of the *best* answer.

1 After eating a sugary dessert, a healthy person experiences a sudden rise of glucose levels in the blood. Receptors of the nervous system detect this increase. They send a signal to cause the liver to remove glucose from the blood and store it for later use. This is an example of how

  A organs make glucose.

  B cells become overactive.

  C organ systems respond to change.

  D tissues differentiate.

2 Keeping the internal environment within the narrow ranges that support life is called

  A active transport.

  B cellular respiration.

  C homeostasis.

  D gas exchange.

3 What is the *best* reason why the body must maintain a stable internal environment?

  A Fewer waste products are produced when the internal environment is stable.

  B Most chemical reactions take place only within a narrow range of conditions.

  C The body cannot grow if the environment is constantly changing.

  D Sensory receptors become confused in an unstable environment.

4 Waste products that result from cellular respiration are transported to organs that remove them from the body. The body system that transports wastes to these organs is the

  A respiratory system.

  B excretory system.

  C digestive system.

  D circulatory system.

5

You exercise.

↓

Nervous system senses
an increase in temperature.

↓

Nervous system signals skin.

↓

Skin produces sweat.

↓

Body temperature decreases.

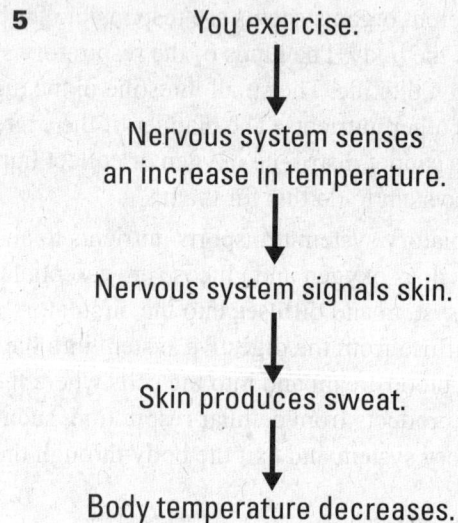

Which of the following is true about the process described above?

  A Organ systems work together to maintain homeostasis.

  B The skin's only role in maintaining homeostasis is sweating.

  C The nervous system requires conscious thought to maintain homeostasis.

  D Homeostasis was not maintained in this example.

REVIEW

CALIFORNIA CONTENT
STANDARD 9.b

Stimulous and Response

STANDARD Students know how the nervous system mediates communication between different parts of the body and the body's interaction with the environment.

Read the summary and answer the questions on the next page.

Living things must be able to respond to their environment to keep the conditions within their bodies stable, a process called homeostasis. The **nervous system** is a highly connected network of specialized cells that helps to maintain homeostasis.

Gathering and Responding to Stimuli

The nervous system has two parts that allow it to gather, interpret, and respond to stimuli. A **stimulus** *(pl. stimuli)* is anything that causes a response. The **peripheral nervous system (PNS)** is the body system that gathers stimuli and delivers signals to other organs of the body. Your five senses—vision, hearing, taste, smell, and touch—are part of the PNS. Each of these senses has sensory receptors that gather stimuli and transmit impulses to the central nervous system. The **central nervous system (CNS)** is the part of the nervous system that includes the brain and spinal cord. Here's an example of how the two systems work together to produce a response:

- Your pencil rolls off your desk. Receptors in your ears detect the sound waves of the pencil hitting the floor.
- A nerve of the PNS generates an impulse and sends it to the CNS.
- The brain interprets the impulse as the sound of the pencil hitting the floor. Then the brain generates a new impulse and sends it down the spinal cord.
- A nerve of the PNS takes this impulse to muscles that allow you to bend over and pick up the pencil.

In some situations, you don't have to think to cause a response. In **reflex arcs,** a sensory receptor sends a signal to the spinal cord. The spinal cord then directs the signal to a muscle, producing a response without having to involve the brain. An example of a reflex arc is when you touch a hot pan and jerk your hand away before you have time to "think."

The Nervous System and Endocrine System

The nervous system sometimes requires the help of the endocrine system, which is another communication system. In response to signals from the brain, endocrine glands produce chemical signals, called hormones. Hormones travel through the bloodstream. When they encounter a cell with a receptor that matches the hormones' shape, they bind to the receptor and change the activity of that cell. The nervous and endocrine systems are connected by the hypothalamus. The hypothalamus sorts the brain's incoming stimuli. In sorting, it might send an impulse to a part of the brain, or it might release hormones that will stimulate another gland to produce its own hormones. Both types of signals will cause other cells to change their activities, producing a response to the initial stimulus.

PRACTICE

CALIFORNIA CONTENT
STANDARD 9.b

Stimulous and Response

DIRECTIONS: Choose the letter of the *best* answer.

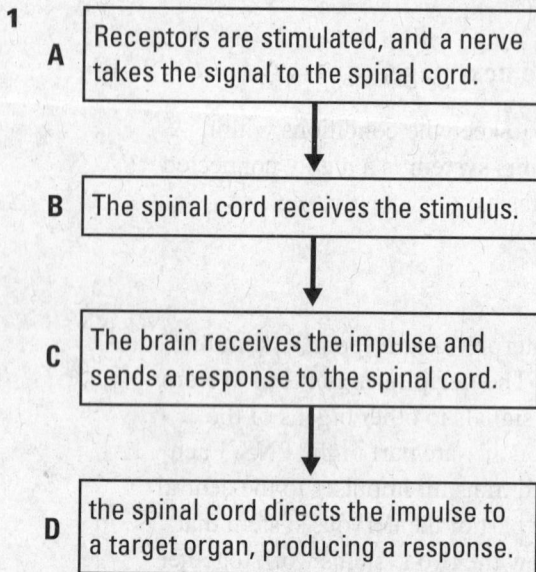

1

A | Receptors are stimulated, and a nerve takes the signal to the spinal cord.

↓

B | The spinal cord receives the stimulus.

↓

C | The brain receives the impulse and sends a response to the spinal cord.

↓

D | the spinal cord directs the impulse to a target organ, producing a response.

The diagram shows the pathway of an impulse, from sensors to response. Which step in the diagram would *not* occur if this process described a reflex arc?

A A

B B

C C

D D

2 What system carries sensory information from the tip of the finger, but also carries impulses to muscles in the foot?

A endocrine system

B peripheral nervous system

C central nervous system

D reflex arcial system

3 A girl walks on a sandy beach, She steps on a sharp piece of shell and quickly jerks her foot up. Her action is an example of a

A conscious decision to move her foot.

B reflex arc.

C response to hormonal stimulation.

D decision by the hypothalamus.

4 How are the roles of the nervous system and the endocrine system similar?

A Both use signals called hormones.

B Both send messages through the spinal cord.

C Both are controlled by reflex arcs.

D Both allow body systems to produce responses.

5 Which of the following is true about the *main* role of the nervous system in the body?

A It interprets stimuli so that the body can interact with its environment.

B It gathers stimuli and prevents the body from maintaining homeostasis.

C It relaxes the endocrine system so that hormones don't overreact.

D It organizes the nerves in the body so that they do not overlap.

REVIEW

CALIFORNIA CONTENT
STANDARD 9.c

Feedback Loops

STANDARD Students know how feedback loops in the nervous and endocrine systems regulate conditions in the body.

Read the summary and answer the questions on the next page

Your environment changes constantly. In order to remain healthy, your body must have ways to monitor, evaluate, and respond to these changes so that the internal environment remains stable. Having a stable internal environment is called maintaining homeostasis. Feedback loops are the key to maintaining homeostasis.

Feedback Loops

Feedback loops are control systems that consist of sensors, control centers, communication systems, and targets. Sensors in the body constantly gather stimuli and monitor internal conditions. They send information, or feedback, to a control center, usually the brain. The brain evaluates incoming information and compares it the ideal value, or set point, for each function. When conditions rise above or fall below the ideal point, the brain signals an endocrine gland, part of the communication system, to release hormones. **Hormones** are chemical messengers that circulate in the blood. They act on specific target cells, causing them to either to speed up, slow down, turn on, or turn off a particular chemical reaction. Changing the activity level of target cells then changes internal conditions in the body to help restore homeostasis. The diagram illustrates a feedback loop.

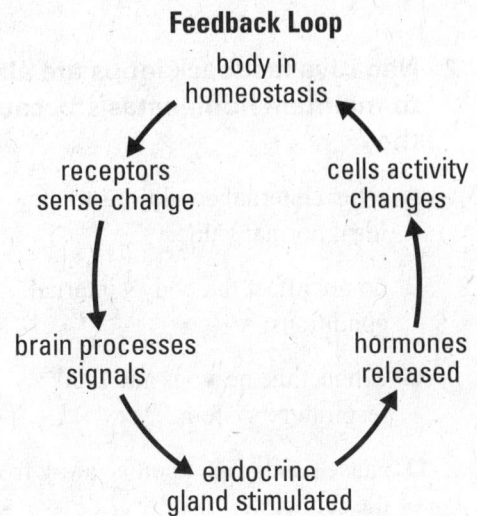

Feedback Loop

body in
homeostasis

receptors
sense change

cells activity
changes

brain processes
signals

hormones
released

endocrine
gland stimulated

Types of Feedback

Most functions in the body are controlled by negative feedback loops. **Negative feedback loops** maintain homeostasis by returning conditions to the set point. The nervous system senses a change in conditions, such as too much water in the blood. It sends a signal to an endocrine gland, which releases hormones that help return the water in the blood to its ideal level. When conditions return to normal, the nervous system "turns off" the endocrine gland, which goes back to its normal level of activity. Body temperature, absorption of nutrients, and the level of glucose (sugar) in the blood are regulated by negative feedback loops.

Only a few functions in the body are controlled by positive feedback loops. **Positive feedback loops** increase change and cause conditions to temporarily move away from homeostasis. When the positive feedback is gone, the body returns to homeostasis. Birth is a positive feedback event. When a woman starts to give birth, contractions in the uterus become progressively stronger. As the contractions continue, the body is under more and more stress until the baby is born. Soon after the birth, contractions stop, and the mother's body returns to homeostasis.

PRACTICE

CALIFORNIA CONTENT
STANDARD 9.c

Feedback Loops

DIRECTIONS: Choose the letter of the *best* answer.

1 Feedback loops are control systems that

  A regulate the expression of genes.

  B allow the body to maintain homeostasis.

  C stimulate the immune system.

  D determine if a particular behavior will occur.

2 Negative feedback loops are able to maintain homeostasis because they

  A return internal conditions to the ideal normal value.

  B do not affect the body's internal conditions.

  C connect the nervous and the respiratory system.

  D cause conditions to move away from the set point.

3 Insulin is a hormone that helps the body use glucose. In some people with Type 2 diabetes, target cells do not respond to insulin. As a result, abnormally large amounts of glucose builds up in the blood. What statement *best* describes what occurred in this example?

  A The insulin had mutated.

  B Homeostasis is not maintained.

  C Type 2 diabetes produces glucose.

  D Glucose receptors stopped functioning.

4

body temperature decreases

↓

receptors send information to the brain

↓

brain signals endocrine system

↓

[?]

↓

cell activity increases

↓

body temperature increases

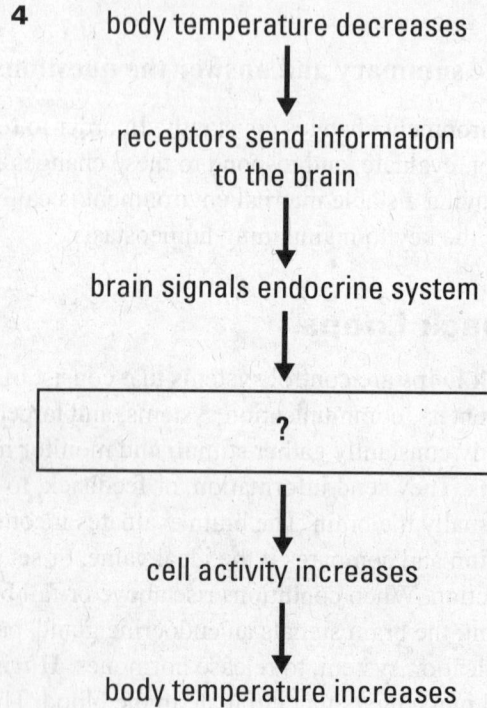

Normal body temperature is 37°C (98.6°F). A hiker is caught in a snowstorm, and his body temperature begins to drop. Which *best* completes the following diagram.

  A Neurons become active.

  B Hormones are released.

  C Homeostasis is maintained.

  D The feedback loop fails.

5 Positive feedback loops move the body

  A back to its original condition.

  B in the direction of less change.

  C toward increased uptake of ions.

  D away from homeostasis.

REVIEW

CALIFORNIA CONTENT STANDARD 9.d

Nerve Impluses

STANDARD Students know the functions of the nervous system and the role of neurons in transmitting electrochemical impulses.

Read the summary and answer the questions on the next page.

The nervous system is made up of billions of specialized cells called neurons. **Neurons** are cells that transmit and receive signals in the form of chemical and electrical impulses.

Neurons

All neurons have three basic parts: a cell body, dendrites, and an axon. The cell body contains the nucleus and other organelles. Dendrites and axons are extensions of the cytoplasm and cell membrane that stretch out from the cell body. **Dendrites** always carry impulses *toward* the cell body. **Axons** always carry impulses *away* from the cell body.

Neuron

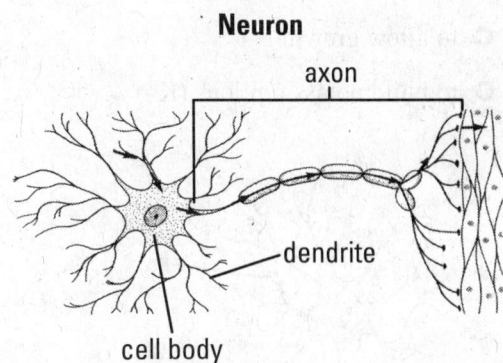

Transmission of Impulses

In order to generate an impulse, a neuron relies on the movement of ions, or charged particles. The two types of ions involved in generating an impulse are sodium ion (Na^+) and potassium ion (K^+).

When the neuron is not transmitting an impulse, there is a small difference in the concentration of ions between the inside and outside of the neuron. **Resting potential** refers to the condition of the neuron when it is not transmitting an impulse. During resting potential, there are more K^+ ions and fewer Na^+ ions inside of the neuron compared to the outside.

When a neuron's dendrite is stimulated, channels in the cell membrane open, and Na^+ ions quickly diffuse into the cell. As positive ions move in, the cell's inner membrane becomes positive compared to the outside. The change in charge causes two things to happen. First, channels in the next section of the membrane open. More Na^+ ions move in, and the impulse moves down the neuron. Second, K^+ channels open, and K^+ ions move out of the neuron, making its inner membrane less positive. This process produces moving electrical impulse is called an **action potential.**

Before an action potential can move into the next neuron, it must cross a small gap, known as a **synapse.** When an action potential reaches the end, or **terminal**, of the axon, the neuron releases chemical messenger molecules, or **neurotransmitters,** into the synapse. Neurotransmitters move across the synapse and stimulate the neuron on the other side to generate an action potential. In this way, an impulse moves through and between neurons.

PRACTICE

CALIFORNIA CONTENT
STANDARD 9.d

Nerve Impluses

DIRECTIONS: Choose the letter of the *best* answer.

1 Cells of the nervous system are called neurons. What is the *most* important function of a neuron?

  A to store sodium ions (Na^+)

  B to transmit signals

  C to allow growth

  D to build potassium ions (K^+)

2

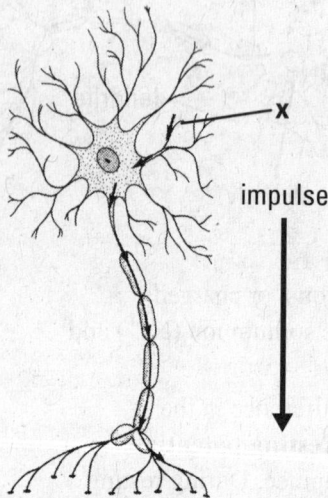

impulse

Above is a picture of a neuron. The part of the neuron marked with an X receives signals from other neurons and generates impulses when it is stimulated. This structure is called a(n)

  A axon.

  B resting potential.

  C dendrite.

  D neurotransmitter.

3 Neurons send signals throughout the body. When an impulse is within a neuron, it is electrical. When the signal moves to the next neuron, it is

  A electrical.

  B chemical.

  C ionic.

  D signals don't move between neurons.

4 The axon is the part of the neuron that carries impulses

  A away from the cell body.

  B across the synapse.

  C toward the nucleus.

  D within neurotransmitters.

5 What allows neurons to generate an action potential and keep it moving through the neuron?

  A presence of a synapse

  B production of neurotransmitters

  C location of the terminal

  D distribution of ions

REVIEW

CALIFORNIA CONTENT
STANDARD 9.e

Roles of Neurons

STANDARD Students know the roles of sensory neurons, interneurons, and motor neurons in sensation, thought, and response.

Read the summary and answer the questions on the next page.

There are three types of neurons, or cells of the nervous system, in the human body: sensory neurons, interneurons, and motor neurons. These neurons have different functions.

Interneurons

Interneurons are only found only in the spinal cord and brain, which together make up the **central nervous system (CNS).** The spinal cord is a bundle of interneurons that carries information between the brain and the rest of the body. The brain is a larger structure within the skull. Interneurons in the brain receive and interpret stimuli, such as heat. The interneurons then send signals that will produce a response, such as moving away from the heat.

Sensory and Motor Neurons

The **peripheral nervous system (PNS)** is the body system that gathers stimuli and delivers signals to other organs of the body. The sensory and motor neurons of the PNS connect the CNS to the rest of the body. Sensory neurons bring signals to the spinal cord, and motor neurons carry signals away from the spinal cord. The PNS produces voluntary and involuntary movements. Responses can occur only when the PNS and CNS work together, as you can see in the diagram.

   A reflex arc is the simplest example of how the CNS and PNS work together. A **reflex arc** describes the path of an impulse for an involuntary reaction, and it involves three neurons. If you step barefoot on a sharp rock, for example, a sensory neuron senses pain and carries this information to the spinal cord. In the spinal cord, an interneuron receives the signal and stimulates a motor neuron. The motor neuron carries the signal to a muscle, which responds by jerking your leg up. Reflex arcs are very fast because the signal does not need to travel all the way to the brain before a response is produced.

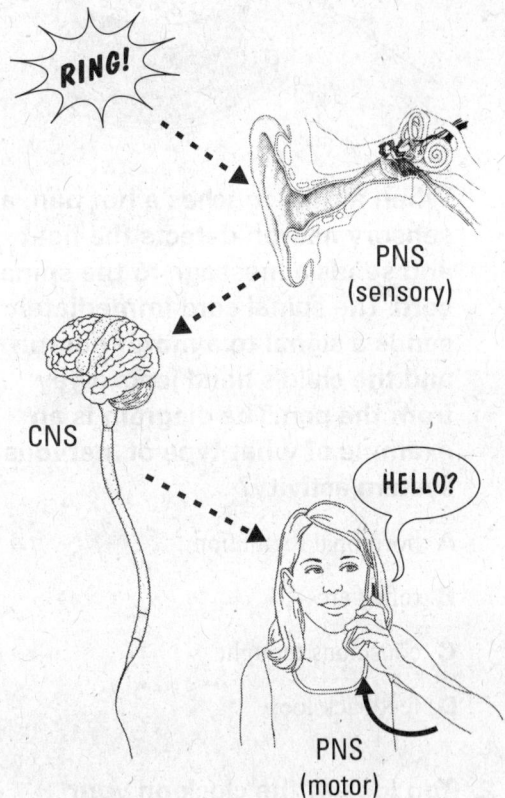

RING!

PNS
(sensory)

CNS

HELLO?

PNS
(motor)

PRACTICE

CALIFORNIA CONTENT
STANDARD 9.e

Roles of Neurons

DIRECTIONS: Choose the letter of the *best* answer.

1

When a child touches a hot pan, a sensory neuron detects the heat and sends a message to the spinal cord. The spinal cord immediately sends a signal to a motor neuron, and the child's hand jerks away from the pan. The diagram is an example of what type of nervous system activity?

A hormonal regulation

B reflex arc

C conscious thought

D feedback loop

2 You look at the clock on your classroom wall and see that it says 1:20. What neuron allows you to interpret what time it is?

A sensory neuron

B motor neuron

C cranial neuron

D interneuron

3 You hear a loud noise that makes you jump up from your seat. What is the role of a motor neuron in this example?

A gathering sound wave stimuli from the air

B transferring impulses from your ear into your brain.

C analyzing impulses to produce one that will cause a response

A stimulating the muscles in your legs to allow you to jump

4 Why are actions produced from reflexes quicker than those that are voluntary actions?

A Voluntary actions require the spinal cord, but reflex actions do not.

B Voluntary actions require motor neurons, but reflex actions do not.

C Voluntary actions require interneurons, but reflex actions do not.

D Voluntary actions require the brain to produce a response, but reflex actions do not.

5 When you touch your hand to a hot stove, you will jerk it away. What type of neuron detects the heat, or stimulus, that produces this response?

A sensory neuron

B motor neuron

C cranial neuron

D interneuron

REVIEW

The Skin

STANDARD Students know the role of the skin in providing nonspecific defenses against infection.

Read the summary and answer the questions on the next page.

Skin provides a physical barrier against disease-causing agents. It is the first line of defense in the body's immune system.

Defense Against Pathogens

Disease-causing agents are called **pathogens.** Pathogens include many different types of viruses and microorganisms, including bacteria and protists. Before a pathogen can make a person sick, it has to enter the body. The skin provides a physical barrier against pathogens getting into the body.

The skin is part of the integumentary system, which also includes hair, nails, and glands. The skin acts as the body's first line of defense by physically blocking invading pathogens. Oil and sweat are secreted by glands in the skin, which make the skin hypotonic and acidic. In a hypotonic environment, cells take in water, swelling to the point of bursting. Many pathogens cannot survive in this kind of environment. When the skin is broken, such as from a cut or scrape, pathogens can enter the body. When this occurs, cells in the immune system are activated to help fight the invading pathogen.

Response to Skin Breaks

You may have noticed that when you scrape your knee or get a cut on your finger, the area around the broken skin swells and turns red. It may also feel warmer than the surrounding skin and itch or hurt. All of these signs are part of inflammation, a nonspecific response that occurs when a pathogen enters the body or when tissues have been damaged. A nonspecific immune response happens in the same way no matter what type of pathogen is invading.

Inflammation begins when certain cells in the immune system release chemicals called histamines. Histamines cause the cells in blood vessel walls to spread out. When this happens, fluids can move out of the blood vessel and into surrounding tissues. White blood cells, cells that find and kill pathogens that have entered the body, squeeze out of the capillary and move toward the site of infection. The white blood cells fight infection by killing pathogens. When the pathogens are defeated, the swelling stops, and tissue repair begins.

During the inflammation response, platelets in the blood form clots to seal the wound. After any pathogens are killed and tissue repair begins, the clot hardens into a scab. The scab eventually falls off the wound when the tissue is completely repaired.

PRACTICE

CALIFORNIA CONTENT
STANDARD 10.a

The Skin

DIRECTIONS: Choose the letter of the *best* answer.

1 When the skin is broken from a cut or scrape, histamines are released, fluids and white blood cells move out of blood vessel and into surrounding tissues, and the white blood cells fight infection. What is this immune response called?

　A clotting

　B swelling

　C inflammation

　D scab formation

2 Which of the following is an example of a role the skin plays in defense against infection?

　A It maintains proper body temperature.

　B It provides a physical barrier against pathogens.

　C It produces a form of vitamin D used by the body.

　D It gathers sensory information about the environment.

3 Oil and sweat make the skin hypotonic and acidic. This provides defense against infection because many pathogens

　A multiply when skin is hypotonic.

　B become dormant in an acidic environment.

　C will penetrate the skin when it is oily.

　D cannot survive in this environment.

4 If a bacterium called *Staphlococcus aureus* gets into the body through a cut in the skin, it can cause an infection. Which of the following terms *best* describes this bacterium?

　A white blood cell

　B inflammation

　C pathogen

　D gland

5

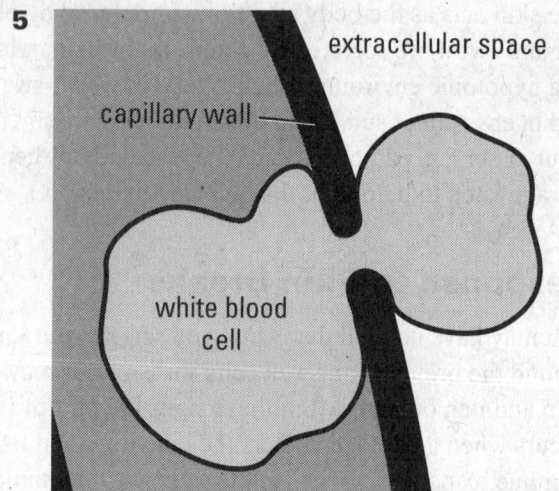

When you get a scrape, white blood cells squeeze out of capillaries and move toward the site of the scrape. How is this response beneficial?

　A Platelets form clots to seal the wound.

　B Histamines fight infection by secreting acids.

　C White blood cells can reach the site and kill pathogens.

　D A scab forms while tissue is repaired.

REVIEW

CALIFORNIA CONTENT
STANDARD 10.b

Antibodies

STANDARD SET 10

STANDARD Students know the role of antibodies in the body's response to infection.

Read the summary and answer the questions on the next page.

Cells in the immune system produce antibodies in response to antigens. Antibodies can inactivate pathogens directly or signal other immune system cells that pathogens are present.

Antibodies' Role in the Immune System

The immune system is the body system that fights off infection and pathogens. Pathogens are agents, such as bacteria or viruses, that cause disease. When the immune system detects a pathogen in the body, it triggers an immune response.

But how does the immune system tell the difference between the body's own healthy cells and pathogens? **Antigens** are protein markers on the surface of cells or viruses that help the immune system identify pathogens or other foreign cells. Each pathogen has uniquely shaped antigens on its surface.

When the immune system recognizes an antigen, it might produce antibodies in response. **Antibodies** are proteins produced by B cells—a type of white blood cell in the immune system. Each antibody has a specific receptor on it so that can attach to a specific pathogen's antigen. Once the antibody attaches to the pathogen, it might affect the pathogen in one of three ways. It might

- cover the pathogen's antigens, preventing the pathogen from infecting body cells.
- cause pathogens to clump together, making it easier for other immune cells to engulf and destroy them.
- activate other immune system proteins that will weaken the pathogen's cell membrane, causing it to burst.

Antibodies and White Blood Cells

Here's how antibodies help the immune system fight infections.

1. When a pathogen enters your body, the immune system recognizes the antigens.
2. The antigens stimulate B cells to divide and differentiate into two types of cells—activated B cells and memory B cells.
3. The activated B cells produce antibodies specific to the pathogen.
4. The antibodies may cause several pathogens to clump together so that phagocytes can engulf and destroy them, as you can see in the picture.
5. The memory B cells will remain in the body. If the same pathogen invades the body again, the memory cells will produce antibodies immediately.

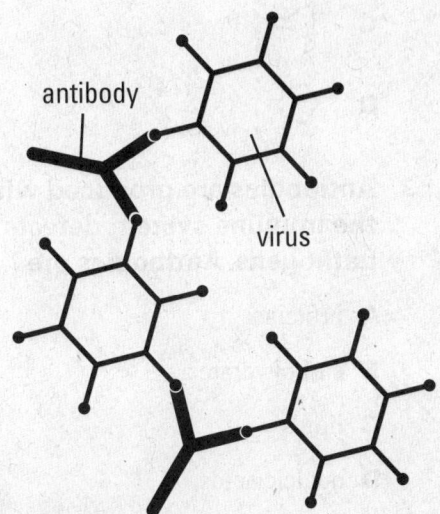

antibody

virus

PRACTICE

CALIFORNIA CONTENT
STANDARD 10.b

Antibodies

DIRECTIONS: Choose the letter of the *best* answer.

1 If a virus that causes a cold enters the body, antibodies are produced in response. Which immune system cells produce antibodies?

  A antigens

  B B cells

  C phagocytes

  D receptor cells

2

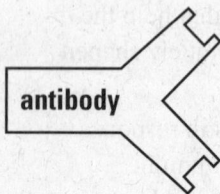

The diagram above shows an antibody with a specific receptor site. Which antigen below would attach to the antibody?

  A

  B

  C

  D

3 Antibodies are produced when the immune system detects pathogens. Antibodies are

  A proteins.

  B carbohydrates.

  C lipids.

  D nucleic acids.

4 Which statement *best* describes the role of antibodies in the immune system?

  A They inactivate pathogens, stopping illness.

  B They engulf pathogens, destroying them.

  C They prevent infection, keeping pathogens out of the body.

  D They release phagocytes, causing pathogens to clump.

5

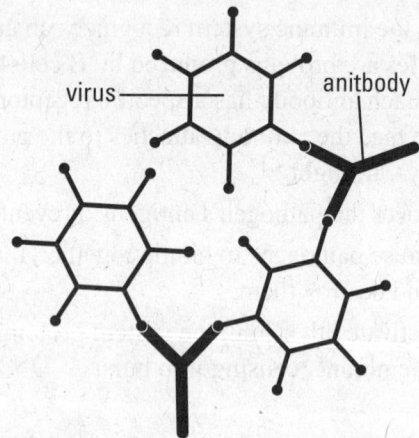

When antibodies bind to the surface of pathogens, sometimes they cause the pathogens to clump. How does this action help the body fight infection?

  A This triggers B cells to form memory cells.

  A Phagocytes can engulf and destroy the pathogens.

  C B cells multiply to fight the infection.

  D The immune system can now recognize the antigens.

REVIEW

CALIFORNIA CONTENT
STANDARD 10.c

Vaccination

STANDARD SET 10

STANDARD Students know how vaccination protects an individual from infectious diseases.

Read the summary and answer the questions on the next page

Vaccines stimulate the immune system to make memory cells and produce acquired immunity in the person receiving the vaccine. Acquired immunity means that a person cannot get sick twice from the same pathogen. This is because the immune system contains B cells that "remember" that pathogen and act quickly to destroy it.

Vaccines

A **vaccine** is a substance that contains the antigen of a pathogen. Vaccines cannot cure a person who is sick; instead, vaccines allow a person to acquire immunity against a pathogen without actually contracting the disease.

Vaccines are made using the same pathogens that they are supposed to protect against. Vaccines contain weakened viruses, antigens, or toxins that bacteria produce. People receiving vaccines do not become sick because the weakened or killed pathogens cannot reproduce or attack cells.

Vaccines and Acquired Immunity

Vaccines produce acquired immunity. Acquired immunity is a type of active immunity that is produced after the immune system responds to a specific pathogen that has infected or is infecting the body. Acquired immunity prevents that same pathogen from making the person sick more than once. Here is how vaccines work:

1. A vaccine is given to a patient either orally or by injection.
2. The antigens in the vaccine stimulate the immune system to produce B cells against the pathogen in the vaccine.
3. B cells divide and differentiate into memory cells and active B cells. **Memory cells** are specialized cells that "remember" the antigens on a pathogen.
4. If the real pathogen infects the body after the patient is vaccinated, memory B cells make antibodies for that pathogen immediately, destroying it before it has a chance to make the patient sick.

PRACTICE

CALIFORNIA CONTENT
STANDARD 10.c

Vaccination

DIRECTIONS: Choose the letter of the *best* answer.

1 Vaccines are beneficial because they prevent

   A illness.

   B infection.

   C pathogens.

   D antibodies.

2 When a patient receives a vaccine against pneumonia, the patient's immune system produces memory cells. How do memory cells prevent illness?

   A They weaken the pneumonia pathogens.

   B They kill the pneumonia pathogens from the vaccine.

   C They produce antibodies quickly the next time pneumonia pathogens invade.

   D They differentiate into B cells that attack the pathogens.

3 A person who gets measles is immune to the disease after he recovers. What type of immunity keeps a person from getting sick from measles more than once?

   A passive immunity

   B acquired immunity

   C B cell immunity

   D memory cell immunity

4 A substance that can stimulate the immune system to produce memory cells without the person getting sick is called a(n)

   A antibody.

   B B cell.

   C pathogen.

   D vaccine.

5

Step 1: A person is vaccinated.

↓

Step 2: The immune system is stimulated.

↓

Step 3:   ?

↓

Step 4: immunity is produced.

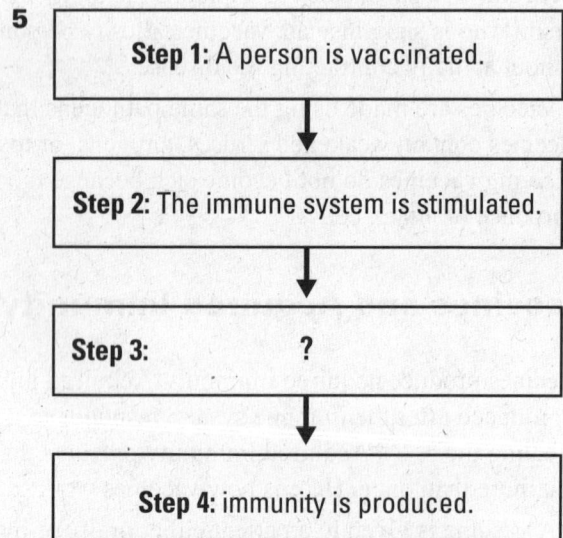

The diagram shows the events that produce immunity after a vaccine. Which of the following statements *best* describes what occurs during Step 3?

   A The person becomes sick from the disease.

   B The pathogens from the vaccine cause an infection.

   C The B cells weaken the pathogens.

   D B cells differentiate into memory cells.

CALIFORNIA CONTENT
STANDARD 10.d

Bacteria and Viruses

STANDARD Students know there are important differences between bacteria and viruses with respect to their requirements for growth and replication, the body's primary defenses against bacterial and viral infections, and effective treatments of these infections.

Read the summary and answer the questions on the next page.

Bacteria and viruses can both cause infections in the body. However, their different structures and reproductive cycles allow them to infect the body in different ways.

Bacteria and Viruses

Bacteria are microorganisms, but viruses are small particles that contain only DNA and RNA. Bacteria and viruses that cause disease in humans are called **pathogens.** Although both types of pathogens cause disease, they have several different characteristics.

- **Cell Wall vs. Protein Coat.** Bacteria have cell walls, but viruses are surrounded by a thick protein, called a protein coat.
- **Living vs. Not Living.** Bacteria are living cells that have organelles, use energy, and reproduce by themselves. Viruses are not living, even though they have a strand of DNA or RNA, because they do not have organelles, cannot reproduce on their own, do not use energy, and cannot make proteins on their own.
- **Self-Reproducing vs. Non-Self-Reproducing.** Bacteria replicate by mitosis, or cell division. Viruses can replicate only if they enter a host cell and cause the host cell to use the virus's DNA to synthesize new viruses.
- **Toxins vs. Stopping Cell Activity.** Bacteria cause illness by releasing toxic chemicals that weaken or destroy body cells. Viruses cause illness by forcing cells to stop their normal activity and spend all of their energy making new viruses.

Controlling the Spread of Pathogens

Different chemicals and medicines can be used to control the spread of pathogens.

- **Antiseptics** are chemicals such as soap, vinegar, and rubbing alcohol that kill pathogens outside the body. Antiseptics weaken cell walls and membranes and poison the pathogens.
- **Antibiotics** are medicines that target specific types of bacteria or fungi and keep them from growing or reproducing once they enter the body. Many antibiotics work by weakening the cell walls of bacteria. With weakened cell walls, the bacteria will burst if they try to divide. Antibiotics cannot treat viral infections because viruses do not have cell walls.

Although antibiotics are very useful in controlling disease, overuse can result in antibiotic-resistant bacteria. **Antibiotic resistance** occurs when bacteria mutate so that they are no longer affected by specific antibiotics.

PRACTICE

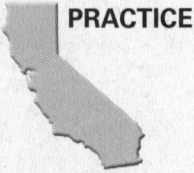

CALIFORNIA CONTENT
STANDARD 10.d

Bacteria and Viruses

DIRECTIONS: Choose the letter of the *best* answer.

1 Which of the following is a difference between bacteria and viruses?

   A Bacteria have protein coats, but viruses have cell walls.

   B Bacteria have genetic information, but viruses do not.

   C Bacteria do not make people ill, but viruses cause disease.

   D Bacteria reproduce on their own, but viruses do not.

2 You are diagnosed with the flu, but your doctor does not give you any antibiotics. The doctor says that antibiotics are not effective against viral infections. Why not?

   A Viruses do not use glucose.

   B Viruses do not need ATP.

   C Viruses do not have DNA.

   D Viruses do not have cell walls.

3 Suppose you get infected with a virus. Which of the following statements *best* describes what the virus will do that will cause you to feel ill?

   A The virus will release toxins that will poison otherwise healthy body cells.

   B The virus will mutate so that antibiotics will not be able to destroy it.

   C The virus will cause body cells to stop their activity and produce viruses.

   D The virus will use ATP to grow large enough so that it can infect and consume body cells.

4 A person cuts her finger and puts an antiseptic on it to kill pathogens. How are antiseptics different from antibiotics?

   A Antiseptics weaken cell membranes.

   B Antiseptics stop the formation of cell walls.

   C Antiseptics are used once the pathogen is inside the body.

   D Antiseptics only target certain types of bacteria.

5

Test Tube	Number of Bacteria Living after 48 hours
Control	4,000,000
A	0
B	4,500,000
C	200
D	0

A scientist tests the effectiveness of an antibiotic against different strains of a bacterium. The scientist placed four strains of the bacterium in separate test tubes along with the antibiotic. The control test tube contained bacteria but no antibiotic. The table shows how the results of the experiment after 48 hours. Which strain is resistant to the antibiotic?

   A Strain A

   B Strain B

   C Strain C

   D Strain D

REVIEW

CALIFORNIA CONTENT
STANDARD 10.e

Weak Immune System

STANDARD Students know why an individual with a compromised immune system (for example, a person with AIDS) may be unable to fight off and survive infections by microorganisms that are usually benign.

Read the summary and answer the questions on the next page.

If the immune system is weak, the body cannot fight pathogens that would normally be easy to destroy. For example, an HIV infection can severely weaken a person's immune system.

When the Immune System Is Weakened

Certain pathogens, usually bacteria and viruses that cause disease, can weaken the immune system by reducing the number of white blood cells. The fewer white blood cells a person has, the less likely that person's immune system can fight off other infections. Sometimes, the immune system becomes so weak that the body is vulnerable to opportunistic infections. **Opportunistic infections** are infections caused by pathogens that a healthy immune system would normally be able to destroy. When the immune system is weakened, a person may have several infections at the same time.

HIV and AIDS

Human Immunodeficiency Virus (HIV) is a virus that attacks and weakens the immune system. HIV is transmitted from person to person through the mixing of blood and other body fluids, such as during sexual intercourse or the sharing of needles used by an infected person.

When HIV enters the body, the virus invades T cells. T cells are white blood cells that trigger the body's immune responses. When HIV enters a T cell, it takes over the cell's functions and uses them to produce more and more HIV. As a result, the T cell can no longer stimulate an immune response. After producing millions of HIV, the T cell dies. Eventually, the body cannot replace the dead T cells quickly enough. The immune system weakens, and opportunistic infections, such as pneumonia and tuberculosis, attack the body.

Acquired immune deficiency syndrome (AIDS) is the condition of having a worn out immune system due to an HIV infection. Unlike HIV, which is a pathogen, AIDS is the collection of symptoms caused by an HIV infection. These symptoms include having several opportunistic infections and very few T cells. AIDS results in death because a person's immune system cannot fight off the body's many infections.

STANDARD SET 10

PRACTICE

CALIFORNIA CONTENT
STANDARD 10.e

Weak Immune System

STANDARD SET 10

DIRECTIONS: Choose the letter of the *best* answer.

1 A patient with an HIV infection has a very low T cell count. The patient also has diseases such as pneumonia and tuberculosis. Which statement *best* describes the patient's condition?

  A The patient's T cells are numerous and very healthy.

  B The patient probably has AIDS resulting from HIV infection.

  C The patient has had an HIV infection for only a few weeks.

  D The patient's B cells are still producing antibodies.

3 Which of the following is *most* likely a characteristic of a person with a weakened immune system?

  A T cells are very active in fighting infections.

  B The body replaces T cells as quickly as those cells die.

  C Opportunistic infections make the person very sick.

  D White blood cells produce many antibodies.

3 Which statement *best* describes AIDS?

  A AIDS is a pathogen that weakens the immune system.

  B AIDS is a retrovirus that contains RNA.

  C AIDS is a condition that results from having an HIV infection.

  D AIDS is a type of opportunistic infection.

4 In which of the following ways can HIV be transmitted?

  A through an insect bite, such as from a mosquito

  B through shaking hands with an infected person

  C through swimming in a pool with an infected person

  D through sexual intercourse with an infected person

5

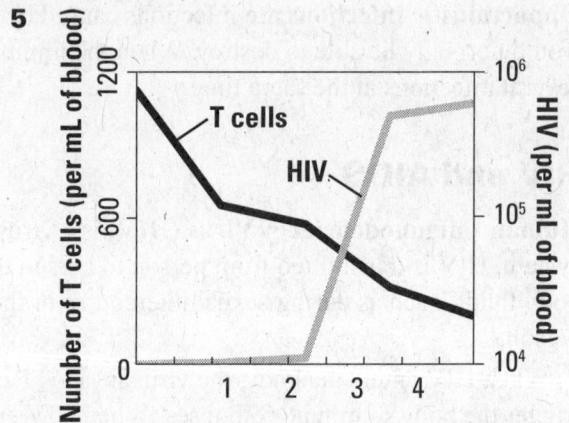

The graph shows how the number of T cells and HIV changes over time in the blood of a person infected with HIV. How does HIV weaken the immune system?

  A HIV destroys T cells faster than the body can replace them.

  B HIV causes T cells to differentiate into different cells.

  C HIV causes no significant changes in T cell numbers.

  D HIV kills T cells without reproducing new viruses.

Introduction to Investigation and Experimentation Standards

Scientific thought and processes are useful for more than just performing your own experiments. At some point, you'll likely want to read a scientific report to decide whether a certain product is safe or to help you form an opinion on an issue during an election year. The standards covered in this section are meant to give you the skills to do these things so that you can make informed decisions. Each of the standards listed below are found in the following pages.

IE.1 Scientific progress is made by asking meaningful questions and conducting careful investigations. As a basis for understanding this concept and addressing the content in the four other strands, students should develop their own questions and perform investigations. Students will:

IE.1.a Select and use appropriate tools and technology (such as computer-linked probes, spreadsheets, and graphing calculators) to perform tests, collect data, analyze relationships, and display data.

IE.1.b Identify and communicate sources of unavoidable experimental error.

IE.1.c Identify possible reasons for inconsistent results, such as sources of error or uncontrolled conditions.

IE.1.d Formulate explanations by using logic and evidence.

IE.1.e Solve scientific problems by using quadratic equations and simple trigonometric, exponential, and logarithmic functions.

IE.1.f Distinguish between hypothesis and theory as scientific terms.

IE.1.g Recognize the usefulness and limitations of models and theories as scientific representations of reality.

IE.1.h Read and interpret topographic and geologic maps.

IE.1.i Analyze the locations, sequences, or time intervals that are characteristic of natural phenomena (e.g., relative ages of rocks, locations of planets over time, and succession of species in an ecosystem).

IE.1.j Recognize the issues of statistical variability and the need for controlled tests.

IE.1.k Recognize the cumulative nature of scientific evidence.

IE.1.l Analyze situations and solve problems that require combining and applying concepts from more than one area of science.

IE.1.m Investigate a science-based societal issue by researching the literature, analyzing data, and communicating the findings. Examples of issues include irradiation of food, cloning of animals by somatic cell nuclear transfer, choice of energy sources, and land and water use decisions in California.

IE.1.n Know that when an observation does not agree with an accepted scientific theory, the observation is sometimes mistaken or fraudulent (e.g., the Piltdown Man fossil or unidentified flying objects) and that the theory is sometimes wrong (e.g., the Ptolemaic model of the movement of the Sun, Moon, and planets).

REVIEW

CALIFORNIA CONTENT
STANDARD IE.1.a

Technology and Data

STANDARD Students will select and use appropriate tools and technology (such as computer-linked probes, spreadsheets, and graphing calculators) to perform tests, collect data, analyze relationships, and display data.

Read the summary and answer the questions on the next page.

Technology helps scientists conduct experiments by making it easier to collect, analyze, and display data. Computer-based technologies, in particular, reduce the time researchers spend on mathematics and decrease computational errors.

Technologies and Tools

During many well-planned scientific experiments, different tools are used to collect and analyze data. For example, various computer-based technologies and computer-linked probes are used to measure pH, radioactivity, heart rate, blood pressure, voltage, and many other factors. There are also specific tools and technologies that scientists use in their experiments.

- **Microscopes** are instruments that provide enlarged images of very small things, such as cells. Without microscopes, we would not be able to see bacteria or cells.
- **Balances** allow scientists to measure mass and determine whether a change in mass occurred during an experiment.
- **Thermometers** give scientists information about the temperature of an environment or organism.
- **Computers and graphing calculators** can be linked to probes and programmed to take and record measurements. With computer-linked probes, a researcher can program the computer, and the system will take measurements without the researcher needing to be present. Computers can also be used to do mathematics that help researchers more easily analyze relationships between variables.

Use of Computers in Analysis

Technology is used to organize, analyze, and plot data. Graphing calculators and computer spreadsheets are both used to organize data. Once the data are in the computer, the computer can put the data into graphs or tables. Computers can use complicated mathematical equations to produce best-fit lines and to statistically analyze data. Best-fit lines are those that show the general trend in the data, as you can see in the diagram. Statistical analysis shows whether an independent variable had an effect on a dependent variable.

Best-Fit Line

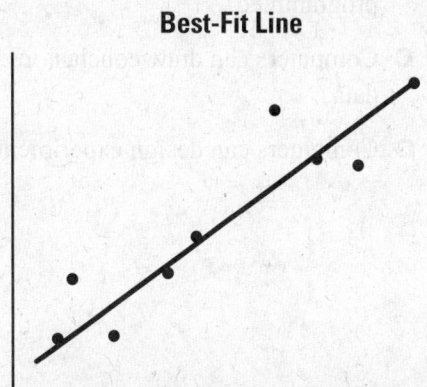

PRACTICE

CALIFORNIA CONTENT
STANDARD IE.1.a

Technology and Data

DIRECTIONS: Choose the letter of the *best* answer.

1

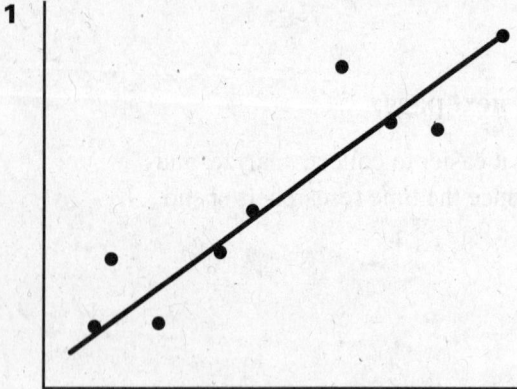

The line on the graph above is
best described as a

A best-fit line.

B linear relationship.

C cause-and-effect line.

D scatterplot.

2 **What is one of the benefits of using computers in scientific research?**

A Computers can do mathematical calculations quickly.

B Computers don't need to be programmed.

C Computers can draw conclusions from data.

D Computers can design experiments.

3 **A scientist would need a microscope to view a**

A housefly.

B skin cell.

C plant root.

D fingernail.

4 **Technology and tools such as computer-linked probes, thermometers, and balances are important in scientific studies because they all**

A measure temperature change.

B analyze data and make charts.

C increase the experiment's time.

D help to collect data.

5 **In an experiment, the temperature of a substance needs to be measured and recorded every two hours for two days. Assuming that the scientists conducting the experiment has all of these technologies in their laboratory, which is the *best* choice for performing this task?**

A a hand-held thermometer

B a graphing calculator

C a computer-linked thermometer

D a pH meter

STANDARD SET IE

REVIEW

CALIFORNIA CONTENT STANDARD IE.1.b

Unavoidable Experimental Error

STANDARD Students will identify and communicate sources of unavoidable experimental error.

Read the summary and answer the questions on the next page.

All scientific studies have some unavoidable errors in them. The best way to deal with unavoidable experimental error is by repeating tests, controlling constants as much as possible, and using a sufficient sample size, or number of subjects. Any factor that could potentially affect the outcome of an experiment is a possible source of experimental error.

Random Error

Scientific investigations do not yield perfect answers. This is especially true in biology because biological systems, such as organisms or ecosystems, are extremely variable and depend on many interacting factors. For example, if a researcher is studying butterflies, some of the butterflies might die due to conditions the researcher could not control, such as genetics, environment, infection, or chance.

Almost no measurement that a scientist takes is absolutely correct. The uncertainty in the accuracy of a measurement is called a **random error.** Random error takes into account the fact that a measuring instrument might yield data that are either higher or lower than the actual values. It also includes the natural variations among living things. However, random error is assumed to affect all measurements, subjects, and groups equally. And, by definition, random error is exactly that—random. There are several appropriate ways to address these unavoidable errors in laboratory investigations.

- Determine a range of values. For example, suppose you measure the pH of a solution three times and get 6.1, 6.7, and 6.4. You can account for this variability by taking the average of the numbers and reporting all of your pH measurements as the measured value +/- the standard deviation of the measurements.

- Conduct many trials to get multiple sets of data. The more data you have, the closer the average, or mean, is to the "actual" value. Additionally, a larger number of measurements or trials decreases the effect of variability on the statistical analysis of the data set.

Systematic Error

In many ways, systematic error is more damaging to data than random error. **Systematic errors** tend to shift data in one direction. It is impossible to perfectly calibrate laboratory equipment, to use every tool exactly how it should be used, or to account for every factor that might throw off a reading. However, systematic errors cannot be taken into account by sample size or statistical analysis.

STANDARD SET IE

PRACTICE

CALIFORNIA CONTENT
STANDARD IE.1.b

Unavoidable Experimental Error

DIRECTIONS: Choose the letter of the *best* answer.

1 Repeating tests is one way to decrease

    A trends.

    B data analysis.

    C random error.

    D instruments.

2 Suppose a researcher is conducting experiments to determine the conditions that allow fish eggs to hatch. The researcher takes water samples three times per day for one month or until the fish eggs in the stream hatch. As part of the study, the researcher must know the temperature of the water. Which of the following would yield the *most* reliable temperature data?

    A Measuring the temperature once during the experiment.

    B Measuring the temperature each day of the experiment.

    C Measuring the temperature two times at the same time every day.

    D Measuring the temperature multiple times each time a sample is collected.

3 The more data points and trials a researcher has, the more likely the means of the data are

    A accurate.

    B the same.

    C important.

    D random.

4

Hen Number	Number of Eggs
1	2
2	0
3	2
4	4

A new farmer wants to know how many eggs hens will lay per day. He studies four hens for one day, and the table above shows his observations. When he tells another farmer that his hens lay an average of two eggs per day, the other farmer says that his hens, which are the same type of hens, lay four eggs per day. What might *best* explain this difference?

    A The farmer has worse hens than his neighbor.

    B The farmer did not collect enough data.

    C The farmer did not study hen number 2.

    D The farmer did not average his data correctly.

5 Which type of error is unavoidable in an experiment?

    A incorrectly counting the number of insects in a jar

    B taking only five data points during the experiment

    C natural variability in living systems

    D designing an experiment without a control

STANDARD SET IE

REVIEW

CALIFORNIA CONTENT
STANDARD IE.1.c

Inconsistent Results

STANDARD Students will identify possible reasons for inconsistent results, such as sources of error or uncontrolled conditions.

Read the summary and answer the questions on the next page.

Reliability in scientific investigations is important. If a researcher completes an experiment and gets a certain result, other researchers should be able to repeat the experiment and obtain that same result. If differences in data exist, the researcher must try to determine what errors or uncontrolled conditions in the experiment might explain the inconsistencies.

Explaining Inconsistent Results

The best way to get reliable data is to run an experimental procedure over and over again until the researcher has many data points. The larger the data set, the better a mean, or average, of the individual data points represents the data set. Sometimes, however, repeating an experiment produces different results each time. There are various reasons that might account for these inconsistent results.

Experimental Error. Experimental error includes random error, such as natural variability among different organisms, and systematic error, such as incorrect measurement of a dependent variable or poorly calibrated instruments. Suppose that researchers are studying the effect of the number of daylight hours on a specific plant species' growth. Random error would include the normal variability in growth among plants, regardless of the amount of light they receive. Systematic error would include giving some plants the wrong amount of water by misreading a graduated cylinder. Having a small sample size increases the effect of experimental error on the analysis of the data. A larger number of data points tends to decrease the amount of variability in a data set.

Uncontrolled Conditions. In an experiment, an independent variable is manipulated to study its effect on a dependent variable. Scientists try to keep all of the other conditions, called **constants**, the same across the different groups in the experiment. Experimental groups are groups that are tested with the manipulation of the independent variable. A control group is exactly the same, except the independent variable, which is not changed, or kept under "normal" conditions.

    Constants are important because they assure that the effect of only one variable is being tested. If the experiment measures the effect of differing amounts of light on plant growth, then all other factors affecting plant growth—such as temperature, soil conditions, amount of water, plant type, age, and fertilizer—must be the same. If inconsistent data result from the investigation, it is possible that an additional, uncontrolled factor is a source of experimental error. Perhaps some of the plants were closer to the laboratory's ventilation source and were cooler than other plants, even though the overall room temperature remained constant. Perhaps the humidity in the lab was not controlled and that affected one experimental group more than another. Uncontrolled conditions such as these may increase variability in an experiment and make it more difficult to attribute growth differences in the plants to the differing amount of light. The uncontrolled factor must be taken into account and the experiment must be repeated before any conclusions can be drawn from the data.

PRACTICE

CALIFORNIA CONTENT
STANDARD IE.1.c

Inconsistent Results

DIRECTIONS: Choose the letter of the *best* answer.

1 Which of the following *best* describes an example of experimental error?

  A data that do not support a hypothesis

  B measuring several dependent variables

  C completely controlling constants

  D random variability

2

Group	Drops of Acid	Percentage of Ants Surviving
1	0	68
2	2	72
3	4	51
4	5	44

The chart above summarizes the results of an experiment testing the effect of acidic soil on a hypothetical ant species. The scientist added a weak acid to the soil, and, after four weeks, calculated the percentage of ants that survived. Which group is the control group?

  A 1

  B 2

  C 3

  D 4

3 Suppose a researcher wants to know the effect of two different types of fertilizer on plant growth. The researcher has three plants of the same species and gives fertilizer A to one plant, fertilizer B to another plant, and no fertilizer to the remaining plant. By the end of the experiment, all three of the plants grew equally well. What should the scientist do next time to decrease experimental error?

  A Use less fertilizer.

  B Use a different control.

  C Use more plants.

  D Use a different plant species.

4 What is the *best* reason why constants are important science?

  A They ensure that only one variable is being tested.

  B They add data points to the variables being studied.

  C They eliminate the need for dependent variables.

  D They guarantee that the experiment is accurate.

5 During a study on bird growth, a researcher accidentally gives one group of birds the wrong food. This is an example of

  A not using a control.

  B experimental error.

  C having too little data.

  D eliminating relationships.

REVIEW

Analyzing Data

STANDARD Students will formulate explanations by using logic and evidence.

Read the summary and answer the questions on the next page.

In order for science to be useful, researchers must collect data and then analyze and interpret their experimental results. Researchers use evidence, in the form of data, and logic to answer questions they have about the world around them.

Scientific Thinking

Scientists use scientific thinking to gather and interpret evidence. First, scientists use observations and data to form a hypothesis, which is a specific and testable proposed answer to a scientific question. Once scientists have a hypothesis, they can develop an experiment to test whether the hypothesis is correct. After the experiment is completed, a scientist must analyze and interpret the data.

Interpreting Evidence

After scientists perform experiments and collect data, they must interpret the data. To do this, scientists use tables and graphs to organize and display data, and they use statistics to analyze whether the data support the hypothesis. Graphs, such as this one, help scientists interpret relationships between variables in an experiment. By looking at this graph a scientist might use logic to conclude that the number of moths increased as time progressed. But what is the extent of the relationship? That is, might the data be due to chance? Statistical analysis of data answers that question. When data are statistically significant, it means that the results are likely not due to chance. Even if statistics show that the data support the hypothesis, scientists have to be careful when explaining and drawing conclusions from their results.

Change in Moths Over Time

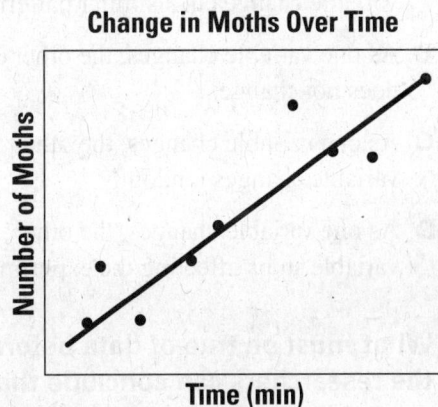

Number of Moths (vertical axis) vs. Time (min) (horizontal axis)

Formulating Explanations

Look at the graph again. What does it tell you? It only indicates that the number of moths increases over time. It also shows that the two variables are related to each other. However, the graph does not tell you why the number of moths increased. Scientists need to be careful to only try to explain their data and what the data mean in the context of the experiment. They should not draw conclusions about factors that were not tested in the experiment. For example, it would be incorrect to look at the graph and conclude that the number of moths increased because the moths that arrived later had to fly a greater distance. There is no evidence to support that conclusion.

PRACTICE

CALIFORNIA CONTENT
STANDARD IE.1.d

Analyzing Data

DIRECTIONS: Choose the letter of the *best* answer.

1 What is the *most* important role of scientific thinking?

   A It can be used to prove a hypothesis.

   B It helps scientists to design experiments that always work.

   C It is used to gather and interpret evidence.

   D It is used to find the results you are looking for.

2 Researchers complete a study and they want to determine if two variables are related. Which statement *best* describes a situation in which variables are related?

   A As one variable changes, the other variable changes in a similar pattern.

   B As one variable changes, the other does not change.

   C As one variable changes, the other variable changes randomly.

   D As one variable changes, the other variable stops affecting the experiment.

3 What *must* be true of data before the researchers can conclude that temperature affects the survival of bacteria?

   A As temperature changes, more bacteria mutate.

   B As temperature changes, so does the number of bacteria.

   C As temperature changes, individual bacteria get larger.

   D As temperature changes, bacteria move faster.

4 How are statistics important in scientific experiments?

   A Statistics allow researchers to develop hypotheses.

   B Statistics help researchers to graph their data.

   C Statistics prevent poorly designed experiments.

   D Statistics determine whether an effect is due to chance.

5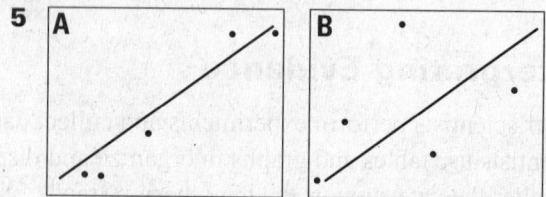

Graph A and Graph B show the results of two different experiments that test different variables. Which of the following is the best conclusion that researchers could draw about the variables in these two graphs?

   A The variables in Graph A are more related than those in Graph B.

   B The relationships between variables in are the same in both graphs.

   C The data in Graph B are much less variable than the data in Graph A.

   D The variables shown in Graph A are affecting those shown in Graph B.

STANDARD SET IE

REVIEW

CALIFORNIA CONTENT
STANDARD IE.1.f

Theory and Hypothesis

STANDARD Students will distinguish between hypothesis and theory as scientific terms.

Read the summary and answer the questions on the next page.

In science, a **theory** is a proposed explanation for a wide range of observations and experimental results that is supported by a wide range of evidence. A **hypothesis** (*pl. hypotheses*) is a proposed answer for one scientific question.

Hypothesis

Sometimes people call a scientific hypothesis an "educated guess." They know something about the question under investigation. Based on what they know, they have a reasonable idea about the answer. The key to a true hypothesis is that it must be specific and testable, and it answers a specific scientific question. A scientist will use observations and data to form a hypothesis. The hypothesis leads to testable predictions of what would happen if the hypothesis is valid.

Suppose a scientist is investigating which soil texture works best for growing a certain species of cactus in a flowerpot. The scientist knows that the soil in many deserts, where cacti naturally grow, is sandy. Therefore the scientist forms a hypothesis that the flowerpot with the sandiest soil will grow the tallest cactus. This hypothesis is the starting point from which the scientist can design an investigation. The investigation will test the hypothesis.

The data from an investigation either supports the hypothesis or fails to support the hypothesis. A hypothesis is never "proven." For scientists, just one test of a hypothesis is usually not enough. Most of the time, it is only by repeating tests that scientists can be more certain that their results are not mistaken or due to chance.

Theory

A hypothesis is a proposed answer to a specific scientific question, but a theory is a proposed explanation for a broader range of observations and experimental results, and is supported by a wide range of evidence. Gregor Mendel spent years in the mid-1800s investigating his hypotheses concerning heredity. It took decades of further study by other scientists, and advances in technology before chromosomes were discovered. Only after a large number of observations and experiments over many years were Mendel's and other scientists' results put together to develop the chromosome theory of heredity in 1902. With further investigations and advances in technology – and the discovery of the structure of DNA in 1953 – revisions to the 1902 theory continue to this day.

Eventually, theories may be broadly accepted by the scientific community. Theories are not easily accepted in science, and by definition they are never proved. Scientific hypotheses and theories may be supported or refuted, and they are always subject to change. New theories that better explain observations and experimental results can replace older theories.

STANDARD SET IE

PRACTICE

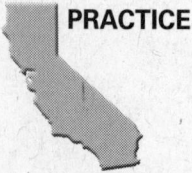

CALIFORNIA CONTENT
STANDARD IE.1.f

Theory and Hypothesis

DIRECTIONS: Choose the letter of the *best* answer.

1 Suppose a scientist thinks: "Organism A lives in a dry climate. The organism probably would not be able to survive in the rainforest." This is a(n)

  A theory.

  B hypothesis.

  C experiment.

  D conclusion.

2 The main difference between a hypothesis and a theory is

  A a theory explains a wide range of observations.

  B a theory can be proved but a hypothesis cannot.

  C a theory is a wild guess.

  D they cannot be tested.

3 What is the role of a hypothesis in a scientific investigation?

  A It gives researchers a specific problem to focus their study on.

  B It uses theories to prove ideas that researchers have.

  C It explains a large amount of data and observations.

  D It analyzes data that researchers gathered during experiments.

4

A observation
B experiments
C conclusion
A hypothesis

Above are some steps scientists take to do investigations and better understand the world around them. Which of the following puts these steps is the proper sequence?

  A A, B, C, D

  B A, B, D, C

  C A, D, B, C

  D A, C, D, B

5

Time through maze	Trial 1 (min)	Trial 2 (min)	Trial 3 (min)
Gerbils	3	4	3.5
Hamsters	4	3.5	4

The data from a student investigation is shown in the table above. The hypothesis was: "Gerbils learn faster than hamsters." Which is the *most* valid conclusion from the data?

  A The hypothesis is supported.

  B The hypothesis is not supported.

  C The theory is inconclusive.

  D The hypothesis is proved.

STANDARD SET IE

REVIEW

CALIFORNIA CONTENT
STANDARD IE.1.g

Limits of Models and Theories

STANDARD Students will recognize the usefulness and limitations of models and theories as scientific representations of reality.

Read the summary and answer the questions on the next page.

A scientific **model** is a representation of the world or a system that explains observations and predicts what might happen if a variable changes. A **theory** is a proposed explanation for a broad field of observations and experimental results. Both are important components of the scientific method. But, as human inventions, they are also imperfect.

Model

Many times, scientists cannot see what they are studying or conduct actual experiments to test a hypothesis. An experiment may be impractical because of cost, ethics, time, or scale. Watson and Crick hypothesized the structure of DNA without looking at it. Instead, they conducted experiments and used their results to build a model.

All good scientific models must do two things: explain existing data and predict new data. The better a job the model does at these two things, the more accepted it becomes. Models help us to explain things we find in nature. For example, some research on global warming is done using mathematical equations. These equations take into account the rates of chemical reactions and how these reactions affect global temperatures. However, no set of mathematical equations can account for every weather pattern.

Models are not perfect. Often, nature is too complicated to be able to take every variable into account. It is very likely that scientists do not even know all of the variables that have a role in a system. It is also likely that scientists do not know exactly how different variables affect each other, thereby affecting the model that is developed.

Theory

Theories explain, and are supported by, wide ranges of observations and experiments, and are widely acceptance in science. They are proposed explanations for broad fields of observations and experimental results.

Still, theories are not perfect. Just as with scientific models, it is difficult to know all of the variables involved and how these variables interact to cause a change. Theories can also take into account observations and experiments that have been done; they are only as good as all of the evidence that supports them. New discoveries and observations can cause scientists to revise theories. For example, when Albert Einstein proposed his general and special theories of relativity, Newton's older theory of motion was revised to exclude very fast-moving objects.

STANDARD SET IE

PRACTICE

CALIFORNIA CONTENT
STANDARD IE.1.g

Limits of Models and Theories

DIRECTIONS: Choose the letter of the *best* answer.

1 **Which of the following *best* describes the role of a scientific model?**

   A to validate observations

   B to explain existing data and predict new data

   C to serve as a visual aid to help older scientists complete studies

   D to revise or throw out old theories

2 **A scientist comes up with a new solar system model that has the planetary orbits shaped like clover leafs. What *must* occur in order for the new model to gain acceptance over the old model?**

   A People must believe it is true and accurate.

   B Scientists must endorse it in journals and at conferences.

   C The scientist must justify the changes.

   D It must do a better job of explaining and predicting data.

3 **Which of the following is a *major* limitation of scientific models?**

   A They do not predict what will occur if there is a change in the system.

   B They do not apply to fast-moving objects.

   C They are based on a limited understanding of the variables involved in the system.

   D They are imaginary and cannot be used to support any sort of hypothesis.

4 **How is a theory similar to a model?**

   A Both are perfect.

   B Both are hypotheses.

   C Both help explain something in nature.

   D Both are unlikely to change.

5

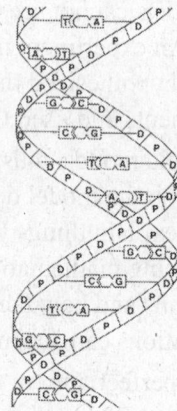

When Watson and Crick were studying the genetic material in cells, they used their data to build a model of DNA. What was the *main* role of the model, similar to the illustration above?

   A to explain DNA's structure

   B to avoid gathering data

   C to predict how DNA stores genetic information

   D to explain DNA's importance

STANDARD SET IE

REVIEW

CALIFORNIA CONTENT
STANDARD IE.1.i

Analyzing Natural Phenomena

STANDARD Students will analyze the locations, sequences, or time intervals that are characteristic of natural phenomena (e.g., relative ages of rocks, locations of planets over time, and succession of species in an ecosystem).

Read the summary and answer the questions on the next page.

Patterns exist within many natural phenomena. Scientists can study the patterns associated with these phenomena by analyzing the locations or time periods in which the phenomena take place. These analyses help scientists make inferences and predictions about natural phenomena even when the phenomena cannot be studied directly.

Patterns in Location

Some patterns in nature can be observed by studying the location of objects. In this case, scientists must carefully analyze a physical, three-dimensional space with a variety of techniques.

For example, sedimentary rock layers provide physical evidence of where, and how long ago, something happened. In layers of sedimentary rock, more recent layers form above older layers. The remains of organisms that lived during a particular time period are preserved within the rock layer that formed during that time. Therefore, a scientist studying fossils embedded in these layers may then infer that fossils found in the upper layers are the remains of organisms that lived more recently than the organisms whose fossils are found in lower layers. The locations of these fossils form a pattern, with the most recent fossils found in the highest layers and older fossils found in the layers below.

Patterns in Time

Some patterns in nature can only be observed if multiple observations are made over time. In order to analyze these phenomena, scientists must carefully observe changes that occur over these time periods, which might extend across many years. Scientists may also study how quickly, and how consistently, the changes take place.

For example, in any ecosystem that has been disturbed, a predictable pattern of ecological succession will occur. No matter how severe the disturbance, this process involves the gradual, predictable reestablishment of soil and plant life that eventually leads to a climax community that is characteristic of the area. To study ecological succession, scientists must visit a disturbed area many times, over the course of many years. By recognizing the types of plant species growing in an area, scientists can infer which stage of ecological succession the area is in, as well as predict how the ecosystem will change in years to come.

STANDARD SET IE

PRACTICE

CALIFORNIA CONTENT
STANDARD IE.1.i

Analyzing Natural Phenomena

DIRECTIONS: Choose the letter of the *best* answer.

1 Ecological succession involves the progression of an ecosystem that occurs

  A without soil or plants.

  B randomly over time.

  C when animals move in.

  D in a predictable way.

2 Suppose a scientist finds a collection of fossils embedded in several layers of sedimentary rock. Samples from each layer of rock are taken back to the laboratory to perform radiometric dating. However, before this analysis is done, the scientist is fairly certain that the largest fossil in the sample is the oldest. What is *most* likely the reason that the scientist would make this conclusion?

  A The large fossil was found in the uppermost layer of rock.

  B The large fossil was found in the lowest layer of rock.

  C Large fossils are usually older than small fossils.

  D Large fossils show more detail than small fossils.

3 The process of ecological succession begins after an ecosystem has been

  A inhabited.   **C** reestablished.

  B disturbed.   **D** colonized.

4

Fossil ID	Depth (cm)
1	20
2	42
3	47
4	111

A scientist collects four fossils from a slab of sedimentary rock. The identification numbers and depths at which these fossils were found are recorded in the table above. Assuming that each fossil was found in a distinct layer of sedimentary rock, which statement is *best* supported by these data?

  A Fossil 1 was formed most recently.

  B Fossils 1 and 2 were formed at about the same time.

  C Fossil 4 was formed the most recently.

  D Fossil 4 was the largest among these fossils.

5 A scientist can best identify the stage of ecological succession that an ecosystem is in by analyzing

  A microclimate data.

  B animal interactions.

  C plant types.

  D rock layers.

STANDARD SET IE

REVIEW

CALIFORNIA CONTENT STANDARD IE.1.j

Statistics and Controls

STANDARD Recognize the issues of statistical variability and the need for controlled tests.

Read the summary and answer the questions on the next page.

When scientists gather data during scientific experiments, they need to have a way to analyze that data to determine if two variables are related. By controlling as many factors, or constants, as possible during experiments, scientists make sure that only the independent variable is being tested and that variability within groups will be limited.

Controls and Constants

In an experiment, scientists must be sure that (1) their work is testing only the independent variable they are interested in and (2) any changes measured in dependent variables are the result of the independent variable.

In experiments, there should only be one **independent variable,** or variable being tested, manipulated, or changed, by the scientists. If scientists want to determine the amount of soil moisture that one species of insect prefers, the researchers might set up four different pans, and each should have different amounts of moisture in them. In this case, moisture is the independent variable. Each pan would be an experimental group or experimental condition. Across all of the pans, all factors other than moisture need to be kept the same. These other factors are **constants.** This means that the number of insects, the temperature, the amount of soil, the amount of light, and other such factors should be the same for each pan.

Experiments also need a control group to compare with the experimental groups. A **control group,** or control condition, is exactly the same as the experimental groups, but the independent variable is constant. Control groups are used to measure what happens under "normal" conditions, when the independent variable is not manipulated. In the insect example, the control pan would have the same soil moisture that is found in the insects' natural environment. Because the moisture is the same as the "normal" amount of moisture, it is a control. When the scientists analyze the data, they can compare the data from the experimental groups with the data from the control group. By tightly controlling the constants across all of the groups, the amount of variability is decreased. Any change that is observed in the data is more likely due to the independent variable rather than random experimental error.

Statistics

Statistics are important in analyzing data, because statistics allows researchers to determine, without bias, whether changes in an experiment are due to chance or due to the independent variable. If there is a statistically significant difference between groups, or conditions, in an experiment, then the change that occurred is not likely due by chance. However, if the results of statistical analysis show that the difference is not significant, then the independent variable did not have an effect on the dependent variable. A large amount of variability in data, which scientists try to eliminate by tightly controlling their experiments, can affect the outcome of statistical analysis.

STANDARD SET IE

PRACTICE

CALIFORNIA CONTENT
STANDARD IE.1.j

Statistics and Controls

DIRECTIONS: Choose the letter of the *best* answer.

1 Which of the following statements *best* explains the importance of keeping all the factors in an experiment constant, except for the independent variable?

A By keeping the factors constant, the scientists can use statistics.

B By keeping the factors constant, the scientists can completely eliminate random error.

C By keeping the factors constant, the scientists make sure that only one variable is being tested.

D By keeping the factors constant, the scientists can use any type of measuring instruments.

2

Group	Dose (mL)	Percent of Patients Cured
A	25	95
B	15	94
C	5	95
D	0	2

Suppose a doctor is conducting experiments to determine whether a new medicine cures patients. The experiment and results are shown in the data table above. Which group is the control group?

A Group A

B Group B

C Group C

D Group D

3 After researchers complete experiments, they use statistics to analyze their results. If the results are statistically significant, this means that the

A results are not likely due to chance.

B data gathered are accurate and precise.

C variables were testable and related.

D results support the hypothesis.

4 What is the *most* important role of control groups?

A They allow scientists to do experiments.

B They prevent experiments from going wrong.

C They provide data that can be used for comparison.

D They help researchers to average their data correctly.

5 Suppose a hotel executive hires a researcher to determine the best amount of light to give an indoor palm tree to keep it green and healthy. The researcher designs an experiment. Which of the following would *best* describe the independent variable in this experiment?

A the species of palm tree

B the amount of light

C the volume of water

D the weight of fertilizer

STANDARD SET IE

REVIEW

CALIFORNIA CONTENT
STANDARD IE.1.k

Cumulative Evidence

STANDARD   Recognize the cumulative nature of scientific evidence.

Read the summary and answer the questions on the next page.

A scientific experiment tests one specific question, or hypothesis. Researchers develop their hypotheses by analyzing experiments that other researchers have completed before them. And, when their experiment is complete, the results of that one test add to the scientific knowledge in that field.

One Experiment, One Hypothesis

A researcher develops a **hypothesis,** or a proposed answer to a scientific question. This hypothesis focuses the researcher's study and helps the researcher design an experiment that will answer that one specific question.

   Although an experiment tests one specific hypothesis, it takes many experiments to fully answer a question. Many different experiments, each adding another small piece of information, are necessary. Natural systems have many variables acting on them, so one experiment that only tests one variable cannot explain such complex systems. This is why many different types of scientific evidence must be gathered and analyzed before people can really understand which variables affect a system and to what extent the variables affect it.

Evidence to Form a Hypothesis

Even before an experiment begins, researchers rely on evidence from other studies, either their own, or those done by other scientists. Scientists can develop their scientific questions by reading scientific journals, which publish other researchers' experiments and results. These journals help researchers to develop their hypotheses because they can use the information from other experiments to give them ideas about what might happen if they performed a similar experiment, or a different experiment on a similar system. One experiment, and its results, leads to another experiment that expands knowledge in that area of science.

Evidence to Form Conclusions

Because biological systems have so many different variables affecting them, one experiment cannot describe everything that is occurring in that system. For example, the causes behind global warming are too complicated to be described in one experiment. And before the causes could even be identified, researchers had to conduct studies to notice that the Earth's temperatures are increasing. Other researchers heard of these studies, and then more studies were done to determine the chemical reactions that take place in the upper atmosphere. Still other experiments had to determine that carbon dioxide (CO_2) in the upper atmosphere traps heat. All of this had to occur before researchers could even pinpoint CO_2 as a greenhouse gas, and that increased levels of CO_2 might cause global warming. By combining many types of evidence, accumulated over many years from many experiments, researchers can better understand these types of complicated systems.

STANDARD SET IE

PRACTICE

CALIFORNIA CONTENT
STANDARD IE.1.k

Cumulative Evidence

DIRECTIONS: Choose the letter of the *best* answer.

1 During which step in scientific thinking will a researcher refer to information in other experiments?

A in forming hypotheses

B in drawing conclusions

C in forming hypotheses and drawing conclusions

D in testing hypotheses

2

Study	Nutrient	Number of Bacteria
1	nitrogen	increases
2	oxygen	none
3	phosphorus	increases
4	iron	decreases

Suppose you find four different studies, described in the chart above. In each of the studies, one nutrient was added in increasing amounts to colonies of bacteria. Then the change in the number of bacteria was recorded. You want to design an experiment to determine a combination of two nutrients that produces to the most bacterial growth. Which two nutrients will be *best* to test in this experiment?

A nitrogen and oxygen

B iron and phosphorus

C oxygen and iron

D phosphorus and nitrogen

3 Which of the following statements *best* explains why it is important that scientists share information about their research with one another?

A Researchers will only receive funding when they share their results.

B Biological systems are too complex to be understood by completing one experiment.

C Results from one study can be used in a new study if the variables are the same.

D Scientists always want to repeat experiments that other researchers already tried.

4 One experiment cannot fully explain a natural system because the experiment tests

A only one variable.

B different systems every time.

C simple chemical reactions.

D more hypotheses.

5 Natural systems, such as streams, are very complex. Which of the following statements *best* explains what is meant by a "complex system"?

A one that has many organisms

B one that has many nutrients

C one that has many variables

D one that has many changes

STANDARD SET IE

REVIEW

**CALIFORNIA CONTENT
STANDARD IE.1.I**

*Applying Concepts from
Different Areas of Science*

STANDARD Students will analyze situations and solve problems that require combining and applying concepts from more than one area of science.

Read the summary and answer the questions on the next page.

Most scientific issues involve more than one area of science. Biology, chemistry, physics, and geology are four major areas of science that are often interconnected. Understanding how different areas of science overlap and affect each other is a necessary component to analyzing scientific problems.

Major Areas of Science

Science is divided into many different fields. Four of the main fields are described below.

Biology is the study of all forms of life. This field includes the study of life at its most basic level, the cell. It also includes genetics, the study of biological inheritance patterns and variations in organisms. At an even larger scale, biology includes the study of how these organisms live, and how they interact with each other and their environment.

Chemistry is the study of the composition and properties of matter. All matter is made up of atoms. Atoms, in turn, make up molecules. Most substances that make up living organisms are molecules. The way in which atoms and molecules interact with each other can be applied to all areas of science, in living systems and in nonliving systems.

Physics is the study of matter and energy and the interactions between the two. Physics explain how the components of matter interact through four fundamental forces. It also describes the many forms of energy, such as chemical and electrical energy, and the way that energy can change from one form to another.

Geology is the study of the origin, history, and structure of the Earth. Physical geology is the study of Earth's materials, such as rocks, mountains, and ice, as well as how these materials change over time. Historical geology is the study of the events that have affected Earth since its origin. Evidence of these events comes from layered rocks and the fossils they contain.

Combining Concepts from Different Areas of Science

Many fields of study are actually combinations of two or more areas of science. For example, geophysics is the study of Earth's physical processes, such as weather. Biochemistry is the study of the chemical substances and processes that occur in living things, such as cellular respiration. Paleontology is the study of life that existed in prehistoric times, based on fossil evidence.

Furthermore, most scientific issues and problems are complex. To fully understand these issues, more than one area of science needs to be applied. For example, the habitat requirements for a plant species may involve the elevation on a mountain range, the chemistry of the soil, and the presence of a certain animal species.

STANDARD SET IE

PRACTICE

CALIFORNIA CONTENT
STANDARD IE.1.I

Applying Concepts from
Different Areas of Science

DIRECTIONS: Choose the letter of the *best* answer.

1 A scientist who studies how life on Earth has changed over time would be applying concepts *most* directly from the areas of

  A chemistry and physics.

  B biology and geology.

  C physics and geology.

  D geology and chemistry.

2

Lake Name	pH
Paradise	3.0
Lily	7.5
Birch	7.3
Diamond	7.9

A study of the fish populations in four lakes shows that Lily, Birch, and Diamond Lakes have healthy fish populations, and Paradise Lake has very few fish. The pH for each lake is shown in the table above. Which statement about Paradise Lake is *best* supported by these water chemistry data?

  A The fish population may be negatively affected by the acidic pH.

  B The fish population may be negatively affected by the basic pH.

  C The higher the pH, the healthier the fish would be.

  D The pH needs to reach at least 7.0 to have healthy fish.

3 A cell is the most basic unit of life. To study cell structure, a microbiologist must be familiar with the most basic unit of all matter, which is called a(n)

  A chemical.

  B organism.

  C molecule.

  D atom.

4 During photosynthesis, oxygen and sugar are produced from carbon dioxide and water in the presence of sunlight. Although this is a biochemical reaction, physics also plays a role because the process involves

  A the four fundamental forces of nature.

  B sunlight being absorbed by chlorophyll.

  C many molecules reacting together.

  D energy changing from one form to another.

5 Geochemistry is a scientific field that involves the overlap between geology and chemistry. A geochemist would therefore *most* likely study the chemical properties of

  A Earth's materials.

  B all life on Earth.

  C matter and energy.

  D atoms and molecules.

STANDARD SET IE

REVIEW

Science-Based Societal Issues

STANDARD Students will investigate a science-based societal issue by researching the literature, analyzing data, and communicating the findings. Examples of issues include irradiation of food, cloning of animals by somatic cell nuclear transfer, choice of energy sources, and land and water use decisions in California.

Read the summary and answer the questions on the next page.

Many topics in biology can be applied to the health and welfare of humans. For example, decisions regarding the regulation of factory emissions have an impact on human health (especially in relation to respiratory-related illnesses), but such decisions also affect a society's economy as well. When researching or reading about a science-based societal issue, it is important to take a number of factors into consideration.

Potential Bias

First, think about who might have an interest in a particular issue. For example, suppose a town is trying to decide where to place a new landfill. In this case, decisions about the issue might include town citizens who need a place for their trash, those people who live in the area where the landfill may be located, the town government, and the landfill company. All of those points of view must be considered.

When reading about an issue, such as a new landfill, you should consider who is writing the article and where the article is published. For example, an article in an environmental magazine might be skewed toward the environmental point of view, while an article in a business magazine might be skewed toward an industry's point of view. When conducting research, it is important to use several different resources to gain the perspective of many different points of view.

Scientific Literacy

Although some reporters for newspapers, popular magazines, or television have a background in the sciences, many do not. When reading articles in magazines or newspapers, or watching news reports on television, it is important to consider the original source used by the reporter. The best original source, and likely the least biased, is an article published in a peer-reviewed scientific journal. Then look at the article's abstract and conclusion sections. The abstract is a summary of the entire experiment and includes general conclusions. The conclusion section gives a more thorough explanation of the experiment's results. By reading these sections, you can determine whether the information reported by the popular press is accurate.

Two common mistakes include taking an experiment's results out of context or applying the results incorrectly. Correlation does not imply causation. For example, in studying the impact of pipelines on caribou populations, it was found that the population of caribou was larger after the pipeline was built. However, what was not taken into consideration was that caribou populations are cyclical, meaning they rise and fall over time. The pipeline construction happened to coincide with a peak in the caribou population.

PRACTICE

CALIFORNIA CONTENT
STANDARD IE.1.m

Science-Based Societal Issues

DIRECTIONS: Choose the letter of the *best* answer.

STANDARD SET IE

1 **Suppose you are writing a research report about the relationship between air quality and the incidence of asthma. Which of the following would be the *most* reliable source of information?**

   A a popular magazine

   B a television news program

   C a book

   D a scientific journal article

2 **Suppose that a news program reports that a scientific study shows that eating vegetables slows mental decline as people age. How could you determine if this report is correct?**

   A Read articles on the Internet about the topic.

   B Find the source of the original study and read it.

   C Conduct a poll to determine if other people believe the study's results.

   D Interview the manager of a local grocery store.

3 **What is meant by "correlation does not imply causation"?**

   A Statistical analysis is not important.

   B Statistics do not help to determine relationships between phenomena.

   C Just because two phenomena are related does not mean that one causes the other.

   D Different resources provide different perspectives.

4 **Why is it important to read the original scientific journal article that is the source of a news report?**

   A to see if the report is accurate

   B to see if the article is correct

   C to see if statistics were used to analyze the data

   D to see if you agree with the article

5

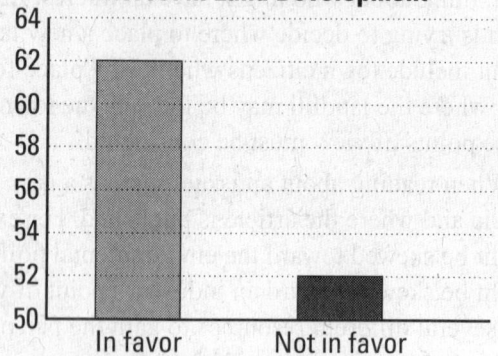

Interest in Land Development

Land developers used the above graph to show that an overwhelming majority of citizens in Coulterville are in favor of land development. What explanation *best* explains why this interpretation of the data is biased toward development?

   A only raw data are shown

   B the number of individuals with no opinion was not included in the graph

   C the surveyed individuals were not asked about their occupations

   D the y-axis scale is misleading

CALIFORNIA CONTENT
STANDARD IE.1.n

Overturning Theory

STANDARD SKnow that when an observation does not agree with an accepted scientific theory, the observation is sometimes mistaken or fraudulent (e.g., the Piltdown Man fossil or unidentified flying objects) and that the theory is sometimes wrong (e.g., the Ptolemaic model of the movement of the Sun, Moon, and planets).

Read the summary and answer the questions on the next page.

A large amount of research must occur before a theory is formed, and even more is needed for a theory to be accepted. Even after a theory has become accepted by the scientific community, new evidence and technology sometimes show that a theory is incorrect or that it needs to change. Other times, the new evidence and observations are mistaken or fraudulent.

Overturning or Changing Theories

A **theory** is an explanation for a large number of observations and experimental results that is supported by a wide range of evidence. In general, theories are accepted until new evidence that the theory cannot explain is presented and accepted. For example, the Ptolemaic model of how planets move in our solar system was one theory that was overturned when new evidence became available. The original theory stated that all of the planets, and the Sun, rotated around the Earth. As telescopes and other instruments became available, however, researchers discovered that all of the planets, including the Earth, move around the Sun.

The theory of disease has also changed over time. Hundreds of years ago, people believed that disease was caused by foul-smelling odors that they observed around sick people. However, the odors caused by some diseases were an effect of the disease and not the cause of it. With the development of the microscope, and through controlled experiments, scientists were able to identify bacteria that actually cause disease. The original theory was overturned, and germ theory, which states that microorganisms cause disease, became the accepted theory of the cause of disease.

Mistaken or Fraudulent Evidence

It is important that scientists continuously review one another's work. This review is meant to prevent scientific mistakes and scientific fraud. The Piltdown Man fossil is a famous example of a fraudulent discovery. In the early 1900s, a man in England discovered a jawbone and claimed that it belonged to an ancient human. The world believed that the fossil was real. Many scientists built careers around trying to locate similar fossils throughout England. However, no one ever found a similar fossil, and no one bothered to examine the existing fossil very closely. In the 1950s, one scientist used a magnifying glass to look at the teeth of the Piltdown Man fossil and found that the teeth had scratch marks on them. After many more scientists examined the teeth, they concluded that the jawbone actually belonged to an orangutan, and that the teeth had been filed down to make them look more similar to human teeth.

PRACTICE

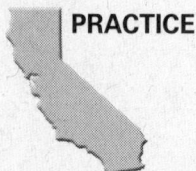

CALIFORNIA CONTENT
STANDARD IE.1.n

Overturning Theory

DIRECTIONS: Choose the letter of the *best* answer.

1 Which of the following statements *best* describes a theory?

  A evidence used to form a hypothesis

  B a proposed answer to a question

  C many experiments that form a study

  D an explanation for a observations

2 Suppose your friends return from vacation and they have digital photos of lights in the sky. Your friends explain that these lights are alien space ships (UFOs). Although you don't think your friends would lie, you don't believe that the lights are UFOs. Which of the following *best* explains why you might be skeptical about this discovery?

  A You have seen UFOs before and the ones in the picture do not look right.

  B You would like to see more evidence before agreeing that these are UFOs.

  C You believe this discovery because you have seen the photos.

  D You think that this evidence definitely supports the existence of UFOs.

3 Sometimes a scientific theory can be changed or completely thrown out. Which of the following *best* describes a condition that would cause a theory to be thrown out?

  A new reliable evidence

  B change in preferences

  C better available technology

  D increased peer review

4

Time (day)	Flowers (number)
1	5
3	12
5	20
7	30

The data table describes a study of the number of flowers blooming in a field. The researcher writes: "It is my theory that the number of flowers will continue to increase as time progresses." Which of the following *best* explains why the statement is not a theory?

  A Theories do not predict what will happen in the future.

  B Theories do not describe data.

  C Theories are based on more evidence than one study.

  D Theories need more data points.

5 Scientists review each other's work and replicate experiments. These measures help to prevent

  A fraudulent data.

  B selfish behavior.

  C throwing out theories.

  D unimportant studies.

Life Science Standards

The biology you learn in high school builds on the life science you have learned earlier. These Life Science standards, listed below, will be assessed on the California Life Science Standards Test.

CELL BIOLOGY

7.1.c *Students know* the nucleus is the repository for genetic information in plant and animal cells.

7.1.d *Students know* that mitochondria liberate energy for the work that cells do and that chloroplasts capture sunlight energy for photosynthesis.

7.1.e *Students know* cells divide to increase their numbers through a process of mitosis, which results in two daughter cells with identical sets of chromosomes.

8.6.b *Students know* that living organisms are made of molecules consisting largely of carbon, hydrogen, nitrogen, oxygen, phosphorus, and sulfur.

8.6.c *Students know* that living organisms have many different kinds of molecules, including small ones, such as water and salt, and very large ones, such as carbohydrates, fats, proteins, and DNA.

GENETICS

7.2.a *Students know* the differences between the life cycles and reproduction methods of sexual and asexual organisms.

7.2.c *Students know* an inherited trait can be determined by one or more genes.

7.2.d *Students know* plant and animal cells contain many thousands of different genes and typically have two copies of every gene. The two copies (or alleles) of the gene may or may not be identical, and one may be dominant in determining the phenotype while the other is recessive.

7.2.e *Students know* DNA (deoxyribonucleic acid) is the genetic material of living organisms and is located in the chromosomes of each cell.

ECOLOGY

6.5.b *Students know* matter is transferred over time from one organism to others in the food web and between organisms and the physical environment.

6.5.c *Students know* populations of organisms can be categorized by the functions they serve in an ecosystem.

6.5.e *Students know* the number and types of organisms an ecosystem can support depends on the resources available and on abiotic factors, such as quantities of light and water, a range of temperatures, and soil composition.

EVOLUTION

7.3.a *Students know* both genetic variation and environmental factors are causes of evolution and diversity of organisms.

7.3.b *Students know* the reasoning used by Charles Darwin in reaching his conclusion that natural selection is the mechanism of evolution.

7.3.c *Students know* how independent lines of evidence from geology, fossils, and comparative anatomy provide the bases for the theory of evolution.

PHYSIOLOGY

7.5.a *Students know* plants and animals have levels of organization for structure and function, including cells, tissues, organs, organ systems, and the whole organism.

7.5.c *Students know* how bones and muscles work together to provide a structural framework for movement.

7.6.j *Students know* that contractions of the heart generate blood pressure and that heart valves prevent backflow of blood in the circulatory system.

INVESTIGATION AND EXPERIMENTATION

IE.6.c Construct appropriate graphs from data and develop qualitative statements about the relationships between variables.

IE.6.e Recognize whether evidence is consistent with a proposed explanation.

IE.7.c Communicate the logical connection among hypotheses, science concepts, tests conducted, data collected, and conclusions drawn from the scientific evidence.

IE.8.b Evaluate the accuracy and reproducibility of data.

IE.8.c Distinguish between variable and controlled parameters in a test.

CALIFORNIA CONTENT
STANDARD 7.1.c

The Nucleus

STANDARD Students know the nucleus is the repository for genetic information in plant and animal cells.

Read the summary and answer the questions on the next page.

Most of the genetic material inside plant and animal cells is contained in an organelle called the **nucleus.** Because it contains the genetic instructions that control all of the cell's activity, the nucleus often is referred to as the control center of the cell.

Genetic Material of Eukaryotic Cells

The genetic information inside the nucleus of plant and animal cells is packaged inside structures called **chromosomes.** Each chromosome consists of tightly coiled molecules of the nucleic acid DNA that are wrapped around proteins. DNA molecules are made up of two strands of chemical units called nucleotides. Each nucleotide contains three chemical subunits—a phosphate compound, a sugar molecule, and a base. There are four types of bases found in DNA: guanine, adenine, thymine, and cytosine. These are abbreviated G, A, T, and C, respectively. The two DNA strands are linked to each other by chemical bonds, forming a ladderlike structure that is twisted into a helix, or coil.

Sequencing and Coding

Each DNA molecule that forms a chromosome can be divided into segments called **genes**. A gene contains instructions for the production of proteins that the cell needs for growth, repair, and other functions. These instructions are determined by the sequence of bases along the length of the gene. The base sequence of a gene forms a coded set of instructions for the production of specific amino acids.

RNA

The instructions encoded in each gene are decoded and translated by another nucleic acid called RNA. Plant and animal cells have three types of RNA. Messenger RNA is found in the nucleus. It decodes the DNA sequence and carries the information to the cytoplasm, where it is translated into proteins by ribosomal RNA and transfer RNA.

STANDARD SET: CELL BIOLOGY

PRACTICE

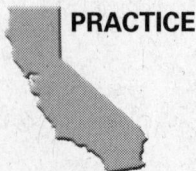

CALIFORNIA CONTENT
STANDARD 7.1.c

The Nucleus

DIRECTIONS: Choose the letter of the *best* answer.

1 The nucleus contains genetic information that is organized into structures called

  A proteins.

  B ribosomes.

  C chromosomes.

  D amino acids.

2 Which of the following are found in chromosomes?

  A DNA and RNA

  B RNA and phosphates

  C DNA and proteins

  D RNA and proteins

3 A gene is a(n)

  A segment of DNA.

  B amino acid sequence.

  C large organelle.

  D RNA segment.

4 Which of the following are *not* found in the nucleus?

  A proteins

  B transfer RNA

  C messenger RNA

  D DNA

5 What are the three subunits of a nucleotide?

  A phosphates, RNA, and sugars

  B phosphates, sugars, and bases

  C phosphates, proteins, and sugars

  D sugars, amino acids, and bases

REVIEW

Mitochondria and Chloroplasts

STANDARD Students know that mitochondria liberate energy for the work that cells do and that chloroplasts capture sunlight energy for photosynthesis.

Read the summary and use answer the questions on the next page.

All cells use chemical energy to fuel the chemical reactions that allow the cells to function and to do work. **Chemical energy** is the energy stored in the bonds that link atoms together to form molecules. The main energy source for most cells is the sugar **glucose.** Animal cells get glucose from their environment. Plant cells manufacture glucose through photosynthesis. For photosynthesis to take place, plant cells must capture light energy from the Sun.

How Mitochondria Work

Most eukaryotic cells break bonds connecting glucose atoms through **cellular respiration,** a process that uses oxygen to free the energy stored in the bonds of glucose molecules. More energy is liberated, or released, from glucose when oxygen is present than when oxygen is not present. Cellular respiration takes place in organelles called **mitochondria.** In the cytoplasm, glucose molecules are broken into smaller molecules. As shown in the diagram, these molecules then enter the mitochondria along with oxygen. Inside the mitochondria, chemical reactions break the bonds connecting the atoms of the glucose fragment. These reactions release energy, and produce carbon dioxide and water.

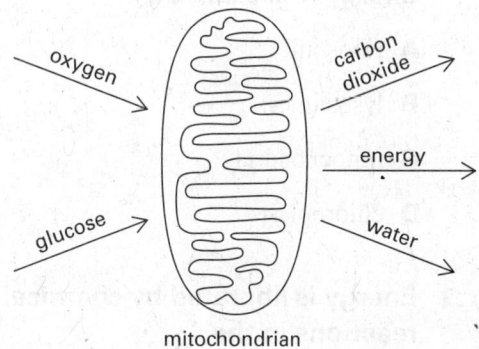

oxygen → / carbon dioxide → / energy → / glucose → / water →

mitochondrian

How Chloroplasts Work

Photosynthesis takes place inside **chloroplasts,** organelles that contain a green-colored pigment called chlorophyll. During photosynthesis, carbon dioxide and water enter the chloroplast from the cytoplasm, as shown in the diagram. The chlorophyll inside the chloroplast absorbs and traps energy from sunlight. This light energy fuels a chemical reaction that changes carbon dioxide and water into glucose and oxygen. This glucose will supply energy for the cell to do work.

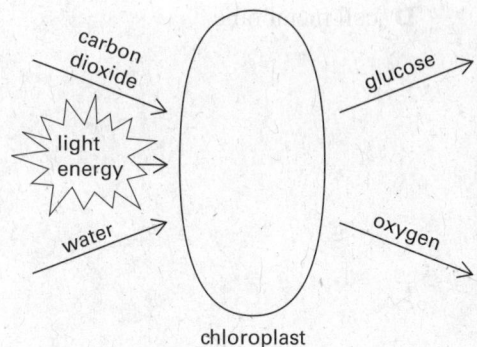

carbon dioxide → / light energy / water → / glucose → / oxygen →

chloroplast

STANDARD SET: CELL BIOLOGY

PRACTICE

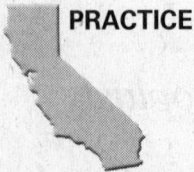

CALIFORNIA CONTENT
STANDARD 7.1.d

Mitochondria and Chloroplasts

DIRECTIONS: Choose the letter of the *best* answer.

1 Which of the following do plant cells need for photosynthesis?

A chemical energy

B oxygen

C light energy

D osmotic pressure

2 During photosynthesis, light energy is captured by

A ribosomes.

B lysosomes.

C mitochondria.

D chloroplasts.

3 Energy is liberated by chemical reactions in the

A mitochondria.

B chloroplasts.

C nucleus.

D cell membrane.

4 Which of the following are found in animal cells?

A mitochondria and cell walls

B mitochondria and chloroplasts

C mitochondria and glucose

D mitochondria and chlorophyll

5 Chemical reactions in mitochondria produce

A energy, glucose, and water.

B energy, carbon dioxide, and water.

C carbon dioxide, water, and glucose.

D energy, glucose, and oxygen.

6 Chemical reactions in chloroplasts produce

A energy, glucose, and water.

B carbon dioxide and water.

C glucose and oxygen.

D water and chlorophyll.

STANDARD SET: CELL BIOLOGY

REVIEW

CALIFORNIA CONTENT
STANDARD 7.1.e

Cell Division

STANDARD Students know cells divide to increase their numbers through a process of mitosis, which results in two daughter cells with identical sets of chromosomes.

Read the summary and answer the questions on the next page.

Mitosis is the process by which a cell divides. Through mitosis, one cell produces two genetically identical cells called daughter cells.

Mitosis

The cell cycle exists as a sequence of events during which the cell first grows and develops, and then divides to produce new cells. Cell division occurs in two parts—mitosis and cytokinesis. During **mitosis** the nucleus divides. This is followed by **cytokinesis,** which is the division of the parent cell's cytoplasm and organelles.

- Before mitosis, the cell's chromosomes duplicate in the parent cell. This produces two copies of chromosomes.
- The chromosome copies separate and move to opposite ends of the parent cell.
- A new nuclear membrane forms around each chromosome set.

Cytokinesis takes place right after mitosis. In animal cells, the cell membrane pinches inward until it divides the whole cell into two daughter cells, each completely surrounded by a cell membrane. In plant cells, a structure called the cell plate grows between the daughter nuclei and forms a new cell wall.

Cytokinesis happens in both plant and animal cells.

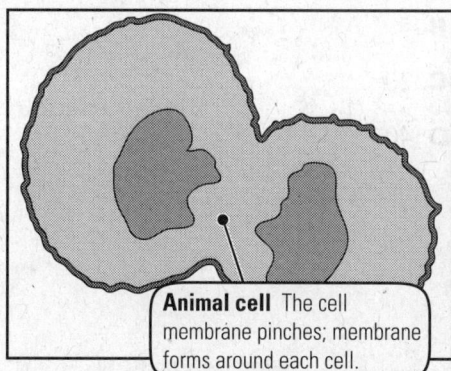

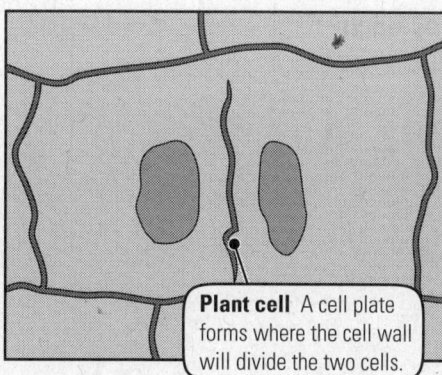

Animal cell The cell membrane pinches; membrane forms around each cell.

Plant cell A cell plate forms where the cell wall will divide the two cells.

Daughter Cells

The processes of mitosis and cytokinesis produce two identical daughter cells from one single parent cell. Each daughter cell has a full set of chromosomes as well as some of the parent cell's cytoplasm and organelles. After mitosis and cytokinesis are complete, the cell cycle begins again for each daughter cell.

PRACTICE

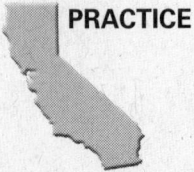

CALIFORNIA CONTENT
STANDARD 7.1.e

Cell Division

DIRECTIONS: Choose the letter of the *best* answer.

1 During which part of the cell cycle does the parent cell's cytoplasm divide?

   A protein synthesis

   B mitosis

   C interphase

   D cytokinesis

2 Which is part of cytokinesis in plant cells?

   A cell plate formation

   B chromosome duplication

   C light energy capture

   D chromosome separation

3 After mitosis, an animal cell with 38 chromosomes will produce two daughter cells with how many chromosomes each?

   A 19

   B 38

   C 76

   D 114

4 Cell division occurs in two stages called

   A cellular respiration and interphase.

   B mitosis and cellular respiration.

   C cytokinesis and mitosis.

   D interphase and cytokinesis.

5 Mitosis is a process in which the

   A organism divides.

   B cytoplasm divides.

   C mitochondria divide.

   D nucleus divides.

6 If you start with 5 cells, how many cells will there be after two cell cycles?

   A 10

   B 5

   C 20

   D 40

STANDARD SET: CELL BIOLOGY

CALIFORNIA CONTENT
STANDARD 8.6.b

Elements in Living Things

STANDARD Students know that living organisms are made of molecules consisting largely of carbon, hydrogen, nitrogen, oxygen, phosphorus, and sulfur.

Read the summary and answer questions on the next page.

Six elements—**carbon, hydrogen, oxygen, nitrogen, phosphorus, and sulfur**—form the bulk of every living organism on Earth. Surprisingly, just one of these elements, oxygen, is also common in the Earth's crust. These six elements, however, can form thousands of very important molecules. Four elements in particular—carbon, hydrogen, oxygen, and nitrogen—are important because of the types of bonds they can form.

Common Elements

The elements carbon, nitrogen, oxygen, and hydrogen each readily forms covalent bonds with each other. These elements can also form bonds with other elements not quite as common in living organisms. The chart shows the types of bonds these molecules can form. Note that triple bonding is much more common in molecules in living organisms.

Element	Single Bond	Double Bond	Triple Bond
Hydrogen	X		
Oxygen	X	X	
Nitrogen	X	X	X
Carbon	X	X	X

The elements carbon, nitrogen, oxygen, and hydrogen are the lightest elements able to form covalent bonds. The lighter the element, the stronger the covalent bond it can form. This means that the molecules found in living organisms have the strongest covalent bonds that can be found in nature.

Less Common Elements

Several other elements can be found in living organisms, although they are not as common as carbon, hydrogen, oxygen, and nitrogen. Phosphorus is found all cell membranes. Sulfur is in some chemicals found in cells called enzymes. Enzymes help speed up essential chemical reactions that keep cells alive. In humans and other animals, calcium is an important element. It makes bones and teeth hard and strong. Other elements, found in very small amounts in living organisms, include sodium, potassium, and chlorine. Traces of other elements found in living organisms include magnesium, manganese, iron, cobalt, copper, zinc, boron, aluminum, vanadium, molybdenum, iodine, and selenium.

PRACTICE

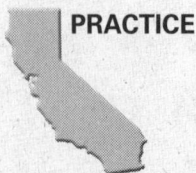

CALIFORNIA CONTENT
STANDARD 8.6.b

Elements in Living Things

DIRECTIONS: Choose the letter of the *best* answer.

1 What are the six main elements found in living things?

A calcium, carbon, hydrogen, oxygen, potassium, and sodium

B carbon, hydrogen, nitrogen, oxygen, phosphorus, and sulfur

C carbon, hydrogen, oxygen, sulfur, magnesium, and iron

D hydrogen, nitrogen, oxygen, calcium, cesium, and boron

2 Which element is common in *both* living things and in Earth's crust?

A carbon

B nitrogen

C oxygen

D sulfur

3 What kind of bonds do the common elements in living things form?

A metallic

B ionic

C covalent

D none

4 What makes the bonds between the common atoms in living things strong?

A They are light nonmetals.

B They are transition metals.

C They are alkaline earth metals.

D The bonds are ionic.

5 Which pair of elements can each form triple bonds?

A carbon and hydrogen

B carbon and nitrogen

C oxygen and nitrogen

D oxygen and phosphorus

6 Which of these organisms is most likely to incorporate the *largest* percentage of the element calcium in its tissues?

A bacteria, because of their cell walls

B moths, because they can fly

C plants, because they grow in soil

D zebras, because of their bones

7 Which element is found in small amounts in the membrane that surrounds each cell?

A carbon

B magnesium

C phosphorus

D sodium

8 Which of the following is a trace element found in living things?

A hydrogen

B iron

C silicon

D uranium

STANDARD SET: CELL BIOLOGY

REVIEW

CALIFORNIA CONTENT
STANDARD 8.6.c

Molecules in Living Things

STANDARD Students know that living organisms have many different kinds of molecules, including small ones, such as water and salt, and very large ones, such as carbohydrates, fats, proteins, and DNA.

Read the information to answer questions on the next page.

Living things rely on many substances. Some of these substances are made of very large, complex molecules. Other substances have far smaller molecules but are still very important.

Molecules

The chart defines and describes four types of large molecules.

Molecule	Examples	Functions
Carbohydrate	Sugars Starch Cellulose	• Energy source • Energy storage (starches) • In plants, form key structural materials
Lipids	Fats Oils Waxes Some hormones	• Energy source • Energy storage—more efficient than carbohydrates • Structural components of cells
Proteins	Enzymes Keratin Hemoglobin	• Control of chemical reactions • Structural materials (e.g., hair) • Transport substances in body
Nucleic acids	DNA RNA	• DNA encodes genetic information • RNA translates genetic code

Several small molecules are essential for living things. For example, water (H_2O) is the basis of life. Cells are 70 to 80 percent water. Carbon dioxide (CO_2) also helps regulate the pH of the blood. Animals release carbon dioxide during respiration. Plants, in turn, use carbon dioxide to make glucose through the process of photosynthesis.

Ions

Several different ionic compounds and ions are essential for living organisms. For example, the ionic compound calcium phosphate ($Ca_3(PO_4)_2$ is the main mineral in bones and teeth. A variety of ions are important for life, as well. Sodium ions (Na^+) and potassium ions (K^+) are involved in nerve transmission. Chloride ions (Cl^-) help with digestion in the body. The body's need for sodium and chlorine is one reason why salt, sodium chloride (NaCl) is an important compound.

STANDARD SET: CELL BIOLOGY

PRACTICE

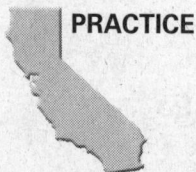

CALIFORNIA CONTENT
STANDARD 8.6.c

Molecules in Living Things

DIRECTIONS: Choose the letter of the *best* answer.

1 What is a function of carbon dioxide (CO_2) in the body?

  A regulate the pH of blood

  B adds structure to hair

  C energy source

  D energy storage

2 What is sodium chloride (NaCl)?

  A a protein

  B a carbohydrate

  C an ionic compound

  D a covalent compound

3 Which type of substance is protein?

  A a small molecule.

  B a large molecule.

  C an ionic compound.

  D an ion.

4 Which type of substance is calcium phosphate ($Ca_3(PO_4)_2$)?

  A It is a small molecule.

  B It is a large molecule.

  C It is an ionic compound.

  D It is an ion.

5 Which small molecule makes up about 70 percent of cells?

  A DNA

  B fat

  C oxygen

  D water

6 Which of these large molecules are important for energy storage?

  A DNA and lipids

  B DNA and RNA

  C lipids and starches

  D RNA and starches

STANDARD SET: CELL BIOLOGY

REVIEW

CALIFORNIA CONTENT
STANDARD 7.2.a

Sexual and Asexual Reproduction

STANDARD Students know the differences between the life cycles and reproduction methods of sexual and asexual organisms.

Read the summary and answer the questions on the next page.

There are two forms of reproduction, asexual and sexual, which are compared in the chart below.

Asexual Reproduction

In **asexual reproduction,** one parent produces offspring that are genetically identical to the parent. This is because the DNA of the offspring comes only from that parent.

Many prokaryotes reproduce through a simple form of cell division called **binary fission.** The cell replicates its DNA and then divides in half, producing two genetically identical offspring cells. Many unicellular eukaryotes reproduce by **mitosis** and **cytokinesis.** During mitosis, the nucleus breaks down. The replicated chromosomes divide and the cell's cytoplasm divides through cytokinesis.

Budding is a form of asexual reproduction found in some yeasts and simple animals such as jellyfish and sponges. In this process, the parent grows a small bud or branch. The bud breaks off of the parent and becomes a separate organism.

Sexual Reproduction

Sexual reproduction involves two parents and the exchange of DNA. Offspring produced through sexual reproduction get about half of their DNA from each parent. Because of this, the offspring is not genetically identical to either parent.

Multicellular organisms that reproduce sexually produce special reproductive cells called **gametes.** Each gamete is a haploid (n) cell—it has half the usual ($2n$) number of chromosomes. The process starts with a diploid ($2n$) cell in the parent's reproductive tissues. The cell's chromosomes are replicated. During **meiosis,** the cell divides, and the resulting cells divide again. This produces four haploid (n) gametes. Gametes from male reproductive tissue are **sperm,** while gametes from female reproductive tissue are **eggs.** An egg and a sperm join together during **fertilization** to form a diploid ($2n$) cell, called a **zygote,** which can develop into a mature individual.

Comparing Asexual and Sexual Reproduction	
Asexual Reproduction	**Sexual Reproduction**
Cell division	Cell division and other processes
One parent organism	Two parent organisms
Rate of reproduction is rapid	Rate of reproduction is slower than rater for asexual reproduction
Offspring identical to parents	Offspring have genetic information from two parents

PRACTICE

CALIFORNIA CONTENT
STANDARD 7.2.a

Sexual and Asexual Reproduction

DIRECTIONS: Choose the letter of the *best* answer.

1 Which of the following statements about meiosis and gametes is correct?

A Meiosis produces two haploid (*n*) gametes from one diploid (2*n*) parent cell.

B Meiosis produces four haploid (*n*) gametes from one diploid (2*n*) parent cell.

C Meiosis produces four diploid (2*n*) gametes from one diploid (2*n*) parent cell.

D Meiosis produces two diploid (2*n*) gametes from one diploid (2*n*) parent cell.

2 Which of the following forms of asexual reproduction is common among prokaryotes?

A meiosis

B mitosis

C binary fission

D fertilization

3 Mitosis and cytokinesis are a form of asexual reproduction for

A jellyfish.

B prokaryotes.

C unicellular eukaryotes.

D sponges.

4 Which of the following statements about forms of reproduction is the *most* accurate?

A Organisms produced by asexual reproduction are genetically identical to their parent.

B In sexual reproduction, offspring get genes from only one parent.

C In asexual reproduction, offspring get about half of their genes from each parent.

D Budding is a form of sexual reproduction used by jellyfish.

5 Which statement about the production of gametes is the *most* correct?

A Gametes are produced by mitosis and contain about half of the genetic material of the parent cell.

B Gametes are produced by mitosis and contain a copy of all of genetic material from the parent cell.

C Gametes are produced by meiosis and contain about half of the genetic material of the parent cell.

D Gametes are produced by meiosis and have a copy of all of the genetic material from the parent cell.

6 How many times do cells divide during meiosis?

A four   **C** two

B one   **D** none

REVIEW

CALIFORNIA CONTENT
STANDARD 7.2.c

Trait Inheritance

STANDARD Students know an inherited trait can be determined by one or more genes.

Read the summary and answer the questions on the next page.

Traits are features that are inherited. Some traits are produced from a combination of one or more genes.

Traits and Genes

All living things have combinations of traits. A **trait** is a characteristic or feature of an individual. Traits may be acquired or inherited. Acquired traits are characteristics that develop during an individual's lifetime. Examples include muscle development as a result of bodybuilding, or the ability to read. Inherited traits are characteristics that are passed from parent to offspring. Some traits, such as eye color, are physical and visible from outside the organism. Other traits, such as blood type, are biochemical and not immediately visible.

Inherited traits are influenced by genes. A **gene** is a segment of DNA at a specific location on a chromosome. Each gene carries a code for information that can affect inherited traits. An organism does not inherit a specific trait from its parents. Instead, it inherits the genes that code for the trait. Each gene may have several variations. For example, a gene for fur color may be for brown fur or black fur. Different forms of the same gene are called **alleles.**

How Genes Form Traits

The chromosomes in most eukaryote cells occur in pairs called **homologs.** The homologs of a pair have the same size and shape and carry the same genes. However, the alleles of the gene may be different. One chromosome of each pair came from one parent, and the other came from the other parent. This means that genes also come in pairs.

Most traits are not coded for by one gene. Some traits are affected by many genes in complicated ways. These traits can show a great deal of variation. For example, hair color in humans is influenced by several genes interacting in complex ways that can produce slightly different outcomes even in closely related individuals. A girl may inherit light brown hair from her parents, but the girl's hair may be slightly lighter or darker than either parent's hair. It may change over time and be influenced by the environment. Because several genes can influence a trait, a change in one gene may have a small effect or a large effect on a trait.

PRACTICE

CALIFORNIA CONTENT
STANDARD 7.2.c

Trait Inheritance

DIRECTIONS: Choose the letter of the *best* answer.

1 An acquired trait is a characteristic that is

　A developed during an individual's lifetime.

　B controlled by several genes and the environment.

　C controlled by one gene.

　D biochemical and therefore not visible.

2 Which of the following statements about traits is the *most* accurate?

　A Inherited traits are acquired over an individual's lifetime.

　B Acquired traits are a result of genes from both parents.

　C Inherited traits are a result of genes from both parents.

　D Each inherited trait is the result of one gene from one parent.

3 Different forms of the same gene are called

　A traits.

　B alleles.

　C codes.

　D characteristics.

4 Which of the following is the *smallest* change that could produce variation?

　A changes in all of the related genes of both parents

　B changes in all of the related genes of one parent

　C changes in one gene in both parents

　D changes in one gene in one parent

5 A characteristic or feature of an individual is known as a(n)

　A homolog.

　B allele.

　C code.

　D trait.

REVIEW

CALIFORNIA CONTENT
STANDARD 7.2.d

Dominant and Recessive Inheritance

STANDARD Students know plant and animal cells contain many thousands of different genes and typically have two copies of every gene. The two copies (or alleles) of the gene may or may not be identical, and one may be dominant in determining the phenotype while the other is recessive.

Read the summary and answer the questions on the next page.

Phenotypes and Genotypes

Plant and animal cells have many thousands of **genes** arranged at specific sites on chromosomes. In most plant and animal species, chromosomes are arranged in pairs called **homologs.** Offspring inherit one chromosome of each pair from one parent, and the other chromosome from the other parent. The homologs are the same size and shape and carry the same genes. Therefore, each cell has two copies of each gene—one on each homologous chromosome. Each of these gene copies is called an **allele.** The alleles for a gene may or may not be identical.

- The way that a trait is expressed—the actual characteristics that are observed—are called a **phenotype.** Eye color, height, and the color of petals on a flower are all examples of phenotypes.
- The phenotype for a trait is determined by the combination of alleles that code for that trait. The combination of alleles that code for a given trait is called a **genotype.**

Dominant and Recessive

The genotype of a trait affects how that trait is expressed in the phenotype. For some traits, one allele may be dominant to the other allele in a gene pair. A **dominant** allele is one that is expressed in the phenotype even if only one copy is present. An allele that is expressed in the phenotype only when two copies are present is called a **recessive** allele.

For example, coat length in domestic cats is a controlled by the genotype of one gene pair at a specific site on a homologous chromosome pair. Short hair length (*S*) is a dominant trait. Long hair length (*s*) is a recessive trait. For a cat to have long hair, both chromosomes in the gene pair must carry the recessive allele. The genotype for this trait may be noted as *ss*. The dominant phenotype—short hair—may result from either of two genotypes. Both chromosomes may have the dominant allele. This genotype can be noted as *SS*. Alternately, one allele may be dominant and the other can be recessive. This genotype is noted as *Ss*.

PRACTICE

CALIFORNIA CONTENT
STANDARD 7.2.d

Dominant and Recessive Inheritance

DIRECTIONS: Choose the letter of the *best* answer.

1 **The observable way traits are expressed is an individual's**

  A genotype.

  B homologs.

  C phenotype.

  D gene pairs.

2 **The combination of alleles that affect a trait is an individual's**

  A genotype.

  B homologs.

  C phenotype.

  D chromosomes.

3 **Which of the following statements about the expression of alleles is the *most* accurate?**

  A The alleles for a gene must be identical for that trait to be expressed.

  B The alleles for a gene cannot be identical; otherwise the trait they affect will not be expressed.

  C The alleles for a gene may or may not be identical.

  D The alleles for most traits are inherited from the mother.

4 **A dominant allele is one that**

  A is expressed even if only one copy is present.

  B must have two copies to be expressed.

  C must be inherited from the female parent to be expressed.

  D is found only in cats.

5 **A recessive allele is one that**

  A is expressed even if only one copy is present.

  B must have two copies to be expressed.

  C must be inherited from the female parent to be expressed.

  D is found only in cats.

6 **Dimples are a dominant trait in humans. Which of the genotypes below could be found in the cells of individuals with dimples? (*D*=dominant allele, *d*=recessive allele)**

  A *DD, Dd*

  B *DD, dd*

  C *dd* only

  D *Dd* only

REVIEW

CALIFORNIA CONTENT
STANDARD 7.2.e

DNA (Deoxyribonucleic Acid)

STANDARD Students know DNA (deoxyribonucleic acid) is the genetic material of living organisms and is located in the chromosomes of each cell.

Read the summary and answer the questions on the next page.

The genetic material in cells is called DNA—deoxyribonucleic acid. **DNA** is a molecule that contains information for an organism's growth and functions. In eukaryotic cells, such as those of plants and animals, most of the cell's **DNA** is located in the **nucleus.**

Structure

A DNA molecule consists of two strands of subunits called nucleotides. A **nucleotide** is a compound that contains three molecules—a phosphate, a sugar, and a nitrogen-containing base. The sugar in DNA is called deoxyribose. There are four types of bases found in a DNA molecule: guanine (G), adenine (A), thymine (T), and cytosine (C). The nucleotides in a DNA strand are linked together by chemical bonds. The two strands also are linked together, forming a ladderlike structure that is twisted into a spiral shape, or helix.

The DNA in the cell nucleus is wrapped around proteins like thread around a spool. The DNA–protein complex is called a **chromosome.** In most plants and animals, chromosomes exist as pairs called **homologs.** One chromosome in each pair comes from one parent, and the other chromosome comes from the other parent. Each species has a characteristic number of chromosomes. Humans have 23 chromosome pairs, or 46 chromosomes. Chimpanzees have 24 pairs of chromosomes, or 48 chromosomes in all. Rye, a cereal grain, has 7 chromosome pairs, for a total of 14 chromosomes.

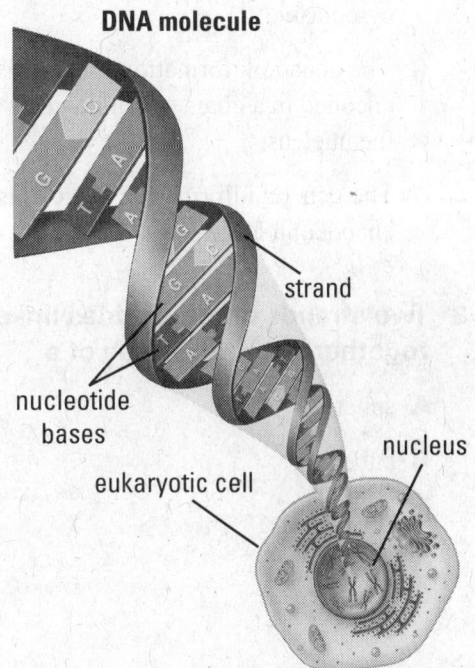

DNA molecule

strand

nucleotide bases

nucleus

eukaryotic cell

Genetic Code

The genetic information in a cell is stored as a code in DNA molecules. This code is determined by the sequence of bases in the molecule. A set of three bases codes for a particular amino acid. For example, the sequence AAG codes for the amino acid lysine. CCT codes for proline. The arrangements of these codes in a segment of DNA are the instructions for the cell to link amino acids in a particular order. These linked amino acids then link together to form a protein needed for cell function.

STANDARD SET: GENETICS

PRACTICE

CALIFORNIA CONTENT
STANDARD 7.2.e

DNA (Deoxyribonucleic Acid)

DIRECTIONS: Choose the letter of the *best* answer.

1 The DNA–protein complex in a eukaryotic nucleus is a(n)

  A allele.

  B chromosome.

  C amino acid.

  D gene pair.

2 Which of the following statements about the location of information in cells is the *most* accurate?

  A In prokaryotes, most of the cell's DNA is found in the nucleus.

  B The genetic information in a cell is encoded in protein molecules in the cytoplasm.

  C The genetic information in a cell is encoded in a chain of amino acids in the nucleus.

  D The genetic information in a cell is encoded in DNA.

3 Two strands of nucleotides linked together form the shape of a

  A sphere.

  B cube.

  C spiral.

  D pyramid.

4 What makes up the code of a gene?

  A the sequence of bases in a DNA segment

  B the sequence of sugars in a DNA segment

  C the sequence of proteins in a DNA segment

  D the sequence of amino acids in a DNA segment

5 How many bases code for one amino acid?

  A 4

  B 2

  C 1

  D 3

REVIEW

CALIFORNIA CONTENT STANDARD 6.5.b

Matter Cycles Through Ecosystems

STANDARD Students know matter is transferred over time from one organism to others in the food web and between organisms and the physical environment.

Read the summary and answer the questions on the next page.

Matter Cycles Through Ecosystems.

In an ecosystem, matter moves through organisms and the physical environment in a **cycle.** A cycle is a series of events that repeat over and over. Like energy, matter does not get used up, or disappear altogether, though it often changes form.

Transfer of Matter Among Organisms

Matter moves from one organism to another when an organism consumes another. In a forest ecosystem, for example, a maple tree uses energy in sunlight, water, and nutrients in the soil. It produces leaves. Caterpillars feed on these leaves. The caterpillars are called **herbivores,** animals that feed on plants. Birds called chickadees eat the caterpillars, but they also eat the seeds and fruit of plants. Organisms that feed on both plants and animals are called **omnivores.** Hawks eat chickadees, and are called **carnivores,** animals that feed on the flesh of other animals. When a hawk dies, its body is consumed by **decomposers,** which are organisms that break down dead plants and animals. Decomposers, such as fungi and bacteria, return matter to the soil and water, where it can be used again.

CYCLING OF MATTER IN AN ECOSYSTEM

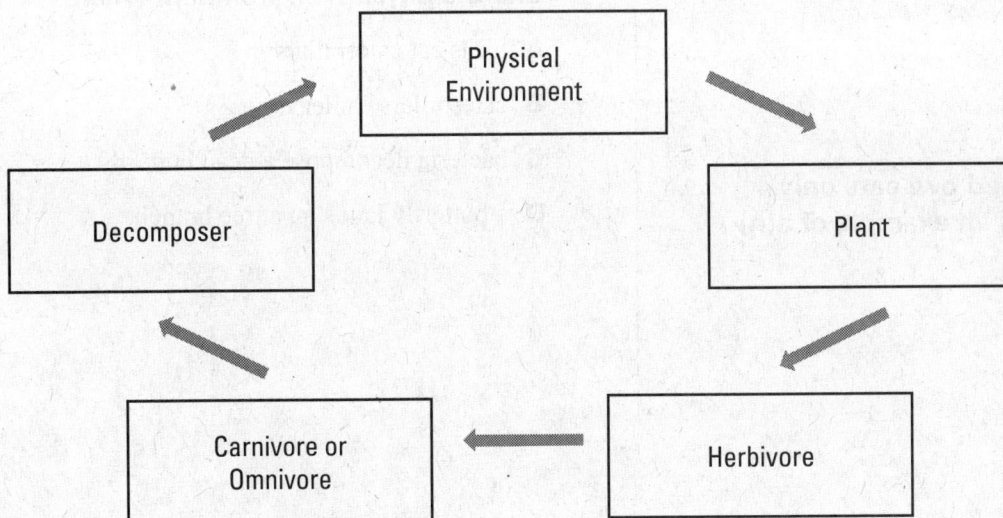

PRACTICE

CALIFORNIA CONTENT
STANDARD 6.5.b

Matter Cycles Through Ecosystems

DIRECTIONS: Choose the letter of the *best* answer.

1   Matter in an ecosystem

   A does not change forms.

   B remains in organisms.

   C stays used up.

   D gets recycled.

2   Matter moves between organisms as one organism

   A eats another.

   B produces its own food.

   C breathes air.

   D grows older.

3   A cottontail rabbit eats only plants. It is an example of a(n)

   A herbivore.

   B carnivore.

   C omnivore.

   D decomposer.

4   A great horned owl eats only animals. It is an example of a(n)

   A herbivore.

   B carnivore.

   C omnivore.

   D decomposer.

5   A raccoon eats both plants and animals. It is an example of a(n)

   A herbivore.

   B carnivore.

   C omnivore.

   D decomposer.

6   An organism that breaks down dead plants and animals and returns matter to the environment is called a(n)

   A herbivore.

   B carnivore.

   C omnivore.

   D decomposer.

7   Matter moves between organisms and the physical environment when

   A birds eat caterpillars.

   B caterpillars eat leaves.

   C bacteria decompose a dead butterfly.

   D a butterfly lands on a tree branch.

REVIEW

CALIFORNIA CONTENT
STANDARD 6.5.c

Categorizing Populations of Organisms

STANDARD Students know populations of organisms can be categorized by the functions they serve in an ecosystem.

Read the summary and answer the questions on the next page.

Different organisms have different roles in an ecosystem.

Populations

A **population** is group of organisms of the same species that lives in an ecosystem. Populations of many species occupy a single ecosystem. An oak-hickory forest, for example, may include a population of white oak trees, a population of gray squirrels, a population of wild turkeys, and so on.

Populations can be categorized by their functions. One of the main functions of a population is the role it plays in a food web. For example, a population mught have a specific diet that few, if any, other populations in the same habitat share.

Types of Organisms

Organisms can be divided into groups based on what they eat. Plants and some microscopic organisms are **producers**—they make their own food. All animals are **consumers**—they eat other organisms for food. There are many types of consumers. Primary consumers feed on producers. Secondary and higher-level consumers feed on other consumers and may be predators, scavengers, or decomposers.

- **Predators** are animals that kill and eat other animals, called **prey.**
- **Scavengers** are animals that feed on dead animals.
- **Decomposers,** which are mainly fungi and bacteria, break down plant and animal remains.

Some consumers fit multiple categories. For example, the American crow eats seeds and fruits, kills and eats insects, and feeds on dead animals. It is a primary and secondary consumer, a predator, and a scavenger!

STANDARD SET: ECOLOGY

PRACTICE

CALIFORNIA CONTENT
STANDARD 6.5.c

Categorizing Populations of Organisms

DIRECTIONS: Choose the letter of the *best* answer.

1 Timber rattlesnakes in a forest kill and eat rodents, small rabbits, and small birds. These snakes are

  A primary consumers.

  B predators.

  C scavengers.

  D decomposers.

2 Watercress is a plant that grows in spring-fed streams and is eaten by ducks, muskrats, and deer. This water plant is a

  A producer.

  B consumer.

  C predator.

  D scavenger.

3 Bison feed on the grasses in a meadow. The bison are

  A producers.

  B primary consumers.

  C predators.

  D scavengers.

4 Turkey vultures living in the cliffs along a river fly over the ground looking for dead animals to eat. These birds are

  A primary consumers.

  B predators.

  C scavengers.

  D decomposers.

5 Common snapping turtles in a pond eat water plants but also kill and eat insects, fish, and other animals. These turtles are *not*

  A primary consumers.

  B secondary consumers.

  C predators.

  D producers.

Carrying Capacity of an Ecosystem

STANDARD Students know the number and types of organisms an ecosystem can support depends on the resources available and on abiotic factors, such as quantities of light and water, a range of temperatures, and soil composition.

Read the summary and answer the questions on the next page.

An environment will only have as many organisms as there are resources for those organisms to use.

Carrying Capacity

The term **carrying capacity** refers to the maximum number of individual organisms within a population that an ecosystem can support. A number of factors affect the carrying capacities of an ecosystem. Some factors are **biotic;** that is, they concern the living parts of an ecosystem. Biotic factors include plants, animals, microorganisms, and the interactions among them. Other factors are **abiotic;** they concern the nonliving parts of an ecosystem. Abiotic factors include how much water is available, how much sunlight the ecosystem receives, what the soil is made of, and what nutrients the soil contains. They also include temperature, wind, altitude, and other environmental conditions.

Some ecosystems can support a greater variety and a larger number of organisms than others. More types of organisms live in the tropics, for example, than live in deserts. The number of organisms that an ecosystem can support also varies with the seasons. More organisms can survive during warm summers than during cold winters.

Pyramid of Biomass

The carrying capacity differs for each population in an ecosystem. In general, ecosystems can support more organisms at lower levels in a food web than at higher levels. A pyramid of **biomass,** mass of organisms, shows this principle. At each step up in feeding level, ecosystems can support fewer organisms. A pyramid of biomass is similar to an energy pyramid, which shows that the amount of available energy decreases with each step up in feeding level.

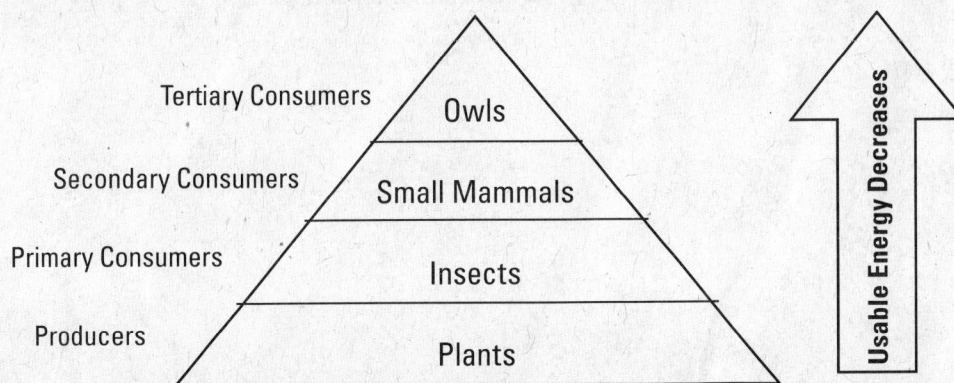

Tertiary Consumers — Owls
Secondary Consumers — Small Mammals
Primary Consumers — Insects
Producers — Plants

Usable Energy Decreases

PRACTICE

CALIFORNIA CONTENT
STANDARD 6.5.e

Carrying Capacity of an Ecosystem

STANDARD SET: ECOLOGY

DIRECTIONS: Choose the letter of the *best* answer.

1 The maximum number of individual organisms that an ecosystem can support is called the

  A pyramid of biomass.

  B biotic factor.

  C abiotic factor.

  D carrying capacity.

2 The number and types of organisms that an ecosystem can support depends on

  A abiotic factors only.

  B biotic factors only.

  C both abiotic and biotic factors.

  D neither abiotic nor biotic factors.

3 For organisms at higher levels on the food web, the number of organisms in an ecosystem generally

  A increases.

  B decreases.

  C doubles.

  D remains constant.

4 In a forest ecosystem, wolves prey on deer. You would expect to find

  A more deer than wolves.

  B more wolves than deer.

  C the same number of wolves and deer.

  D one deer for every two wolves.

5 In any ecosystem, which of the following groups of organisms would you expect to be most numerous?

  A plants

  B herbivores

  C carnivores

  D omnivores

6 Which of the following is a biotic factor that could affect the carrying capacity of an ecosystem?

  A arrival of migrating birds

  B building of a new road

  C delay in spring rains

  D erosion of topsoil

REVIEW

CALIFORNIA CONTENT
STANDARD 7.3.a

Causes of Evolution and Diversity

STANDARD Students know both genetic variation and environmental factors are causes of evolution and diversity of organisms.

Read the summary and answer the questions on the next page.

If there is a large variety of genes in a population, the population will have many different traits. This variety will allow some members of a population to survive, if the environment changes.

Evolution and Natural Selection

Evolution is the process through which species change over time. These changes result from changes in the DNA of an organism that are passed from one generation to the next. Evolution can occur through **natural selection.** The theory of natural selection states that organisms with the best traits will survive and reproduce more successfully than organisms without these traits. Natural selection is based on four principles: overproduction, variation, adaptation, and selection, which are described in the chart.

PRINCIPLES OF EVOLUTION BY NATURAL SELECTION	
Overproduction	Organisms produce more offspring than can be supported by the environment, leading to competition for resources.
Variation	Within a population, there is genetic variation among individuals.
Adaptation	Different traits can be advantageous in different environments. Such traits are called **adaptations**.
Selection	Individuals with an adaptation for their environment tend to survive and produce offspring at a higher rate than individuals that lack this adaptation.

Environmental Factors and Genetic Variation

Environmental factors such as resources, space, and energy affect the population. In order to survive a change in environmental factors, a population must have genetic variation for natural selection to take place. Individuals must have differences that can be passed on to offspring. A population without genetic variation may not survive a crisis.

Individuals have traits that may help them to survive and reproduce in a particular environment. These individuals are more likely to produce more offspring. Over time, the traits that are useful in that environment become more common. This process is called selection. A population in a different environment will have different traits. When two populations become too different to interbreed, they are considered different species.

PRACTICE

Causes of Evolution and Diversity

DIRECTIONS: Choose the letter of the *best* answer.

1 Which of the following statements *best* defines the term evolution?

A a key cause of fossilization

B the process through which species change over time

C the movement of organisms in and out of an area

D a form of overpopulation

2 What are the four principles of natural selection?

A overproduction, adaptation, speciation, and selection

B overproduction, speciation, variation, and adaptation

C overproduction, variation, adaptation, and selection

D overproduction, variation, adaptation, and extinction

3 Natural selection is a(n)

A natural law that describes events such as hurricanes.

B theory of how evolution occurs.

C important environmental factor.

D process that describes how fossils are formed.

4 Which of the following statements *most* accurately describes the term adaptation?

A a trait that is advantageous under any environmental circumstance

B a trait that is beneficial only in catastrophic events such as earthquakes

C a trait that is advantageous in a particular environment

D the process by which a species changes over time

5 A bird species that feeds on large, tough seeds has large, heavy beaks. Another species that feeds on insects has long, slender beaks. What term *best* describes the beak traits?

A speciation

B environmental factors

C selection

D adaptation

6 A single bacterium divides and begins a new population. All of the resulting bacteria have copies of the same DNA. This population has no

A traits.

B overproduction.

C genetic variation.

D environmental factors.

STANDARD SET: EVOLUTION

REVIEW

CALIFORNIA CONTENT
STANDARD 7.3.b

*Charles Darwin and
Natural Selection*

STANDARD Students know the reasoning used by Charles Darwin in reaching his conclusion that natural selection is the mechanism of evolution.

Read the summary and answer the questions on the next page.

Charles Darwin synthesized his theory of **natural selection** based on information from three sources: his own observations of living things, an essay on human population growth, and animal breeding practices.

Darwin and His Observations

Before he came up with his theory of natural selection, Charles Darwin made many observations.

Natural Variation in Traits

Darwin had observed that there was always variation in certain traits among members of a population, and that offspring usually resembled their parents. He reasoned that these inherited traits first appeared in a population by chance.

Populations Limited by Resources

In an essay on human population growth, the economist Thomas Malthus had noted that human populations tended to grow in size too rapidly, given the limited resources on Earth. To Malthus this suggested that only a fraction of the individuals born on Earth could survive, while those remaining were doomed to starvation and disease.

Animal Breeding and Artificial Selection

Darwin knew that breeders produced new varieties of animals over time by selecting animals with desirable traits and mating those individuals, then repeating the process over many generations to eventually produce a distinctly new breed that displayed the desired trait.

Natural Selection

Darwin's theory of natural selection proposed that different traits would be beneficial in different environments, and that individuals with those traits might be more successful at competing for certain resources, especially when those resources were scarce. Organisms that were best suited to their environment would survive and reproduce at a higher rate than other individuals in the environment. The successful individuals would pass on their advantageous traits, or **adaptations,** to their offspring. Darwin called this mechanism natural selection because environmental conditions selected for the advantageous trait, just as a breeder would select for a desirable characteristic. Over time the adaptation would become more common in the population. In a different environment, a different set of traits would become common. Two populations that started out the same would become different as they became adapted to different environmental factors.

STANDARD SET: EVOLUTION

Name _____ Period _____ Date _____

 **PRACTICE**

CALIFORNIA CONTENT
STANDARD 7.3.b

Charles Darwin and
Natural Selection

DIRECTIONS: Choose the letter of the *best* answer.

1 Natural selection is a mechanism for evolution in which

A breeders choose a desirable trait by interbreeding organisms that have it.

B environmental factors influence a beneficial trait found among individuals of a population.

C individuals select traits that better meet their needs.

D populations quickly outgrow their resources.

2 Which statement *most* accurately reflects Darwin's views about variation in populations?

A Variations in traits first appear in a population by chance.

B Variations in traits are acquired by organisms during their lifetimes.

C Variations in traits cause individuals to outgrow their resources.

D Variations in traits are a result of selection.

3 How does a population become adapted to its environment?

A Individuals learn changes and pass them on to their offspring.

B A population chooses new traits to help it survive environmental conditions.

C Traits that give advantages become more common in the population over time.

D Variation becomes an adaptation as the organisms learn how to use it.

4 What were the sources of ideas and information that Darwin used to develop his theory of natural selection?

A his own observations, laboratory experiments, and animal breeding practices

B laboratory experiments, Malthus's essay about human populations, and animal breeding practices

C his own observations, Malthus's essay about human populations, and laboratory experiments

D his own observations, Malthus's essay about human populations, and animal breeding practices

5 A population of nut-eating birds experiences a sudden change in its food supply. There are fewer nuts and most of these are very large and have rough shells. Which trait would be an adaptation in this scenario?

A sharp talons (claws)

B a strong beak

C a long, slender beak

D strong wings

STANDARD SET: EVOLUTION

McDougal Littell Biology

REVIEW

CALIFORNIA CONTENT
STANDARD 7.3.c

Evidence for Evolution

STANDARD Students know how independent lines of evidence from geology, fossils, and comparative anatomy provide the bases for the theory of evolution.

Read the summary and answer the questions on the next page.

Evolution is the process by which organisms change over time. Scientists find evidence for evolution in geology, fossils, an comparative anatomy.

Geologic and Fossil Evidence

In an undisturbed sequence of sedimentary rock, the more recent rock layers are at the top of the sequence and the older rock layers are at the bottom. The characteristics of rock layers provide information about changes in climate and other aspects of the environment over time. Organisms may leave fossils as each sediment layer is deposited. More recently evolved organisms are found in younger rock layers, and more ancient species are found in older rock layers.

The information from **fossils** and their location in rocks is called the **fossil record**. Scientists use the fossil record to identify periods during which different species existed. The geographic location of many fossils provides evidence that two species with a common **ancestor** can develop differently in different locations.

Evidence from Comparative Anatomy

Similar structures with different functions in different species are another form of structural evidence for evolution. The forelimbs of vertebrates such as reptiles, birds, and mammals contain similar bones, yet the size and shape of these bones differs in species that use their forelimbs differently. The similarity in limb structure is evidence that these organisms shared a common ancestor. During early development, the embryos of different species closely resemble each other, even though as adults they have distinct characteristics. The genes controlling early development in these species were inherited from a common ancient ancestor.

Vestigial organs are physical structures that were fully developed and used in an ancestral group of organisms but are reduced and unused in later species. Small but unused leg bones in whales and in snakes are examples of vestigial organs.

STANDARD SET: EVOLUTION

PRACTICE

CALIFORNIA CONTENT
STANDARD 7.3.c

Evidence for Evolution

DIRECTIONS: Choose the letter of the _best_ answer.

1 **Evidence for evolution is found**

  A mostly in fossils.

  B mostly in the structures of living things.

  C in both fossils and the structures of living things.

  D in neither fossils nor the structures of living things.

2 **Fossils tend to be found in which type of rock?**

  A metamorphic

  B igneous

  C sedimentary

  D embryonic

3 **Which statement regarding vestigial organs is the _most_ accurate?**

  A They are tiny structures that developed for unknown reasons.

  B They are structures that once were fully developed and functional in an ancestral species.

  C They are found only in vertebrates.

  D They are found only in embryos.

4 **Species X became extinct about 50,000 years before Species Y evolved. Both species lived in the same location. In which arrangement would you _most_ likely find their fossils in a rock sequence?**

  A Species X would be in a deeper layer than Species Y.

  B Species Y would be in a deeper layer than Species X.

  C Both species would be in the same rock layer.

  D Species X would be inside Species Y.

5 **Similarities in the embryos of two very different species, such as chickens and lizards, are evidence that both species**

  A had similar vestigial organs.

  B used the same limb structures.

  C inherited genes from a common ancestor.

  D developed in mothers that are in a similar environment.

6 **The combination of fossils and their location in rocks is called the**

  A fossil record.

  B rock sequence.

  C geologic time scale.

  D law of superposition.

STANDARD SET: EVOLUTION

REVIEW

CALIFORNIA CONTENT
STANDARD 7.5.a

Organization of Living Things

STANDARD Students know plants and animals have levels of organization for structure
and function, including cells, tissues, organs, organ systems, and the whole organism.

Read the summary and answer the questions on the next page.

Animals and plants have different structures that do the many tasks needed to stay alive.
The structures represent different levels of organization, from cells to the complete organism.
Cells make up tissues, which make up organs, which make up organ systems, which make up
the organism.

Levels of Organization

Cells

The basic unit of structure for all living things is the cell. **Cells** are the smallest level
of organization for multicellular organisms, such as plants and animals. Many cells are
specialized. Specialized cells perform specific tasks. Humans have specialized cells such as
nerve cells, muscle cells, and skin cells.

Tissues

A **tissue** is a group of similar cells that work together to perform a specific function. There
are many examples of tissues in organisms. In humans, a group of muscle cells makes up
a muscle tissue that produces movement. In vascular plants, specialized cells form phloem
tissue, which transports sugars from the leaves to the rest of the plant.

Organs

An **organ** is a structure made up of two or more types of tissue that work together to carry
out a function. For example, a heart is an organ made of muscle tissue and nerve tissue. A
leaf is an organ that includes dermal tissue and ground tissue.

Organ Systems

An **organ system** is a group of organs that together perform a function. For example, the
human digestive system is made of the mouth, esophagus, stomach, intestines, liver, gall
bladder, and pancreas. The digestive system breaks down foods into nutrients and prepares
them so the body can use them. The shoot system of a plant is an organ system. This system
produces and stores the sugars a plant needs for food. All of the organs in an organ system
depend on each other. If one organ fails, the whole system is affected.

The Complete Organism

Animal and plants have many different organ systems that carry on different life functions.
The organ systems in an animal or plant work together to keep the organism alive. Organ
systems work together to allow an organism to grow, repair itself, and reproduce.

PRACTICE

Organization of Living Things

DIRECTIONS: Choose the letter of the *best* answer.

1 Every living organism is made of one or more

A cells.

B organ.

C organ systems.

D tissues.

2 What makes a cell specialized?

A It reproduces.

B It uses energy.

C It is the only one of its kind.

D It performs specific tasks.

3 What is a tissue?

A a group of similar cells that do a specific job

B a group of similar organs that do a specific job

C a specific structure inside a single-celled organism

D the largest type of structure in a multicellular organism

4 Which of the following is made of two or more tissues and performs a specific function?

A a cell

B an organ

C an organism

D an organelle

5 A group of epithelial cells in a gland all produce the same fluid. These cells make up a(n)

A tissue.

B organ.

C organ system.

D organism.

6 The heart pumps blood. Arteries, veins, and capillaries carry blood through the body and allow it to exchange materials with other cells. Together the heart, arteries, veins, and capillaries make up a(n)

A tissue.

B organ.

C organ system.

D organism.

STANDARD SET: PHYSIOLOGY

Bones and Muscles

STANDARD Students know how bones and muscles work together to provide a structural framework for movement.

Read the summary and answer the questions on the next page.

Vertebrates are animals that have a skull and backbone, or an internal support system. Birds, amphibians, reptiles, fish, and mammals, including humans, are vertebrates. Movements in animals result from the interactions of the skeletal system, the muscular system, and the nervous system. The **skeletal system** includes bones, ligaments, cartilage, and tendons. The **muscular system** includes the muscles are attached to the skeleton. The nervous system signals muscles to contract and relax.

Skeletal System

The main function of the skeletal system is to support and protect the body. **Bones** are living tissue that provides support and protection, produce and store blood cells, and store calcium for the body. Bones are made of cells and minerals. **Ligaments** are a type of connective tissue that connects bones together and cartilage to bones. **Cartilage** is a tough but flexible connective tissue. It acts as a cushion between two bones, such as the bones of your leg at the knee joint. **Tendons** are a type of connective tissue that connects muscles to bones. In the skeletal system, bones meet at joints.

Muscular System

Skeletal muscle tissue is attached to bones and helps give the body shape. These voluntary muscles contract and relax in ways that make an animal move. Muscles can produce pulling force when they contract, or shorten.

A skeletal muscle contracts and pulls on the tendon that is attached to a bone. The bone is pulled in the direction of the contraction. Often the bone rotates, or pivots, around a joint. To produce the opposite movement, a different muscle and tendon pulls the bone in the other direction.

Most skeletal muscles work in coordinated groups to produce smooth, controlled movements. For example, the human biceps and triceps together control the movement of the upper arm. When the biceps contracts, the triceps relaxes and the forearm rotates at the elbow toward the shoulder. When the triceps contracts, the biceps relaxes and the forearm rotates at the elbow as the arm straightens. Other muscles work to stabilize the joints and the body's movements.

STANDARD SET: PHYSIOLOGY

PRACTICE

CALIFORNIA CONTENT
STANDARD 7.5.c

Bones and Muscles

DIRECTIONS: Choose the letter of the *best* answer.

1 What system provides a framework to support the body?

A the muscular system

B the skeletal system

C the nervous system

D the digestive system

2 The connective tissue that connects muscles to bones are called

A cartilage.

B ligaments.

C tendons.

D organs.

3 Bones in the skeletal system meet at

A joints.

B tendons.

C minerals.

D muscles.

4 What happens when you bend your leg?

A All of the muscles attached to your leg bones contract together.

B All of the muscles attached to your leg bones relax together.

C One group of muscles contracts while the other relaxes.

D One group of tendons contracts while the other relaxes.

5 Muscles produce force by

A contracting.

B growing.

C pushing.

D relaxing.

REVIEW

CALIFORNIA CONTENT
STANDARD 7.6.j

The Pumping Heart

STANDARD Students know that contractions of the heart generate blood pressure and that heart valves prevent backflow of blood in the circulatory system.

Read the summary and answer the questions on the next page.

The circulatory system is the body system that moves blood throughout the body. **Blood** is a fluid that transports materials, such as oxygen and wastes, to and from most body cells. Veins, arteries, and capillaries are **blood vessels,** or tube-shaped, flexible structures of different diameters.

Parts of the Circulatory System

The **heart** is an organ that pumps blood through the circulatory system. Contraction of muscle increases the pressure of the blood. When more materials are needed or more wastes must be carried away from cells, the heart pumps faster and harder. As a result, the blood flows faster and moves materials faster.

Blood travels through different types of blood vessels, which are described in the chart. **Arteries** carry blood from the heart to the lungs and other locations. The arteries nearest the heart have the largest diameters. They have strong walls that withstand the high pressure produced by the heart. Arteries branch into smaller and smaller blood vessels. The smallest blood vessels are **capillaries,** which have thin walls that allow materials to move out of the circulatory system and back into it. **Veins** carry blood from capillaries back to the heart. Veins have one-way valves that prevent blood from flowing backwards. Without valves, the blood in the veins of your legs would flow back down to your feet due to gravity and would not circulate back to your heart

Blood Pressure

Pressure is force spread over an area. Blood moves away from areas of high pressure toward areas of lower pressure. One-way **valves** within the heart prevent blood from moving backward. Blood pressure and other pressures are given as the amount of force per unit area, such as newtons per square meter. One joule is equal to one newton per square meter. Pressure can also be given in millimeters of mercury or inches of mercury, due to one method of measuring pressure.

THE CIRCULATORY SYSTEM

Structure	Function
Heart	Pumps blood through the circulatory system by contracting muscle tissue
Blood	Transports materials within the body
Artery	Carries blood away from the heart toward other locations
Capillary	Allows blood to exchange materials with cells in the body
Vein	Carries blood from different locations toward the heart
Valve	Lets blood flow in one direction only

STANDARD SET: PHYSIOLOGY

PRACTICE

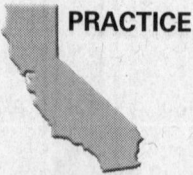

CALIFORNIA CONTENT
STANDARD 7.6.j

The Pumping Heart

DIRECTIONS: Choose the letter of the *best* answer.

1 What body system moves blood throughout the human body?

A circulatory system

B digestive system

C muscular system

D respiratory system

2 Which of the following moves blood throughout the circulatory system?

A gravity

B pressure

C flowing fluids

D skeletal muscles

3 How does a runner's circulatory system respond when his or her muscle cells need more oxygen?

A His or her heart beats faster and harder, making blood transport oxygen faster.

B His or her heart beats slower and conserves blood to meet the need for oxygen.

C His or her blood increases its volume and so increases its pressure to move more oxygen.

D His or her heart beats more gently and gives the blood more time to deliver oxygen.

4 The function of valves in the circulatory system is to

A exchange materials with cells.

B maintain a steady heartbeat.

C prevent blood from flowing backward.

D push blood through arteries.

5 What is the function of veins?

A to bring blood toward the heart

B to carry blood away from the heart

C to allow blood to exchange materials

D to produce blood pressure

6 Which structures have one-way valves?

A veins and capillaries

B arteries and veins

C the heart and arteries

D the heart and veins

REVIEW

CALIFORNIA CONTENT STANDARD IE.6.c

Constructing and Interpreting Graphs

STANDARD Students will construct appropriate graphs from data and develop qualitative statements about the relationships between variables.

Read the summary and answer the questions on the next page.

Researchers use graphs because graphs are much easier to read than a paragraph full of numbers. Knowing how to construct and read graphs will help you quickly understand scientific data.

Data Tables

You gather data by conducting an investigation. In order to analyze the data and draw conclusions from them, you need to arrange them in some kind of order. Data tables allow you to organize numerical data by variable. The data table here shows the number of days of air quality rated poor for Bakersfield, California, by year from 1993 to 2002.

Line Graphs

It would be easier to see any trend in the information if you showed it in the form of a graph. The line graph below shows the data from the table. The vertical axis (y-axis) shows number of days, starting with 0. The horizontal axis (x-axis) shows the years. You can tell from the graph that there is a gradual trend over the time period toward more poor quality days per year. The trend isn't perfect, for there was a dip in 1997 and 1998, but you can clearly see it in the graph.

DATA TABLE

Year	Days with Poor Air Quality
1993	97
1994	105
1995	107
1996	110
1997	58
1998	78
1999	144
2000	132
2001	125
2002	152

Air Quality in Bakersfield, California, 1993–2002

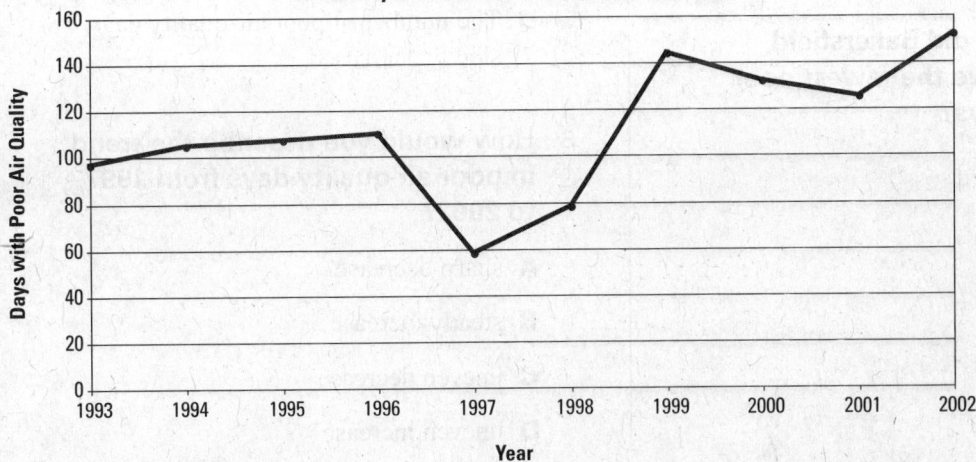

When you describe this trend you are making a qualitative statement about the relationships between the variables. A **qualitative statement** is one that describes the quality of something. If you wanted to make a **quantitative statement**, by contrast, you would describe the actual numbers involved. A quantitative statement would be: There were 20 more days labeled poor in 1998 than in 1997.

STANDARD SET: INVESTIGATION
AND EXPERIMENTATION

PRACTICE

CALIFORNIA CONTENT
STANDARD IE.6.c

Constructing and Interpreting Graphs

DIRECTIONS: Choose the letter of the *best* answer.

1 In constructing a line graph, which of the following steps would you do first?

A Mark the scale on each axis.

B Draw line segments connecting the points.

C Draw and label the axes.

D Graph the points.

Use the line graph on page 167 to answer questions 2–6.

2 What are the two variables shown on the graph?

A time and location

B poor air quality and year

C poor air quality and weather

D air quality and location

3 In which year did Bakersfield, California, have the *fewest* poor air-quality days?

A 1995

B 1997

C 1999

D 2001

4 In which year did Bakersfield, California, have the *most* poor air-quality days?

A 1993

B 1996

C 1999

D 2002

5 Which of the following is an accurate qualitative statement about the data from 1993 to 1997?

A The number of poor air-quality days slowly increased and then dramatically dropped.

B The number of poor air-quality days steadily increased and then decreased slightly.

C The number of poor air-quality days slowly increased.

D The number of poor air-quality days slowly decreased.

6 How would you describe the trend in poor air-quality days from 1997 to 2002?

A sharp decrease

B steady increase

C uneven decrease

D uneven increase

McDougal Littell Biology

REVIEW

CALIFORNIA CONTENT
STANDARD IE.6.e

Evaluating Evidence and Explanations

STANDARD Students will recognize whether evidence is consistent with a proposed explanation.

Read the summary and answer questions on the next page.

Scientists conduct experiments in attempt to answer a question. They gather evidence in the form of data, and use this evidence to explain the answer to their question.

Evidence

Evidence is what you use to make a conclusion or form a judgment. You find evidence in many ways, including experimenting and observing. A wet sidewalk, for example, may be evidence that it recently rained.

Scientists support their explanations of natural processes by citing evidence. To evaluate an explanation, you need to consider whether the evidence is consistent with it, that is, whether the evidence supports the explanation. Ask yourself these questions:

- Does the explanation fit all the evidence?
- Does the explanation fit known natural processes?

Evaluation

As an example, suppose a large boulder weighing several tons is lying in an open field in Wyoming.

Question	How did the boulder get in the field?
Proposed Explanation	A glacier that covered the region long ago left the boulder when it melted.
Evidence	• The boulder is a different type of rock than the bedrock in the area. • A long, high ridge several kilometers away separates the field from a river.

Evaluating the Explanation

The explanation fits the evidence and known natural processes. Glaciers did cover the northern United States long ago, and Wyoming is in the northern United States. Glaciers can transport huge amounts of debris, including large boulders. Glaciers can also transport rock from far away, and then the rock might not match the bedrock in an area where it is deposited.

PRACTICE

CALIFORNIA CONTENT
STANDARD IE.6.e

*Evaluating Evidence
and Explanations*

DIRECTIONS: Choose the letter of the *best* answer.

Suppose a park in rural Missouri has two old statues with similar dates.

Question	Why does one statue show the effects of weathering and the other does not?
Proposed Explanations	1. Acid rain has worn away one of the statues but not the other. (Acid rain results from air pollution that makes rainwater more acidic.) 2. Limestone weathers, or breaks down, faster than granite so the limestone statue has weathered faster. 3. Earthquakes damaged one of the statues but not the other. (Earthquakes are ground vibrations caused by sudden movement of rock along a fault.)
Evidence	• The statues are next to each other. • One statue is made of limestone, and the other is made of granite. • One statue is heavily pitted, and the details have almost worn away. • The other statue is smooth, and the details are clear.

1 How does the first explanation conflict with the evidence?

 A Acid rain does not occur in Missouri.

 B Acid rain does not affect rocks.

 C Statues side by side would be equally affected by acid rain.

 D Rural areas do not have acid rain.

2 How does the second explanation fit with a known natural process?

 A Rainwater breaks down different types of rocks at different rates.

 B Many statues are made of granite or limestone.

 C Mechanical weathering occurs when plant roots grow in the cracks of rocks.

 D Ocean waves can wear down rocks along a shoreline.

3 How does the third explanation conflict with the evidence?

 A Earthquakes do not occur in Missouri.

 B Earthquakes affect everything close their epicenters equally.

 C Earthquakes do not affect rocks on the surface of the ground.

 D Earthquakes do not cause the kind of weathering described in one of the tombstones.

4 Suppose you offered this explanation: the more weathered statue is older. Which evidence conflicts with this explanation?

 A The statues are next to each other.

 B The statues are both granite.

 C The statues are the same age.

 D The statues have been moved.

REVIEW

CALIFORNIA CONTENT
STANDARD IE.7.c

Scientific Logic

STANDARD Students will communicate the logical connection among hypotheses, science concepts, tests conducted, data collected, and conclusions drawn from scientific evidence.

Read the summary and answer questions on the next page.

Scientists try to solve problems and answer questions in a logical fashion. Scientific processes used by all scientists include asking questions, determining what is known, investigating, interpreting the results, and sharing the results with others.

Observations, Questions, and Inferences

Scientists observe the physical world, or the world of matter and energy. Observations are information gathered by the senses, perhaps with instruments that expand the senses. For example, a biologist uses a microscope to view the tip of an onion root. Some cells are smaller, some have dark strings along the center, and some have dark strings near the ends. The scientist records these and other observations in diagrams and notes, and may make an inference to explain the observations. An **inference** is a tentative conclusion based on observations and logic. The scientist might infer that the cells are in different stages of cell division.

Forming and Testing a Hypothesis

A scientist often forms a **hypothesis,** or a possible, testable explanation for a set of observations. An inference from past observations may become a hypothesis to be tested by future observations. A scientist may use a hypothesis to make a specific prediction, and then test the prediction. A biologist might predict that quickly-growing onion roots will show more cells with dark strings than slowly-growing onion roots. A scientist might design an experiment to test a prediction. An **experiment** is an organized procedure to study something under controlled conditions. It can provide evidence for or against a hypothesis. A biologist might design an experiment to make onion roots grow at different speeds and then compare the resulting cells.

Analyzing Data and Making Conclusions

During an experiment, scientists collect data, which includes measurements and other observations. They analyze their data using computers and other tools and by using calculations, graphs, charts, and other methods. For example, a biologist might put diagrams or photographs of cells into a sequence that shows the process of cell division. The results of the analysis may help a scientist draw conclusions. A **conclusion** is an ending or summary, such as an explanation, based on logic and convincing evidence. After enough tests, a biologist might conclude that the cells with dark strings represent different stages of cell division.

PRACTICE

CALIFORNIA CONTENT
STANDARD IE.7.c

Scientific Logic

DIRECTIONS: Choose the letter of the *best* answer.

1 An astronomer who notices a faint light near the planet Neptune is making a(n)

A conclusion.

B hypothesis.

C inference.

D observation.

2 Which is an example of making an inference?

A After studying paw and hoof prints, a biologist thinks that deer are hopping fences at night to escape neighborhood dogs.

B A biologist spends several weeks in the Canadian woods watching grey wolves and taking notes.

C An ecologist places pictures of hawks on a set of glass windows to find out if it will prevent songbirds from flying into the windows.

D A chemist publishes a description of experiments, data, and results about photosynthesis in a scientific journal.

3 An explanation of a set of observances that can be tested is called a(n)

A conclusion.

B hypothesis.

C inference.

D observation.

4 Before making conclusions from the data from an experiment, a scientist must first

A analyze the data.

B write a procedure.

C revise the hypothesis.

D make a new prediction.

5 A marine biologist makes an inference about the effect of pesticides on corals and then tests this idea using an experiment. The results convince the biologist that their idea is correct. The biologist has reached a(n)

A hypothesis.

B conclusion.

C prediction.

D theory.

REVIEW

CALIFORNIA CONTENT
STANDARD IE.8.b

Accuracy and Reproducibility in Experiments

STANDARD Evaluate the accuracy and reproducibility of data.

Read the summary and answer questions on the next page.

When designing experiments, it is important that the experiment yeilds accurate and reproducible data.

Accurate Measurements

Science depends on accurate measurements. A measurement is **accurate** when it is very close to the actual value. When a measurement is accurate, there is a very small difference or no difference between the measured value and the actual value.

For example, suppose you are measuring the volume of two different liquid samples. Before giving you the samples, your teacher carefully pre-measured each sample and recorded the volume. Your teacher's measurements agree with those given on the bottles that originally contained the samples. You can assume they are accurate.

You measure and record the volume of each sample. For one sample, your measurement agrees with that of your teacher. That measurement is accurate. For the other sample, your measurement is 3 mL lower than your teacher's measurement. Your teacher's measurement is 100 mL. Your measurement is 97 mL. As scientific measurements go, 3 mL is a significant difference. Therefore, your volume measurement is not accurate.

Reproducibility of Results

Science experiments are most valuable when the results are **reproducible.** This means that, when an experiment is repeated, the results are the same or almost the same. One scientist may claim to have made a certain measurement or observed a certain result from a particular experiment. If the scientist's results are not reproducible by others, very few will take them seriously. Reproducibility depends on several things:

- The equipment and materials used to repeat the experiment must be identical to those used in the original.
- The experimental procedure must be detailed and precise. The scientists repeating the experiment need to follow the exact same procedure as the original scientists did.
- The conditions under which the experiment is carried out have to be the same or very similar. Conditions might include the temperature, humidity, or amount of sunlight in the laboratory. If the experiment was done outside, conditions might include the weather or the season. When conditions vary, the results of the experiment can vary as well.

PRACTICE

CALIFORNIA CONTENT
STANDARD IE.8.b

*Accuracy and Reproducibility
in Experiments*

DIRECTIONS: Choose the letter of the *best* answer.

1 A lead mass came from the factory labeled as 1 kilogram. You use a scale to measure it and find that it has a mass of 1.4 kilograms. How accurate was your measurement?

A Your measurement was accurate enough, because a kilogram is small.

B Your measurement was not accurate; you should check the scale and try again.

C Your measurement was accurate enough, because factories often mislabel masses.

D Your measurement was not accurate; all scales do not measure accurately.

2 What is one thing a scientist can do to ensure an experiment will be reproducible by others?

A Use materials that are difficult to obtain.

B Write notes in a shorthand used only in a particular lab.

C Write very detailed steps that clearly explain what was done.

D Do the experiment on a bright, sunny day.

A scientist does an experiment to see how water temperature affects the breathing rate of frogs. The scientist puts a frog in distilled water at 27°C and measures the frog's breathing rate. Then, over the next few hours, the scientist places the frog in identical containers each with water 3°C lower than that in the previous container and measures the frog's breathing rate. The last container has water at 15°C.

3 If you were repeating the experiment, which of these questions would you have to ask the scientist? [Hint: You simply want to repeat the experiment.]

A What type of water did you use?

B How did you measure the frog's breathing rate?

C Why did you first place the frog in water that was 27°C?

D Why did your last container have water at 15°C?

4 Which of the following would make your repetition of the experiment invalid?

A recording the frog's initial breathing rate on a graph

B observing how the frog's behavior changed when it was placed in cooler water

C using a toad instead of a frog

D washing your hands with soap and water after completing the experiment

REVIEW

CALIFORNIA CONTENT
STANDARD IE.8.c

Variable and Controlled Parameters in Experiments

STANDARD Distinguish between variable and controlled parameters in a test.

Read the summary and answer questions on the next page.

When scientists design an experiment, they usually test how one thing affects another. They keep all other conditions of the experiment exactly the same, or constant. The conditions of an experiment are called **parameters.**

Description of Experiment

Imagine that a group of students decide to design an experiment to test the effects of water temperature on plant growth. They predict that if they keep the water near room temperature, then plants will grow better. They have hypothesized that room temperature water will not damage plant tissues.

Controlled Parameters

The students are testing one parameter: water temperature. They must make sure all other parameters remain the same for all plants. They make a list of all other parameters they must keep constant.

- plant species
- plant age
- soil type
- flowerpot size
- light conditions
- temperature of the room
- amount of water
- type of water (distilled)

The parameters that remain the same for all the plants in this experiment are called **controlled parameters.** They are also sometimes called **constants.** The experimenters hold them constant. In other words, they keep them exactly the same for all subjects of the experiment.

Variable Parameters

Reread the students' hypothesis and prediction for this experiment. Students will change or vary the water temperature. They expect then the growth of the plants to vary as well. Plant growth and water temperature in this experiment are the **variable parameters.** These parameters change during the experiment.

Independent and Dependent Variables

The two variable parameters in the experiment differ from one another. The students change the temperature of the water in a planned way: this parameter is called the **independent variable.** The students hypothesized that plant growth depends on water temperature. For this reason, plant growth is called the **dependent variable.**

STANDARD SET: INVESTIGATION AND EXPERIMENTATION

PRACTICE

CALIFORNIA CONTENT
STANDARD IE.8.c

Variable and Controlled Parameters in Experiments

DIRECTIONS: Choose the letter of the *best* answer.

1 **What are the parameters of an experiment?**

  A what scientists learn from an experiment

  B why scientists do an experiment

  C observations made before the experiment

  D constant and variable conditions during an experiment

2 **What are two controlled parameters in the experiment described on the previous page?**

  A plant height and size of the pot

  B size of the pot and air temperature

  C air temperature and plant height

  D plant height and plant species

3 **Why is the temperature of the distilled water a variable parameter in the experiment described on the previous page?**

  A Students change this parameter to see if it affects how plants grow.

  B Students hold this parameter constant to see if it affects water quality.

  C By keeping this parameter the same, students control plant growth.

  D By varying this parameter, students can control air temperature.

A class wants to see if unripe bananas will ripen faster if placed in a bag with very ripe bananas. They get seven (unripe) green bananas and two (very ripe) brown bananas. The bananas are all the same size. They get three identical brown paper bags. In one bag, they place three green bananas. In each of the other two bags, they place two green bananas and one brown banana. They seal each of the bags with masking tape and place the bags on a small table at the front of the classroom. The bags remain undisturbed and sealed for two days.

4 **What is a variable parameter in this experiment?**

  A bag size

  B banana size

  C exposure to ripe bananas

  D bag color

5 **What are two controlled parameters in this experiment?**

  A number of ripe bananas in each bag; placement of bags in the room

  B number of bananas in each bag; degree bananas ripened in two days

  C number of bananas in each bag; placement of bags in the room

  D humidity of room; number of ripe bananas in each bag